Garry MacKenzie has a PhD in poetry from the University of St Andrews, and was awarded a New Writers Award by the Scottish Book Trust. He teaches literature and publishes articles on modern poetry and Scottish literature. Originally from Glasgow, he lives in Fife with his wife and cat. This is his first book.

'Clear, concise, and companionable, the prose is engagingly readable, and the learning worn with admirable lightness. Garry MacKenzie's *Scotland* is a delight.'

Robert Crawford, author of *Scotland's Books*
and *The Bard: Robert Burns, a Biography*

'"Scotland small? Our multiform, our infinite Scotland small?" Hugh MacDiarmid once expostulated. Many other nations are larger than Scotland, but its cultural achievements and influences have by far exceeded its geographical size and demography. Its literature – Robert Burns, Sir Walter Scott, Robert Louis Stevenson and many others – from earliest times to the present day, as well as visitors from abroad, have inscribed Scotland as a literary land, balladic, sung, and dramatised. Garry MacKenzie's *Scotland* will be invaluable to literary visitors, and for those who live in Scotland a catalyst to explore further its literature and its places.'

Douglas Dunn, editor of
The Oxford Book of Scottish Short Stories

Scotland

A LITERARY GUIDE FOR TRAVELLERS

Garry MacKenzie

I.B. TAURIS
LONDON · NEW YORK

Published in 2016 by
I.B.Tauris & Co. Ltd
London • New York
www.ibtauris.com

ISBN: 978 1 78453 641 1
eISBN: 978 0 85772 863 0
ePDF: 978 0 85772 836 4

A full CIP record for this book is available from the British Library
A full CIP record is available from the Library of Congress

Library of Congress Catalog Card Number: available

Typeset by JCS Publishing Services Ltd, www.jcs-publishing.co.uk
Printed and bound in Sweden by ScandBook AB

For Vicky, with all my love

Literary Guides for Travellers
Listed in Fathom's 24 Best Indie Travel Guides

Andalucía by Andrew and Suzanne Edwards

Berlin by Marcel Krueger and Paul Sullivan

Florence and Tuscany by Ted Jones

The French Riviera by Ted Jones

Sicily by Andrew and Suzanne Edwards

Tangier by Josh Shoemake

Venice by Marie-José Gransard

CONTENTS

Illustrations

Credits: All photographs were taken by Garry MacKenzie, except 3, 4 and 8 by Alistair MacKenzie and 23, 24, 25 and 26 by Vicky MacKenzie. The map of literary Scotland is by Leo Mewse, of the Print and Design department at the University of St Andrews. All images used with permission.

ACKNOWLEDGEMENTS

Writing a literary travel guide means I've accrued many debts, not least to those travelling companions who have accompanied me throughout Scotland. My first literary journey was taken aged about five or so, when my grandparents James and Jean Preston took me to Burns's Cottage in Alloway. More recently my wife Vicky has explored much of Scotland with me and has been an endless source of encouragement and love, as well as the most eagle-eyed of first readers. Vicky, you've my deepest thanks and all my love, and this book is for you. Thanks also to my parents, Alistair and Annette, for all the childhood holidays in Scotland, for your support over many years, and for undertaking your own literary tour to supply some much-needed photographs. Some of the places in this book were visited with friends, including Euan and Anna Cuthbert, Will and Alison Gray and Marco Dees. Thanks to you all, especially to Euan for undertaking a risky turn on the road near Ben Dorain, in the name of literary endeavour.

I'm immensely grateful to Shirley McKay, Neil Rhodes and John Beaton for suggesting that I write this literary guide and helping me get it as far as the drawing board. Thanks also to Neil for pointing me in the direction of some surprising gems, including the medieval leper colony at St Andrews and Dorothy Sayers's connections with the Borders. Conversations over many years with teachers, including Robert Crawford and Douglas Dunn, have unearthed a store of treasures, some of which may have found their way into the book in one form or another. My thanks also go to Christine Rauer for her unstinting help as I got my head around Old English and the mysteries of the Ruthwell Cross; and to Peter Mackay for help with translating Duncan Ban Macintyre's Gaelic. For sage advice and enjoyable chat about translation more generally, my thanks go to Boris Dralyuk. Gordon Jarvie, himself a dedicated literary traveller, has been another fount of knowledge and supplied some of the books my own shelves lacked. I'm very grateful to Ellen Cranitch for casting her eye over parts of the book and inevitably making them more stylish. Special thanks go to my cat, Geoffrey, for adding his own keystrokes when he felt something was lacking from my prose. Finally, my heartfelt thanks go to Tatiana Wilde and David Campbell, my editors at I.B.Tauris, and Jessica Cuthbert-Smith, for their help and guidance from start to finish.

I am indebted to the researchers, biographers and literary travellers who have come before me and done much of the groundwork that has inspired this book. These authors are listed in my bibliography, and the books which I have found particularly invaluable are included within the Select Bibliography under the heading 'Useful Resources'. Throughout the book I have modernised, and very occasionally Anglicised, spellings when I deemed this helpful for clarity. Translations, unless otherwise stated or listed as such in the bibliography, are my own.

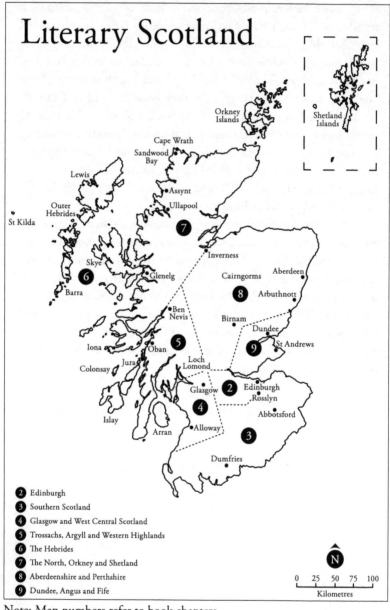

Literary Scotland

Shetland
Islands

Orkney
Islands

Cape Wrath

Sandwood
Bay

Lewis

●Assynt

●Ullapool

Outer
Hebrides

St Kilda

7

Skye

●Inverness

Cairngorms

Aberdeen

6

●Glenelg

8

●Arbuthnott

Barra

Birnam

●Ben
Nevis

●Dundee

Iona

Oban

5

St Andrews

Colonsay

Jura

Loch
Lomond

9

Glasgow●

2

Edinburgh●
,Rosslyn

4

Islay

Arran

●Alloway

Abbotsford

3

Dumfries●

2 Edinburgh
3 Southern Scotland
4 Glasgow and West Central Scotland
5 Trossachs, Argyll and Western Highlands
6 The Hebrides
7 The North, Orkney and Shetland
8 Aberdeenshire and Perthshire
9 Dundee, Angus and Fife

N

0 25 50 75 100

Kilometres

Note: Map numbers refer to book chapters

❧ 1 ❧

Introduction

Scotland wasn't always part of Great Britain. In the distant reaches of geological time, the landmass that roughly corresponds with modern Scotland was on a separate tectonic plate from modern England and Wales. Eight hundred million years ago it was south of the equator; 600 million years ago it was part of North America, separated from England and the rest of the European continent by an ocean. Over time, despite modern appearances, Scotland was a desert, a swamp and a rainforest. About 410 million years ago the gap between Scotland and England closed. Collisions and tectonic movements caused volcanic eruptions which brought islands such as Skye and St Kilda into being. This long pre-history of separation means that Scotland's geology is different from the rest of Britain, and its distinctive landscape of deep glens, dramatic mountains and fragmented coastlines has produced a culture different from that in other parts of the landmass it now shares. Scotland's landscape is one of the most important influences on its culture today, with millions visiting the Highlands and Islands each year, or at least climbing the slope to Edinburgh Castle, perched on an extinct volcano in the middle of the capital city. It was to the scenic glens of the southern Highlands, rich in the history and legends of their fiercely independent clans, that tourists flocked in the nineteenth century, guided by the novels and poetry of Sir Walter Scott. For a present-day literary traveller there are countless places to explore, from rugged mountains to bustling city streets, from islands with Viking heritage to the quiet farming communities that produced some of the world's most famous writers.

The history of Scotland is a story of repeated waves of immigration and emigration, of languages and cultures informing one another to produce what the contemporary Scottish novelist William McIlvanney has called 'a mongrel nation'. Perhaps surprisingly, the people known as the Scots weren't the original inhabitants of Scotland: they came in relatively late in the country's history. Evidence of widespread human inhabitation in Scotland dates from around 9,000 years ago, and by the Neolithic period around 5,000 years ago substantial civilisations existed, wealthy and extensive enough to build large monuments such as Maeshowe and the Ring of Brodgar in Orkney. These sites still stand today and have been wondered over and celebrated by generations of writers; in some cases the stones have even been written on. Scotland was the northern frontier of the Roman Empire, and its patchwork of Celtic tribes, collectively named 'Caledonians' by the Roman historian Tacitus, were never fully conquered by the legions. It was only after the Roman Empire declined that the Scots arrived. They were a Gaelic-speaking tribe from Ireland, whose gradual conquest of the west coast of Scotland culminated in the establishment of the kingdom of Dál Riata, which had its heyday in the sixth and seventh centuries and ruled much of the Hebrides and the Argyll peninsula. Saint Columba, an Irish prince, led a mission to spread Christianity on the west coast at this time. He arrived in 563 and soon founded a monastery on the small island of Iona. This was to become the religious and cultural centre of medieval Scotland, a place of art and learning: the illuminated Book of Kells, now one of Ireland's historic treasures, was started there.

In the middle of the ninth century Kenneth MacAlpin unified the western kingdom of the Scots with an eastern kingdom ruled by a people called the Picts, forging a single country whose territory covered much of modern-day Scotland. Kenneth and his successors were under constant threat from the Vikings, who ruled the northern archipelagos of Orkney and Shetland and frequently raided both coasts of Scotland. Orkney and Shetland only became part of Scotland in the fifteenth century, and their Norse heritage is still important to their modern inhabitants, one of whom was writer George Mackay Brown, whose poetry and fiction hark back to the Norse sagas written and set on Orkney. Among the kings of the early Scottish state was the eleventh-century Macbeth, maligned in later centuries as the archetype of the bloodthirsty tyrant, but in reality a more pious and generous king than Shakespeare allows.

As Scotland established itself as a unified country, it increasingly came to blows with its larger, more powerful neighbour, and many of Scotland's castles date from the medieval period, when a succession of English kings tried to incorporate Scotland into their dominions. The Scots, in turn, made repeated incursions into England. Matters came to a head in 1290 when a royal succession crisis led the thirteen candidates for the Scottish throne to ask Edward I of England to decide who had the strongest claim. Edward's choice, John Balliol, failed to assert his autonomy from the English king, and by the end of 1295 Scotland and England were at war. Within a few months Edward had annexed Scotland, in the process earning himself the nickname 'Hammer of the Scots'. The Scottish resistance was led by William Wallace. In one of the first books to be printed in Scotland, the sprawling poem *The Wallace*, written by a bard known only as Blind Harry, Wallace was portrayed as a near-legendary freedom fighter. Harry's patriotic interpretation of history stuck, and one modern legacy of the poem is Mel Gibson's 1995 film *Braveheart*. In 1297 Wallace won the Battle of Stirling Bridge, but his campaign was ultimately unsuccessful and he was executed in London in 1305. Scotland's decisive victory in the Wars of Independence came in 1314 at the Battle of Bannockburn, when the Scots were led by Robert the Bruce: the victory cemented his claim to the title of Robert I, king of an independent Scotland.

Robert I's victory ensured the continuing survival of the cultures and languages that existed in Scotland. The Celtic language of Gaelic was the dominant tongue in the Highlands and the Western Isles, the regions where it still survives today. In the lowlands, Scots was more common and in time it became the language of court. The debate about whether Scots is a separate language from English or merely a dialect of it has gone to and fro for centuries. Scots and English evolved from a similar Anglo-Saxon source, but Scots grew apart from English in the Middle Ages until, by the Renaissance, it was markedly different from its southern cousin. John Barbour's fourteenth-century poem *The Bruce*, written a generation after the Battle of Bannockburn, is one of the oldest surviving works written in Scots. In the fifteenth and sixteenth centuries poets – including William Dunbar, Robert Henryson and Gavin Douglas – were at the forefront of a golden age for verse in Scots. Many of the Border ballads, the narrative poems that are the mainstay of the Scots oral tradition, also date from this time. Gaelic and Scots, along with English, remain the three literary languages of Scotland today.

Scotland and England enjoyed a tempestuous relationship until the Union of the Crowns in 1603 when, after the death of Queen Elizabeth I, James VI of Scotland was crowned James I of England. For a century the two countries shared a monarch but remained technically separate from each other, with different churches and legal systems. However, when James's son, Charles I, was executed, the Civil Wars affected Scotland as well as England. Among the warring factions were the Covenanters, hard-line Protestants who opposed Catholic and Anglican influences upon Scottish souls (the Reformation left an indelible mark on Scotland's religious and political life). After the Catholic King James II was deposed in 1688, the Highland clan chiefs, many of whom remained loyal to the King and didn't share the Protestantism of southern Scotland, were involved in an unsuccessful Jacobite rising to re-establish James's Stuart dynasty. Pro-Jacobite unrest culminated in further risings in 1715 and 1745; both failed to bring back James or his descendants.

A further change came to Scotland in 1707 with the Act of Union. A disastrous attempt to found a colony at Darien, in modern Panama, bankrupted the country and the only solution was full union with England. Scotland was no longer an independent country, but a part of the United Kingdom. In 1746 the Battle of Culloden, where Jacobite forces were led by Prince Charles Edward Stuart, known as 'Bonnie Prince Charlie', proved to be a decisive defeat, and the British government's subsequent crackdown on dissent in the Highlands brought an end to the traditional clan system and the power of clan chiefs.

Access to English trade markets proved a windfall for Scottish merchants, and the wealth of the rapidly expanding cities of Edinburgh, Glasgow, Aberdeen and Dundee was founded on colonial trade and industry. As these cities grew in the eighteenth and nineteenth centuries, the country's northern rural areas faced waves of emigration, some forced and some voluntary, a process of depopulation known today as the Highland Clearances. Scotland changed immensely in the Industrial Revolution, and one of the results of this was a flowering of Scottish literature as writers explored the nation's past and tried to come to terms with its present.

Robert Burns, Scotland's national bard, whose worldwide fame is partly a result of his popularity among emigrating Scots, was inspired by the country's traditional songs. For example, in 'Auld Lang Syne', now the universal marker of New Year, Burns combines his own words with an older Scots melody. A generation after Burns, Sir Walter Scott became the most successful novelist of the early nineteenth century. Although his writing is often concerned with Scotland's historical events, including the Jacobite risings, Scott captivated an international readership and his striking depictions of Scotland's landscape brought large numbers of tourists to the country for the first time. In the late nineteenth century another giant of Scottish literature, Robert Louis Stevenson, also turned to pivotal moments in national history; *Kidnapped*, one of his best-loved novels, is set in the aftermath of Culloden.

The Act of Union and the quashing of Jacobite unrest made travel in the Highlands and Islands easier and safer than ever before, bringing writers and artists as well as regular tourists. James Boswell and Samuel Johnson toured the Western Isles in 1773. In the early nineteenth century Romantic writers, including William and Dorothy Wordsworth, Samuel Taylor Coleridge and John Keats, sought inspiration beside Scotland's lochs and glens. Famous writers in their own right, they were also among the first literary travellers to Scotland, visiting locations such as Burns's Cottage and the folly where the mythical Celtic bard Ossian was supposed to have dwelled.

Scotland faced the twentieth century's ups and downs as part of the United Kingdom, but in some ways its culture diverged from the rest of the country as the century progressed. In the 1920s and 1930s the 'Scottish Renaissance', a period in which Scottish writers and artists increasingly asserted a distinct Scottish national identity, was led by figures including the poet Hugh MacDiarmid and the novelist Lewis Grassic Gibbon. Whilst aware of Scotland's history, they were also concerned with its future, engaging in critiques of society, technology, gender and other pressing issues. They sought to show that Scottish literature was not only about misty glens and ancient clans, and that Scots had more to take pride in than the whisky, tartan, bagpipes and haggis that are their most famous cultural exports. These writers and artists gave birth to contemporary Scotland's cultural nationalism, and it's partly because of the Scottish Renaissance that the country evolved into the dynamic and vibrant society it is today. Scotland boasts a world-class arts scene, with international festivals, traditional, classical and contemporary musicians, filmmakers, poets, novelists, playwrights, computer games designers, visual artists and many more making it an exciting and confident twenty-first-century nation.

Any literary travel guide to a country as large and old as Scotland is bound to feel like a whistle-stop tour, with so many places rich in literary and cultural history to visit. There isn't the space here to include every location that every writer has lived in, visited or been inspired by: figures such as Scott and Burns travelled and wrote widely about their country, and tourists like Boswell and Johnson likewise covered a great deal of ground. In selecting the places and writers mentioned in this guide, I have sometimes turned off the beaten track in the hope that readers will discover new locations and writers to explore further. There are writers here from every era, natives of Scotland, visitors, émigrés and those who have made the country their adopted home. As a result, a diverse range of genres and styles sit side by side, from hard-boiled crime writing to lyric poetry and from urban realism to meditations upon mountains. I hope that there will be something for every reader and that you will come to think of the literature mentioned here as an essential part of what makes each place unique and enticing. Works of literature, like places, can be inhabited by those who spend time getting familiar with them. And in time both can come to inhabit the reader, or visitor, too.

❦ 2 ❦

EDINBURGH

City of Literature

Arriving in the City

Edinburgh wastes no time in proclaiming its literary credentials. Arriving in the city by train you disembark at Waverley Station, named after Sir Walter Scott's hugely influential novel, *Waverley*. Stepping out of the station onto Princes Street, one of the first landmarks you see is the Scott Monument, built after the author's death in 1832. The monument is a testament to Scott's influence on Scottish and world literature, but also to the vital role he played in the formation of Scotland's modern cultural identity. Although his reputation as a poet and novelist has diminished since he was a nineteenth-century bestseller, it's fitting that a literary tour of Scotland should begin with the writer nicknamed the 'Wizard of the North', and Scott will be a presiding spirit as we travel around Edinburgh and throughout the country.

Like a volcano on a fault line, the Scott Monument marks a boundary, in this case between the Old and New Towns of Edinburgh. When the monument is approached from Waverley Station the focal points of the medieval Old Town – Castle Rock and the Royal Mile – loom above and to the south; to the north lies the elegant New Town, an eighteenth-century masterpiece of urban planning. At over 60 metres high, the Scott Monument is the tallest memorial in the world dedicated to a writer. It's hard to think of any other city that has honoured one of its writers in so physical

1 The Scott Monument, ready for lift-off

a way. It's as if the Albert Memorial in London was dedicated to Shakespeare instead of the Prince Consort, and its primary station was King Lear rather than King's Cross.

Scott was born in 1771, the son of an Edinburgh lawyer. He followed his father into law but in 1802 began his literary career when he compiled and published the first volume of *The Minstrelsy of the Scottish Border*, an anthology of ballads and folk songs. Between 1805 and 1810 he published his own long narrative poems *The Lay of the Last Minstrel*, *Marmion* and *The Lady of the Lake*. These were phenomenally successful, selling by the thousand and garnering praise from contemporaries, including Lord Byron. The 1,000-guinea payment Scott received for *Marmion* was the first literary 'advance', and in 1811 he used his literary earnings to buy a farm in the Scottish Borders which he developed into the Abbotsford estate. It was when Scott turned to writing novels, however, that he became a literary colossus. In 1814 his anonymously published

Waverley was a sensation. The novel is an engrossing yarn filled with rugged landscapes, dangerous outlaws and charismatic clan chiefs, set during the 1745 Jacobite rising. Scott was astonishingly prolific – over the next 17 years he wrote a further 26 novels, as well as plays and non-fiction – and his work gained an international readership.

Some of Scott's most popular books, including *The Lady of the Lake* and *Waverley*, are set in the Scottish Highlands, and these kick-started the Scottish tourist industry as people flocked to experience the sublime landscapes, tranquil lochs and brooding castles that Scott evoked. In 1820 he was knighted by King George IV, and two years later organised the King's landmark visit to Edinburgh, the first by a reigning British monarch since 1650. For the occasion Scott choreographed a tartan pageant (even the King wore a kilt), accompanied by bagpipes and Highland dancing. Walking about Edinburgh today, with its barrage of busking pipers, whisky-and-shortbread gift shops, kilt-makers and pseudo-Celtic souvenirs, you could be forgiven for thinking that Scott's pageant has never come to an end.

The Scott Monument was opened in 1846, 14 years after the author's death. Seen from Princes Street Gardens, it's spectacular: a central spire tapers into the Edinburgh sky, supported by four smaller spires connected in the style of a Gothic cathedral's flying buttresses. When Charles Dickens (whose wife was a native of Edinburgh) saw the monument, he quipped that 'it is like the spire of a Gothic church taken off and stuck in the ground.' Modern commentators can seldom resist comparing it to a space rocket. The cathedral effect is enhanced by the monument's 64 statuettes in alcoves, which represent characters from Scott's novels as well as historical figures such as Robert the Bruce, Mary Queen of Scots and Bonnie Prince Charlie, and literary luminaries ranging from Robert Burns to Paisley-born 'Weaver Poet' Robert Tannahill. There are several viewing decks, the highest reached by a claustrophobic climb up 287 steps, but it's worth the effort for the panoramic views of the city: Princes Street and its gardens below; the River Forth and Fife to the north; the observatory and Greek-style folly on Calton

Hill to the east; the rugged crags of Arthur's Seat to the south-east; Edinburgh Castle to the south.

Central Edinburgh is a jumble of architectural styles, comprising townhouses, department stores, churches, galleries, gardens and rocky outcrops. It has made a vivid impression on many writers arriving in the city. In the early 1920s the Czech writer Karel Čapek, who is remembered today for coining the term 'robot', toured Britain and published a record of his travels as *Letters from England* (a title guaranteed to rile Scottish and Welsh readers – Čapek wrote his 'letters' from these countries too). He was immediately captivated by the architecture, history and grandeur of Edinburgh:

> An English friend of mine was almost right when he declared Edinburgh to be the finest city in the world. It is a fine place, stonily grey and strange of aspect. Where in other cities a river flows, there a railway runs; on one side is the old town, on the other side the new one, with streets wider than anywhere else, every vista showing a statue or a church; and in the old town the houses are appallingly high.

Čapek isn't the only visitor to have been struck by Edinburgh's dramatic skyline. In 1850 Charlotte Brontë, perhaps showing a bias towards northern parts of Britain, wrote fondly of Edinburgh in a letter to her editor, W. S. Williams:

> My dear Sir, do not think I blaspheme when I tell you that your Great London as compared to Dun-Edin 'mine own romantic town' is as prose compared to poetry, or as a great, rambling, heavy Epic – compared to a lyric, bright, brief, clear and vital as a flash of lightning.

Brontë, like many a nineteenth-century visitor to Edinburgh, was seduced at least in part by Scott's fiction and its romanticisation of all things Scottish: for her, walking in the footsteps of her literary hero was clearly a sublime experience. And for Brontë, as for the modern visitor, the Edinburgh landmark that above all else takes your breath away is the imposing Castle, perched almost 100 metres above Princes Street Gardens on Castle Rock.

Edinburgh Castle

Standing on the castle ramparts, surveying the city on a cold Edinburgh day, it's easy to appreciate that this building has played a pivotal role in Edinburgh's, and Scotland's, history. St Margaret's Chapel, the oldest remaining building in the castle complex, was built around 1140 by King David I. Since that time the castle has played host to royal power struggles and sieges, to the fractious reign of Mary Queen of Scots in the sixteenth century, and to the Jacobite rising in 1745. By the time that it was occupied by Bonnie Prince Charlie's forces, the castle's heyday as a royal residence was over. And from the time of Scott onwards, it became the flagship of Scotland's heritage industry. Today the castle is an incredibly popular tourist attraction, with visitors flocking to its complex of historic buildings.

As so often in Edinburgh, evidence of Walter Scott's hand can be seen in this reinvention of the castle. In Scott's day, the castle was primarily a garrison and military prison. However, its role began to change in 1818 when the Prince Regent, soon to be George IV, granted Scott permission to search the castle for the lost Honours of Scotland – the crown, sceptre and sword worn by monarchs of Scotland before the Act of Union which joined England and Scotland. This royal regalia had an almost legendary status in Scott's day. Dating from the fifteenth and sixteenth centuries, the items were hidden under a church floor during Oliver Cromwell's rule before being returned to Charles II following the Restoration of the monarchy. After the Union they fell out of use, were locked safely away in an oak chest in Edinburgh Castle, and promptly forgotten. When the team led by Scott found them over a century later, they were put on display and have remained so ever since: they are now given pride of place in the castle's exhibition on Scottish history.

For a while the castle retained its military function. In the First World War Eric Linklater was among the soldiers stationed there, and he later described the place vividly in his fiction. In *Magnus Merriman*, his satirical skewering of Scottish nationalism (Linklater was himself a nationalist candidate in 1933), he captures the nature of its modern-day besiegers:

> It is a castle of moods, now merely antiquated, now impregnable, now the work of giants and now of dreams; a fairy castle, a haunted castle, a castle in Spain, a castle you may enter with a twopenny guide in your hand [. . .] it is Scotland's castle, Queen Mary's castle, and the castle of fifty thousand annual visitors who walk through it with rain on their boots and bewilderment in their hearts.

Linklater's description, written in 1934, is still accurate: the only amendments a contemporary writer would make would be to add several zeros to the number of annual visitors, and to place audio guides and smartphones in their hands.

Castle Rock is a steep crag on three sides, and the only way to approach the castle is from the shallower, western side. Here the esplanade at the castle entrance meets the Royal Mile, the street – or rather, series of adjoined streets – that runs downhill to Holyrood Palace and the Scottish Parliament. This is the centre of Edinburgh's Old Town, and is such a gold mine of literary, political and social history that this chapter can only scratch its sooty, weathered surface.

The Upper Royal Mile: The Lawnmarket

To walk down the Royal Mile is to stroll through history. Much of the Old Town's medieval street plan remains, and many of the buildings date back to the Reformation. Architecturally, it's eclectic:

gables jut out above the road; spires bristle from churches; medieval stonework sits awkwardly beside 1960s concrete. Many closes – the alleyways and courtyards named after famous inhabitants and long-closed marketplaces – have their entrances on the Royal Mile. For centuries the city's population lived in this cluster of winding alleyways and tall dark buildings, and the smoke from their hearths and industries earned Edinburgh the nickname 'Auld Reekie', which means 'Old Smoky' in Scots. Conditions were cramped, dingy and pretty unpleasant. In 1727 in *A Tour Through the Whole Island of Great Britain*, Daniel Defoe commented that it seemed 'as if the People were not as willing to live sweet and clean as other Nations, but delighted in Stench and Nastiness'. He drew attention to the Old Town's 'mountainous Situation, throng'd Buildings, from seven to ten or twelve storeys high' and concluded 'that in no City in the World so many people live in so little Room as at Edinburgh'. Defoe, it should be noted, wasn't necessarily an impartial observer; he worked as a spy and propagandist for the English government in the lead-up to the 1707 Act of Union.

In the eighteenth and nineteenth centuries new bridges and buildings changed the look and layout of Edinburgh. The spacious Georgian terraces of the New Town became fashionable residences and many Old Town closes fell into disrepair, becoming slums. These slums have since been cleared, and the Royal Mile is now a mix of housing, pubs, arts venues, hotels, museums, shops and offices. Each August during the Festival the streets teem with thousands of budding playwrights, actors, comedians, musicians, magicians and artists.

Few writers who have lived in or visited Edinburgh can resist engaging with this combination of history, dark and atmospheric alleyways, grand buildings and the juxtaposition of wealth and poverty. In his 1968 poem 'Old Edinburgh', Norman MacCaig envisages a personification of history leaning against the dark doorway of a close, muttering about the pity and poverty of the past. Robert Louis Stevenson, another Edinburgh-born writer, was a master of bringing this past to life and gives an immersive sense of the bustling eighteenth-century Old Town in *Catriona*, his novel of political intrigue. In Stevenson's story the Royal Mile is populated by lawyers, notaries, merchants, aristocratic ladies and renegade Highlanders. Set in 1751, soon after the quashing of the Jacobite rising, the book characterises a city on the cusp of modernising and becoming an important part of the emergent British Empire. Contemporary Edinburgh's greatest chronicler is the crime writer Ian Rankin, whose Detective Inspector John Rebus walks the same Old Town streets and finds no shortage of underworld secrets to investigate in this claustrophobic cityscape.

The top section of the Royal Mile is the Lawnmarket, a short street containing old closes in which numerous literary celebrities and notorious figures have lived. David Hume, born in 1711 and regarded by some as the greatest and most readable English-speaking philosopher, lived first in Riddell's Close – his residency is marked by a plaque – and from 1762 in James Court, on the opposite side of the Lawnmarket. During his lifetime Hume's scepticism of religion was socially unacceptable in his native city, in which the Presbyterian Church of Scotland was a powerful cultural and political force, and despite his intellect and his influential treatises, he was passed over for the Chair of Moral Philosophy at the University of Edinburgh. Nevertheless Hume was a popular figure in the Old Town, frequenting taverns and gaining the affection of contemporaries such as Adam Smith who praised his wisdom, virtue and affability.

Hume was a principal figure in what is now known as the Scottish Enlightenment, the period in which Scotland's intellectual and scientific achievements flourished. A statue of Hume, completed in 1995, now sits near to his old Royal Mile residences outside Edinburgh High Court. Half a mile away in the University Quarter the David Hume Tower, built in 1970, houses many of the University of Edinburgh's lecture theatres. It is best visited in the imagination only, as in Jennie Erdal's 2012 novel *The Missing*

Shade of Blue, in which a French translator of Hume's works visits Edinburgh and describes his impressions of the building:

> I had imagined that a building bearing the name David Hume Tower would be an elegant eighteenth-century affair, with an ornate roof and a grand entrance, something like the Château de Bagatelle in Paris. But no, it was a huge block of concrete, whose ugliness made me gasp. Of course, there are tower blocks like it in any metropolis, even in complacently beautiful cities like Munich, but generally they are hidden away on the outskirts, housing the disadvantaged high above ground level and protecting the civic conscience. By contrast, the David Hume Tower seemed like a terrible blemish in the heart of Edinburgh, and brazen with it.

James Court was a late addition to the Old Town, and a prestigious address; its other famous resident was James Boswell. Boswell was born in 1740, the eldest son of Lord Auchinleck, an Edinburgh judge. As a young man he travelled widely in Europe, gaining a reputation as a libertine, and was friends with famous intellectuals including Voltaire and Jean-Jacques Rousseau, with whose mistress he had a brief affair. Although he practised law, his reputation today rests almost entirely on his friendship with London's pre-eminent man of letters, Dr Samuel Johnson, and on his ground-breaking biography *The Life of Samuel Johnson*, published in 1791. Boswell published many political and cultural essays in his lifetime and first wrote about Johnson in his *Journal of a Tour to the Hebrides*, the account of a journey they took together in 1773. Johnson's opinion of Edinburgh was, at best, ambivalent. Boswell tells of their first evening together in the city:

> Late in the evening, I received a note from him, that he was arrived at Boyd's Inn, at the head of the Canongate [. . .] before I came in, the Doctor had unluckily had a bad specimen of Scottish cleanliness. He then drank no fermented liquor. He asked to have

his lemonade made sweeter; upon which the waiter, with his greasy fingers, lifted a lump of sugar, and put it into it. The Doctor, in indignation, threw it out of the window.

Johnson stayed in Edinburgh for four nights as Boswell's guest and Boswell records Johnson's endless sardonic comments about the Scottish capital.

A few steps down the Lawnmarket from Boswell's old home is Lady Stair's Close. Robert Burns, on his first visit to Edinburgh, stayed in a house on the east side of this close, in a dark poky room with thin walls and ceilings, under the watchful eye of a landlady, Mrs Carfrae, whom he immortalised as 'a flesh-disciplining, godly Matron' with a 'staid, sober, piously-disposed, sculduggery-abhoring' manner. Whether this is a fair description or not will never be known, but as a personification of her city, Mrs Carfrae is perfect. Excited by the critical success of his first volume of poetry, *Poems, Chiefly in the Scottish Dialect*, Burns arrived in Edinburgh in November 1786 and met the city's movers and shakers, including his future publisher, William Creech. Burns relished playing the cosmopolitan man-about-town. He was welcomed into the Crochallan Fencibles, a laddish drinking club that met in a tavern on nearby Anchor Close, where they sang bawdy songs and engaged in 'rough banter'. Dressed in a ruffled shirt, dark coat and buckskin breeches, with his unpowdered hair casually strewn over his forehead, Burns cut a dashing figure in the rowdier parts of the Old Town.

Although the building in which Burns stayed is now demolished, Lady Stair's Close has a fitting afterlife. Lady Stair's House, a seventeenth-century townhouse with many period features, now serves as a museum dedicated to Burns, Scott and Stevenson. It holds original manuscripts, early editions of their works, portraits and artefacts, including Scott's rocking horse (one footrest is higher than the other to compensate for his crippling childhood polio), the sword-stick carried by Burns when he worked as an exciseman, and the ring given to Stevenson by a Samoan chieftain. Outside the house in what is now called Makars' Court – 'makar' being the Scots word for a poet – the flagstones are engraved with quotes by many of Scotland's greatest writers, from the fourteenth-century poet John Barbour to Muriel Spark, who died in 2006.

Brodie's Close is across the road from Lady Stair's, and is named after Francis Brodie, the father of the notorious William Brodie. William, who lived in Edinburgh at the time of Hume, Boswell and Burns, inherited his father's role as Deacon of Wrights, a position which gave him responsibility for the installation of doors and locks for the city's businesses. Such was the respect he garnered in this position that he was granted a seat on the town council. However, following a spate of high-profile robberies in 1787, it transpired that he was also the leader of a criminal gang blessed with a seemingly miraculous ability to open locked doors. Deacon Brodie was tried in Edinburgh and, found guilty, was hanged on a gibbet made in his own workshop.

Brodie's story is that of a man who appeared genteel and respectable by day, but who engaged in criminal and immoral acts under the veil of night. Unsurprisingly, his character has inspired Edinburgh writers to examine the concept of the split personality. Most famously, Stevenson's *The Strange Case of Dr Jekyll and Mr Hyde* tells of a well-regarded professional man with a sinister and violent alter ego. More than a few critics have noted that although the novella claims to be set in London, its dark, narrow lanes and Georgian terraces bear close resemblance to Stevenson's hometown of Edinburgh. More recently, in Muriel Spark's psychological novel *The Prime of Miss Jean Brodie*, about the relationship between a group of schoolgirls and their charismatic but manipulative teacher, the eponymous Miss Brodie dubiously claims her descent from this infamous criminal: 'I am a descendant, do not forget, of William Brodie, a man of substance, a cabinet maker and designer of gibbets, a member of the Town Council of Edinburgh and a keeper of two mistresses who bore him five children between them. Blood tells.'

Spark, crafting her masterpiece about a contradictory woman living in a city of contrasts, finds in Deacon Brodie a perfect image of this complexity. Blood tells, but so does the desire of a teenager to shake off the influences of childhood. Miss Brodie is 'betrayed' by Sandy, the most perceptive of her pupils, who has grown indignant about the extent of her teacher's control over the girls of the 'Brodie Set' and informs her headmistress of Brodie's flirtation with fascism. Brodie loses her job and with it her *raison d'être* while Sandy, perhaps consumed by guilt, becomes a nun and writes a psychological treatise that she later claims was influenced by 'a Miss Jean Brodie in her prime'.

George IV Bridge and the Grassmarket

Leading off to the south of the Lawnmarket is George IV Bridge, an elevated road constructed in the 1830s to connect the Old Town with the southern New Town extension of the city. The National Library of Scotland, one of Britain's five copyright libraries, is located here. Opposite it is the Elephant House café, decorated on one wall with newspaper clippings about the writers who have frequented it. Ian Rankin and Alexander McCall Smith have spent time writing at its coffee-stained wooden tables, and the café features in brief scenes in Rankin's *Fleshmarket Close* and Smith's *Love Over Scotland*. But by far the most famous patron of the café is J. K. Rowling, who was a regular customer when she began working on the Harry Potter books.

Rowling moved to Edinburgh in 1993 and completed *Harry Potter and the Philosopher's Stone* while living in a one-bedroom flat in Leith, to the north-west of the city centre. The idea for a young wizard called Harry Potter came to Rowling on a train journey from Manchester to London. If this was where he was 'born', then he spent his infanthood in Edinburgh. Harry and his friends don't actually spend any time in Edinburgh, although it's easy to imagine the Old Town's closes, medieval buildings and narrow flights of stairs inspiring Rowling's Diagon Alley. In recent years The Elephant House has become a pilgrimage site for Potter fans, and its toilets have a secondary role as message boards, scrawled with countless messages about the books. The café makes no secret of its wizarding connections: a sign in the window proclaims it to be the 'birthplace of Harry Potter'. It's also not hard to find alternative cafés in the city which boast that 'J. K. Rowling *didn't* write here.'

A couple of doors down from the Elephant House is the Frankenstein theme bar, which cheekily claims to have been established in 1818, the year that Mary Shelley's novel was first published. The bar itself has no connections with Shelley or her novel, but is a reminder that Victor Frankenstein spent a week in Edinburgh on his way north in search of a remote location in which to build his monster a mate. Like many visitors, Victor and his friend Clerval are impressed by the unique atmosphere of the city:

> I visited Edinburgh with languid eyes and mind; and yet that city might have interested the most unfortunate being. Clerval did not like it so well as Oxford [. . .] But the beauty and regularity of the new town of Edinburgh, its romantic castle, and its environs, the most delightful in the world, Arthur's Seat, St Bernard's Well, and the Pentland Hills, compensated him for the change.

George IV Bridge ends at the junction with Candlemaker Row, opposite the National Museum of Scotland. On this corner is a plinth raising the statue of a Skye Terrier called Greyfriars Bobby. The story goes that Bobby belonged to John Gray, an Edinburgh nightwatchman, who died in 1858 and was buried in Greyfriars Kirkyard, across the road from the present-day statue. For 14 years Bobby is said to have guarded his master's grave and won fame and plaudits for his loyalty. In a quintessentially Victorian fit of sentiment, the lord provost of Edinburgh paid for Bobby's licence and collar (the collar is now in the Museum of Edinburgh). Bobby died in 1872 and was buried just inside the graveyard; a year later Lady Burdett-Coutts, a philanthropist, had the statue erected – originally it doubled as a drinking fountain, with an upper section for humans and a lower section for dogs. The dog's story has inspired several books, most notably Eleanor Atkinson's 1912 novelisation *Greyfriars Bobby*. Bobby remains the most popular dog in Scottish folk culture, and his statue is so well handled by schoolchildren and tourists that in 2013 Edinburgh Council attempted to restore his nose, which they deemed had become too shiny.

The graveyard from which Bobby takes his name has no shortage of famous two-legged inhabitants, including the poets George Buchanan, Allan Ramsay, Duncan Ban Macintyre and William McGonagall, all of whom played significant roles in Scottish literary history. Also buried here is William Creech, the bookseller-*cum*-agent who helped establish Robert Burns as Scotland's leading poet, and James Hutton, the eighteenth-century geologist whose *Theory of the Earth* and *An Investigation of the Principles of Knowledge* were seminal in proving that the Earth is millions of years old.

Follow Candlemaker Row downhill past Greyfriars Kirkyard and you arrive at the Grassmarket, which gets its name from its former use as a market for grazing animals. Broad and open, like a pedestrianised boulevard or an elongated square, it's lined with pubs, restaurants, cafés and hotels, and in the summer musicians and street performers play here, overlooked by the magnificent southern crags of Castle Rock. Compared with the rest of the Old Town, with its narrow closes and steep flights of steps, the Grassmarket feels positively European. It's a place to sit outside with a long drink while the world hurries by, and indeed the area has long been the site of inns and hostelries. William and Dorothy Wordsworth stayed here during their 1803 tour of Scotland, with Dorothy describing their surroundings as 'not noisy, and tolerably cheap', a glowing recommendation compared to her comments on many of the rural hotels she had endured on their Scottish journey. The Wordsworths lodged at the White Hart Inn, as Robert Burns did on his 1791 visit to the city. The White Hart still sits on the northern side of the Grassmarket, a small traditional pub and an Edinburgh institution. It claims to be the city's oldest pub, with cellars dating back to 1516, and perhaps because of this long history it has also been proclaimed the most haunted pub in Edinburgh.

It's easy to see why drinkers hunched over their whisky and ale two centuries ago might have seen ghosts here. The Grassmarket doubled as a place of execution, and at the eastern end a saltire on rose-coloured cobblestones marks the spot where many Protestant Covenanters were put to death in the 'Killing Time' between 1661 and 1688. Beside this memorial the shadow of a gibbet is outlined in dark cobbles. One of James Boswell's first criminal clients was hanged here in 1775, and in 1829 Sir Walter Scott witnessed the execution of William Burke. With his fellow criminal, William Hare, Burke had sold the corpses of his 16 murder victims to an anatomy professor, Robert Knox, for dissection in lectures. Their tale resembles that that of Deacon Brodie in its combination of Knox's professional respectability and underworld criminality. Burke and Hare have captivated writers and filmmakers, including Stevenson again (in his story 'The Body Snatcher', later made into a film starring Boris Karloff), Dylan Thomas (in his screenplay *The Doctor and the Devils*) and Simon Pegg and Andy Serkis in their 2010 comedy film *Burke & Hare*.

When Scott saw Burke hanged he was part of a crowd 25,000 strong. In his 1818 novel *The Heart of Midlothian* he tells the story of another Grassmarket execution. The novel is loosely based on the events of 1736, when the brutal Captain John Porteous fired a musket into the crowd at the hanging of a popular smuggler. Porteous was found guilty of murder but received a royal reprieve, provoking a mob to storm the Tolbooth Prison on the Royal Mile, convey Porteous to the Grassmarket, and lynch him. These events form the opening of Scott's novel, although its primary focus is on the plight of its heroine, Jeanie Deans, whose sister is imprisoned in the Tolbooth at the same time as Porteous, having been wrongly accused of infanticide. The novel has an epic sweep: Jeanie, a woman of humble means but characterised by honesty, faith and determination, travels to London on foot and eventually secures an audience with Queen Caroline to intercede for her sister. Jeanie is Scott's strongest female character, and the popularity of the book led to many Scottish pubs, ships and trains being named 'Jeanie Deans'. The Grassmarket itself is the other dominant presence in the novel, and Scott evokes it vividly:

[F]ew of the houses which surround it were, even in early times, inhabited by persons of fashion; so that those likely to be offended or over deeply affected by such unpleasant exhibitions were not in the way of having their quiet disturbed by them [. . .] The fatal day was announced to the public, by the appearance of a huge black gallows-tree towards the eastern end of the Grassmarket. This ill-omened apparition was of great height, with a scaffolding surrounding it, and a double ladder placed against it, for the ascent of the unhappy criminal and the executioner. As this apparatus was always arranged before dawn, it seemed as if the gallows had grown out of the earth in the course of one night, like the production of some foul demon.

Scott's description of a down-at-heel Grassmarket held true for a long time. In Muriel Spark's *The Prime of Miss Jean Brodie*, set in the 1930s, the teacher leads her middle-class pupils through here on their way to the Royal Mile. For Sandy, her most observant pupil, it's a culture shock:

It was Sandy's first experience of a foreign country, which intimates itself by its new smells and shapes and its new poor. A man sat on the icy-cold pavement; he just sat. A crowd of children, some without shoes, were playing some fight game, and some shouted after Miss Brodie's violet-clad company, with words that the girls had not heard before, but rightly understood to be obscene.

The Grassmarket itself is now home to less vindictive forms of recreation than jeering at hangings or lynching the city guard; its inhabitants are more likely to be browsing its record shops and bistros than fighting. From its south-west corner runs the West Port, home to many of Edinburgh's best second-hand bookshops. The Traverse Theatre and the Usher Hall, the city's main concert hall, are nearby. Nevertheless, this is Edinburgh, and as its writers and readers know well, respectability by day goes hand-in-hand with shady goings-on under cover of darkness. Beyond the West Port lies the so-called 'pubic triangle' of strip clubs and showbars, which in Ian Rankin's crime books are frequented by sleazy punters, dodgy businessmen, crooks, councillors and politicians. To the east of the Grassmarket, on the other hand, lies the long, dark, dingy Cowgate. Again Rankin, writing in *Dead Souls*, is the best guide to this road: 'There were clubs still open down there, teenagers spilling on to the road. The police had names for the Cowgate when it got like this: Little Saigon; the blood bank; hell on earth. Even the patrol cars went in twos.'

In the fifteenth century aristocrats lived on this road. Gavin Douglas, appointed provost of St Giles' Cathedral around 1501, lived in an episcopal palace on the Cowgate. His was a turbulent time for the clergy: in 1515, the year he was promoted to bishop of Dunkeld, the Duke of Albany imprisoned him in Edinburgh Castle. Douglas is best remembered as a poet, one of the 'makars' of the first golden age of Scottish poetry. Douglas's *Eneados*, a Scots translation of Virgil's *Aeneid*, was one of the first full translations of a Classical epic into a vernacular language and has been described by some writers – including Ezra Pound – as better than the original. The highlights of Douglas's translation are the prologues of his own creation, which give a distinctly Scottish feel to the Mediterranean story. The prologue to Book VII contains a suitably grim image of medieval Edinburgh's streets in winter:

> The plane street is, and every hie way,
> Full of floshis [bogs], dubbis [puddles], mire and clay.

Ironically, Douglas's lines may now be best applied to the Cowgate, which has fallen from favour since his time.

The Royal Mile: High Street

From the Grassmarket, a series of short streets in the north-east corner snake uphill to George IV Bridge and lead back to the Royal Mile, where the Lawnmarket becomes High Street and continues its journey downhill to Holyrood. St Giles' Cathedral is the first major landmark on the right. The present building dates from the fourteenth century, although an earlier church on this site was destroyed by fire; its crown-topped steeple was added a little over 100 years later. The cathedral is in some ways the paradigm of an Edinburgh church: imposingly bulky and not exactly beautiful, with aggressive rather than ornamental flourishes, now soot-stained. On Miss Brodie's tour of Edinburgh, Sandy reflects that 'the outsides of old Edinburgh churches frightened her, they were of such dark stone, like presences almost the colour of the Castle rock, and were built so warningly with their upraised fingers.'

The interior of St Giles' is less daunting but nevertheless grand. Medieval heraldic carvings and modern stained-glass windows are dazzling in their different ways. A window from 1985 pays tribute to Robert Burns and is crowned with a sunburst that resembles the 'red, red rose' of one of the bard's most popular poems. Another colourful window, designed by Edward Burne-Jones and made in William Morris's workshop, features Old Testament heroines. On one aisle wall is a bronze memorial to Robert Louis Stevenson. He is swathed in blankets and holding a pen in his right hand, a late alteration as the sculptor, Augustus St Gaudens, had originally depicted him holding a cigarette.

St Giles' sits on a section of High Street that widens into Parliament Square. On the south side of the square is Parliament House, where the Scottish Parliament convened until the Act of Union of

1707, and where the Court of Session, Scotland's highest civil court, still sits. Parliament House boasts a grand hammer-beamed roof made of Scandinavian oak and there is also a statue of Sir Walter Scott, who was a clerk to the court. These halls have long been a hive of lawyers and judges. Thomas Carlyle, the Victorian essayist and social commentator, was struck by the bustling atmosphere on his first visit and reflected upon it in his *Reminiscences*, published after his death in 1881:

> An immense Hall, dimly lighted from the top of the walls [. . .] filled with what I thought (exaggeratively) a thousand or two of human creatures; all astir in a boundless buzz of talk, and simmering about in every direction [. . .] Higher up on the walls, stuck there like swallows in their nests, sat other humbler figures: these I found were the sources of certain wildly plangent lamentable kinds of sounds or echoes which from time to time pierced the universal noise of feet and voices, and rose unintelligibly above it, as if in the bitterness of incurable woe; – Criers of the Court, I gradually came to understand.

The Old Tolbooth, the prison which is stormed in Scott's *The Heart of Midlothian*, sat adjacent to Parliament Square until it was demolished in 1817 – Scott's novel takes its title from the Tolbooth's nickname. Its massive lock and key came into Scott's possession and form part of his collection of Scottish historical artefacts on display at Abbotsford. On the pavement near St Giles' is a red heart-shaped mosaic that indicates the Tolbooth's former location. There's a long tradition of Edinburgh's citizens spitting on this symbol of authority.

In Tobias Smollett's 1771 novel *The Expedition of Humphry Clinker*, a travelling Welsh squire called Matthew Bramble writes that High Street 'would be undoubtedly one of the noblest streets in Europe, if an ugly mass of mean buildings, called the Lucken-Booths, had not thrust itself, by what accident I know not, into the middle of the way'. Fortunately for the modern-day tourist, but perhaps unfortunately for historians, Edinburgh's town planners agreed with Bramble, and 30 years after the novel was published they demolished the Luckenbooths, which were a row of timber-fronted buildings that ran downhill from St Giles' in the middle of High Street. The Luckenbooths had been erected in about 1440 and effectively blocked the street. One of the most famous shopkeepers here was Allan Ramsay, who in 1726 opened a bookshop trading under a sign with the heads of Ben Jonson and William Drummond of Hawthornden on it. Ramsay was a key figure in the Scottish arts world of his day: in 1728 he established Scotland's first circulating library, and in 1736 he opened Edinburgh's first regular theatre in Carrubber's Close on the Royal Mile. Ramsay was also a poet, playwright, translator and publisher. His Scots-language poetry is often riotously bawdy, but has a satirical edge and inventiveness that won him admirers including Alexander Pope, John Gay and Robert Burns.

William Creech, the publisher and bookseller who made a handsome profit from the popularity of Burns's poetry (to which he owned copyright), also traded from the Luckenbooths. Like many successful and well-connected Edinburgh men, his influence extended into politics and the law. Notoriously mean with money, Creech had a quarrelsome relationship with his star poet: Burns's letters tell of his prolonged attempts to recoup money owed him by the bookseller. During one such wrangle, Burns dashed off a poem titled 'On William Creech', which begins:

> A little upright, pert, tart, tripping wight,
> And still his precious self his dear delight.

Burns goes on to lambast Creech's 'meddling vanity' and 'selfish craft'. Eventually their dispute was resolved and Creech paid Burns, though it seems he retained the upper hand. When the poet tried to get his own back by delaying to provide his publisher with corrections for a new edition of his poems, Creech simply went ahead and published the book without them.

This central stretch of High Street, from St Giles' to John Knox House, one of Edinburgh's oldest surviving houses, is considerably less cramped and smelly than it was when Ramsay and Creech traded here from the Luckenbooths. The modern road is now lined with pubs, hotels, restaurants and the ubiquitous souvenir shops hawking tartan, whisky, shortbread, haggis and Loch Ness Monster toys. There are, however, many narrow closes leading off High Street into the dark underbelly of the Old Town, and some of these are worth exploring. Mary King's Close, for example, is the entrance to a warren of underground streets that was closed up in 1645 in order to prevent the spread of plague; the legend goes that the council incarcerated the diseased here to die a slow and claustrophobic death. It's now preserved as a tourist attraction. This is the atmospheric site of a murder in Iain Banks's 1993 novel *Complicity*. Further down is Fleshmarket Close, so called because it used to lead to a slaughterhouse. With a name like that, however, it's little wonder that Ian Rankin named one of his crime thrillers after this steep close. In an early scene of the book, the skeletons of a woman and child are found in a pub cellar here, and while the police investigate, tour guides and landlords plan how they can turn this grisly find into a profitable tourist attraction.

In the eighteenth and nineteenth centuries, Edinburgh rivalled London as the hub of British publishing, and much of this trade was based on or near the Royal Mile. Arguably the two most significant nineteenth-century literary magazines, the Tory-supporting *Blackwood's Edinburgh Magazine* and the Whiggish *Edinburgh Review*, were published in the city, selling thousands of copies of each issue, and being read in London, America and throughout the British Empire. The *Edinburgh Review*, based in Trunk's Close, was run by an advocate called Francis Jeffrey (yes, another Edinburgh lawyer), an authoritarian editor whose reviews provoked lawsuits and even on occasion duels. Lord Byron

2 The entrance to Fleshmarket Close, inspiration for Ian Rankin

described the magazine's contributors as 'a coward brood, which mangle as they prey' on the authors whose work they tear to sheds (victims included Wordsworth and Goethe). The *Edinburgh Review* published essays and fiction as well as reviews; among its stellar list of contributors were Thomas Carlyle, William Hazlitt, Leigh Hunt, Thomas Babington Macaulay, John Stuart Mill, Bertrand Russell and Walter Scott. *Blackwood's*, based in the New Town, was established to rival the *Review*. One of its early editors was John Gibson Lockhart, Walter Scott's son-in-law and biographer. Among the authors it published were the Brontës, Charles Dickens, Arthur Conan Doyle, George Eliot, Edgar Allan Poe (who even satirised the magazine in 'Loss of Breath: A Tale à La *Blackwood*'), Thomas De Quincey and Margaret Oliphant. Joseph Conrad's *Heart of Darkness* was first published in *Blackwood's* in 1899 in serial form.

The Royal Mile: Canongate and Holyrood

Soon after John Knox House, High Street narrows and becomes the Canongate, a stretch of the Royal Mile that somehow feels off the beaten track despite its location between major destinations like the castle and the parliament. Indeed, until 1856 the Canongate was a separate burgh and a haven for those in financial or legal trouble. At the far end lies Holyrood, site of an elegant royal palace and the stunning, audacious modern parliament building. Holyrood Abbey stands in the grounds of Holyrood Palace; it was founded in 1128 but has been ruined since the seventeenth century.

As a young and aspiring author Thomas De Quincey moved to Edinburgh in 1820 in the hope of writing essays for *Blackwood's*, but after falling out with its proprietor, William Blackwood, he relocated to Grasmere in the Lake District. In the same year he published *Confessions of an English Opium Eater* in the *London Magazine*; the argument cost Blackwood a considerable coup. De Quincey returned to Edinburgh in 1830 and was soon pursued by creditors: 35 debtor's suits were filed against him over the next ten years. He sought refuge in a house at the Holyrood Sanctuary near the abbey and lived there on and off for several years. This sanctuary was an area indicated by a white line painted on the Canongate pavement – once a debtor crossed the line he was safe, but if he left the sanctuary area he could be arrested and imprisoned. Debtors had to register with the governor of Holyrood and pay a small fee. After this they were free to live in the precinct and enjoy its shops, taverns, parkland and lochs without fear of prosecution.

De Quincey still worked as an essayist during his residence in the sanctuary, relying on his children and the occasional policeman to deliver proofs and manuscripts to him. The 'catch-poles', the court officers whose duty it was to arrest debtors, patrolled outside the white perimeter line but weren't permitted to work on Sundays. As a result, crowds of debtors would wait for midnight each Saturday to cross back into the city proper and would be sure to return before the clocks struck midnight on Sunday. De Quincey struggled in poverty for most of his adult life, and after he died in 1859 he was buried in St Cuthbert's Kirkyard on Princes Street.

Percy Bysshe Shelley, another Romantic writer with a colourful life, also spent time in the Canongate district (though not the sanctuary). He arrived in Edinburgh in 1811, having eloped with the 16-year-old Harriet Westbrook, and they took out a marriage licence immediately: on the marriage register he is listed as 'Farmer, of Sussex'. They were married at 225 Canongate, in the house of Reverend Joseph Robertson. On their wedding night, Shelley stood on the threshold of his residence and drew his pistols on a group of well-wishers, promising to fire on anyone who followed him and his wife indoors. The Shelleys stayed in Edinburgh for several weeks, though Shelley was to chafe at his lack of funds and complained in a letter of being 'chained to the filth and commerce' of the city. Three years later, Shelley, who was disinclined to spend any length of time with one woman, eloped again, with Mary Godwin, whom he married in 1816 after Harriet drowned herself in London's Serpentine Lake in Hyde Park.

Today the Canongate is home to the Scottish Poetry Library, which is tucked down Crichton's Close, on the right-hand side as you proceed downhill. The bright, modern but cosy building is sheltered from the bustle of the Royal Mile. It has an impressive collection of over 40,000 items to do with poetry: books, pamphlets, magazines, manuscripts, newspaper clippings, recordings and much more. As you might expect, its Scottish poetry holdings are comprehensive, and this is as good a place as any to encounter Scottish writing beyond the usual household names. But this isn't a parochial library and its collection includes a great deal of poetry from around the world, from the present as well as the past. Roughly opposite it is Dunbar's Close, the location of a hidden gem of a garden in the heart of Edinburgh. Laid out in the style of a seventeenth-century garden, it is open to the public, invariably quiet, and is the perfect place to sit on a sunny day and read a volume from the Poetry Library.

Also on this stretch of the Royal Mile is Canongate Kirkyard, whose residents include Adam Smith, economist and author of *The Wealth of Nations*, and Agnes McLehose, who under the pen name Clarinda enjoyed a passionate and largely epistolary affair with Robert Burns. Upon finding out in 1791 that Clarinda planned to sail to Jamaica to reunite with her estranged husband, Burns travelled to Edinburgh to bid her farewell and lodged in the White Hart Inn on the Grassmarket. After this final meeting he posted her a poem expressing his sorrow at her emigration, his enduringly popular 'Ae Fond Kiss':

> Ae fond kiss, and then we sever!
> Ae fond kiss, and then forever!
> Deep in heart-wrung tears I'll pledge thee,
> Warring sighs and groans I'll wage thee.

Burns has another connection to Canongate Kirkyard. On arriving in Edinburgh in 1786, he paid for a headstone for the pauper's grave of Robert Fergusson, a brilliant but troubled poet and major influence on Burns, who died in the Edinburgh Bedlam in 1777 aged 24. Four tender lines by Burns are inscribed on the headstone:

> No sculptur'd Marble here nor pompous lay
> No storied Urn nor animated Bust
> This simple Stone directs pale Scotia's way
> To pour her sorrows o'er her Poet's Dust.

Despite Burns's admiration, Fergusson's reputation remains dwarfed by that of the later poet. Since 2004 he has gained attention because of a jaunty statue of him sited at the entrance to the kirkyard. Passers-by may now, briefly, look upon a poet whom Scotland has almost forgotten.

At the foot of the Royal Mile are the Scottish Parliament and Holyrood Palace. Work on the palace building was begun by King

James IV in the early sixteenth century, and it was a seat of the Scottish royal court. As the hub of feudal Scotland it attracted nobles, bureaucrats, courtiers and poets; among the most lauded of these was William Dunbar. Born in East Lothian, Dunbar served James IV first as an ambassador to Denmark and Norway (which was a single entity at the time) and France; later he became a court poet and was a leading light in the 'golden age' of James's cosmopolitan and cultured reign. Dunbar's masterful Scots poetry ranges from bawdy satires of corrupt Edinburgh society to haunting elegies. His 'Lament for the Makars' is a tribute to Scotland's dead poets, including many of his friends, with its liturgical-sounding Latin refrain *'Timor mortis conturbat me'* ('The fear of death disturbs me'). This is the poem for which he is now remembered. Other court poets whose work survives today include Sir David Lyndsay, aristocratic companion to the future King James V; George Buchanan, tutor to the teenage Mary Queen of Scots; and Mary herself, who was an accomplished sonneteer.

Holyrood is once again the political centre of Scotland, but the secretaries, civil servants and officials are now located a few steps away at the Scottish Parliament. This arresting building was completed in 2004 and is home to the devolved government of Scotland. Spanish architect Enric Miralles designed it to appear as if it was 'growing out of the land', inspired by the Scottish landscape and the shape of upturned boats on a shore. On the parliament's Canongate wall are 26 inscriptions, including quotations from proverbs, poetry and prose works in English, Gaelic and Scots. Each is carved on a different Scottish mineral, such as Iona marble or Lewisian gneiss, and each gives a distinctive comment on the Scottish people, their political identity and their aspirations for a future society. Many of the country's most famous writers and thinkers, from the pro-establishment unionist Walter Scott to the left-wing nationalist Hugh MacDiarmid, are represented. Less famous figures also feature, such as the mill worker and trade unionist Mary Brooksbank whose 'Jute Mill Song' laments that 'the warld's ill-divided' between rich and poor. The Canongate wall is an extraordinary gesture, an example of a country not only giving pride of place to its writers, but also laying itself bare, reflecting both on its strengths and on the failings that need to be corrected. It's as if the building is calling the politicians to account, affording them no opportunity for complacency.

The parliament building may be striking, but so are its surroundings. The cluttered and busy streets of the Old Town give way to Holyrood Park, a former royal hunting estate. This isn't a park in the sense of lush, verdant lawns, fountains, boating ponds and flowerbeds. Instead, it's an assortment of crags, ridges, cliffs, lochs and gorse moor, and is dominated by Arthur's Seat, which, like Castle Rock a mile away, is an extinct volcano. Although it's only 251 metres high, the dramatic incongruity of the hill makes it feel higher; Stevenson was right when he observed that, despite its low stature, it is 'a mountain by reason of its bold design'. Needless to say the views of Edinburgh from here are spectacular. In a country that draws on the scenery and wild species of the Highlands for much of its national iconography, it's appropriate that the Scottish Parliament has this miniature Highland landscape on its doorstep.

In Elspeth Davie's 1971 novel *Creating a Scene*, Arthur's Seat is depicted as a lunchtime retreat for harried workers. Mr Foley, an art teacher, thinks longingly about it during his morning classes and when the bell rings he wastes no time in heading there. He enjoys its relative solitude: 'no mountain slope could have seemed more remote.' And yet, despite this, it's oddly domestic, a site for picnics as well as 'pagan rites'. The narrator adds that 'in the summertime visitors searched for heather here and found none. The maddest expected eagles.' It might seem like the Highlands, but it isn't: Foley soon encounters every relaxing teacher's worst nightmare, picnicking parents wanting to talk about pupils and school plays.

The definitive literary depiction of Arthur's Seat, however, is James Hogg's 1824 novel *The Private Memoirs and Confessions of a*

Justified Sinner. Hogg's book is simultaneously a Gothic horror story, an early example of psychological crime fiction, a proto-modernist metafiction (it was championed by André Gide in the 1940s) and a satire of religious fundamentalism. The middle section of the book is a mysterious document, a memoir by a young, intensely devout Calvinist called Robert Wringhim, and this account is framed by a fictional editorial narrative that provides an unreliable commentary of Wringhim's story. Wringhim's early life is shaped by the religious upheavals, politics and preaching of seventeenth-century Scotland. He follows a particularly extreme interpretation of the doctrine of predestination that leads him to believe that he is one of the 'elect', destined for heaven, regardless of any crimes he commits on earth. He falls under the influence of an elusive, charming and urbane figure called Gil-Martin. The reader is led to suspect that Gil-Martin is the Devil, whispering evil thoughts in Wringhim's ear and encouraging him to commit fratricide in the name of God. He also describes himself as Wringhim's 'second self', a split in the young man's personality.

In a climactic scene in the book, Wringhim stalks his half-brother George through the streets of Edinburgh. Determined to have some peace from Robert's menacing presence, George climbs Arthur's Seat. It's a cloudy morning, and in the gloom his thoughts turn to his brother:

> The idea of his brother's dark and malevolent looks coming at that moment across his mind, he turned his eyes instinctively to the right, to the point where that unwelcome guest was wont to make his appearance. Gracious heaven! What an apparition was there presented to his view! He saw, delineated in the cloud, the shoulders, arms, and features of his brother, but dilated to twenty times the natural size. Its dark eyes gleamed on him through the mist, while every furrow of its hideous brow frowned deep as the ravines on the brow of the hill. George started, and his hair stood up in bristles as he gazed on this horrible monster.

This is a wonderfully atmospheric scene, unforgettable for anyone skirting the hill's rocky outcrops on a cloudy day. What's most frightening is that the phenomenon Hogg describes is real: it's a 'Brocken spectre', a trick of the light that causes one's shadow to be magnified ghoulishly on the clouds below. In a novel all about split personalities and the supernatural, this is a haunting image of the self conjured up in a distinctively Edinburgh location, the tame-but-wild Arthur's Seat.

The New Town

In contrast to the Old Town's medieval warren of closes, churches, castles, graveyards and higgledy-piggledy buildings, Edinburgh's New Town follows a thoroughly rational design: its broad streets, neat squares and geometric layout positively scream (or rather, enunciate elegantly) the Age of Enlightenment. In the 1760s, town councillors, in a bid to alleviate the overcrowding of the Old Town, agreed to extend the city to the north and drain the Nor' Loch, the polluted body of water lying in the hollow that is now Princes Street Gardens and Waverley Station. The New Town was built in stages from the 1760s to the middle of the nineteenth century and is less an extension than a reinvention of the city. It's dominated by three parallel thoroughfares, Princes Street, George Street and Queen Street, which run from Charlotte Square to St Andrew Square. Originally these were intended as residential streets, but today they are Edinburgh's main shopping destination. Between these three arteries of the New Town are two narrower streets, Rose Street and Thistle Street.

Dominating the eastern end of Princes Street is the Balmoral Hotel, formerly known as the North British. This grand, square, faintly municipal building with its bulky clock tower is only a few steps from Waverley Station, and as a result has long been the accommodation of choice for the rich and famous when they arrive in the city. Elizabeth Taylor has sashayed along its corridors. Royals and prime ministers have sipped whiskies beside its roaring fires. In 2007 J. K. Rowling completed *Harry Potter and the Deathly Hallows*, the final book in the series, in a suite at the Balmoral and inscribed a marble bust with the date, her name and the title of the book. The suite has been renamed the J. K. Rowling Suite, and its tariff has soared as high as any broomstick. In fiction, too, the Balmoral is the Edinburgh residence of the powerful: in Ian Rankin's *The Naming of the Dead*, diplomats, gangsters and shady businessmen do deals here in the run-up to the Gleneagles G8 summit.

One side of Princes Street is crammed with high-street retailers and department stores; on the other, the lawns of Princes Street Gardens slope down towards the railway line and add an element of grace to the busy shopping street. Thomas Carlyle wrote in his *Reminiscences* that 'the chosen Promenade of Edinburgh was Princes Street', and that 'all that was brightest in Edinburgh seemed to have stept out to enjoy, in the pure fresh air, the finest city-prospect in the world and the sight of one another.' The walk is perhaps less elegant now than it was in Carlyle's day, though the views of the city remain as glorious as ever.

Uphill and to the north of Princes Street is Rose Street. Little broader than a lane, in days gone by it had the reputation of being the New Town's seediest thoroughfare, lined with bars with sawdust floors and disreputable punters. Two of these, Milne's Bar and the Abbotsford, are stalwarts of Edinburgh's literary pub tour scene. Milne's was the watering hole of choice for the poets in the vanguard of the Scottish Renaissance, the twentieth-century movement that saw the publication of innovative, often distinctively Scottish writing. Hugh MacDiarmid, poet and polemicist, frequented Milne's when he was in Edinburgh. There he would meet Sydney Goodsir Smith and Robert Garioch, two leading Scots-language poets. Norman MacCaig, a much-loved poet whose best poems are affectionate but metaphysically daring studies of Highland landscapes and wildlife, was another regular at these gatherings of the group that became known as the Rose Street Poets. Visitors from further afield came to Milne's: Stevie Smith and W. H. Auden talked poetry with the regulars here, and Dylan Thomas also slaked his prodigious thirst at the bar. Eventually Milne's proved too small for the numbers attending these gatherings, and the poets migrated to the larger, more ornate Abbotsford. On the fringes of this group was the Orcadian poet George Mackay Brown, at the time an awestruck student watching the famous bards from afar. Brown records an early experience of these gatherings in his autobiography *For the Islands I Sing*:

> The Abbotsford is a handsome spacious bar, a relic of the Victorian age. The circular counter is an island in the centre of the bar, richly gantried with all the drinks of the western world, especially whiskies. And there, one Friday night, they were, in a cluster at one corner of the counter, Norman MacCaig and Sydney Goodsir Smith and a few of their friends. Simply to be there, watching that famous huddle, was a delight. I drank my beer but dared not go near them.

Beyond Rose Street is George Street, the heart of the New Town development. At its western end lies Charlotte Square, which is transformed for a few weeks every summer into a tented, literary metropolis when the Edinburgh International Book Festival brings the great and the good of world literature to the city. The Book Festival is part of Edinburgh's holy trinity of annual gatherings, along with the International Festival and the Edinburgh Fringe. These attractions, together with the city's literary heritage, led to Edinburgh's appointment in 2004 as the world's first UNESCO City of Literature.

Before heading along George Street it's worth turning on to Young Street at the north-east corner of Charlotte Square. The narrow, cobbled, nondescript street has achieved fame as the location of the Oxford Bar, or the 'Ox', in which Ian Rankin's Detective Inspector

Rebus spends most of his nights. An old-fashioned, 'talking-shop' pub, where regulars put the world to rights while sitting on bar stools, the Oxford is where Rebus achieves a measure of anonymity among his cronies.

George Street itself is much broader and grander than either Rose or Young Street. About halfway along is the Assembly Rooms, a conference venue built in 1787 which has a columnar façade like a Greek temple. It has long been a centre of Edinburgh social life, hosting dances, performances, lectures and readings. In the 1840s and 1850s Charles Dickens made regular appearances, reading works including *A Christmas Carol* to sell-out audiences. William Makepeace Thackeray also gave several lectures at the Assembly Rooms, although he lost his audience's sympathy when he insulted Mary Queen of Scots and was subsequently hissed and booed.

North, and downhill, lies the third of the New Town's original main thoroughfares, Queen Street. Like Princes Street, one side of it is taken up with gardens, and beyond these are impressive views over the city to the River Forth and the distant hills of Fife. Oscar Wilde lectured in Edinburgh at the now-defunct Queen Street Hall. Another, more interesting, connection between Wilde and Edinburgh is St Peter's Church in the affluent suburb of Morningside. Designed in the style of an Italian–Byzantine church with a campanile and forecourt, St Peter's was built for Father John Gray, who as a young man hung around the Rhymers' Club in London, wrote decadent poetry and became a friend and disciple of Wilde. In 1893 Wilde paid for the publication of Gray's poetry collection *Silverpoints*. Dorian Gray, the beautiful, vain hero of Wilde's novel *The Picture of Dorian Gray*, is rumoured to be modelled on John Gray. Although Dorian never actually takes holy orders, John Gray entered the Church after Wilde's arrest in 1895 for 'gross indecency'. Gray employed a barrister to attend the trial and ensure that there was no incriminating mention of his name.

Much of this Edinburgh literary tour has been about streets and buildings. For those wanting to come face-to-face with Scottish literature, however, the Scottish National Portrait Gallery on Queen Street is worth a visit. It's a neo-Gothic building of red sandstone and features arts and crafts embellishments inside and out, including stained-glass windows and murals of figures from Scottish history. Its permanent collection offers a visual who's who of Scottish writers. Inevitably there are portraits of Scott and Burns, as well as Boswell, Robert Fergusson, Stevenson, Carlyle, Muriel Spark, Kathleen Jamie, Ian Rankin, Irvine Welsh and many more. The poets of the Scottish Renaissance are well represented; a highlight is Alan Thornhill's wonderfully craggy bronze bust of Hugh MacDiarmid. Now-neglected writers share wall space with more famous names: an affecting pencil drawing captures the demure but thoughtful expression of Margaret Oliphant, who published around 125 novels, short stories, biographies and other works of non-fiction in the nineteenth century. A cosmopolitan writer whose productivity was in part due to her need to support her family (she was widowed young), Oliphant produced writing that was critically and commercially successful on several continents.

The University Quarter

To the south of the Royal Mile lies another New Town extension of Edinburgh, the University Quarter, centred on George Square, where the University of Edinburgh is based. Walter Scott was born in this district and from 1778 to 1797 lived with his parents at 25 George Square, a newly built townhouse. The university itself, founded in 1582, is one of Britain's oldest and it has long been renowned for its departments of medicine, natural sciences, philosophy and law. This reputation continues today: its most recent world-famous scientist is the Nobel laureate Peter Higgs. In 1771 Tobias Smollett, in *The Expedition of Humphry Clinker*, noted that 'Edinburgh is a hot-bed of genius', and the city's pre-eminence as a seat of learning in the eighteenth and nineteenth centuries led to it becoming known as the 'Athens of the North'. Thomas Carlyle, who at the age of 13 walked the 80 miles from his home in the village of Ecclefechan to study at Edinburgh, twice left without taking a degree. Walter Scott and Robert Louis Stevenson both studied law here: Scott had a successful legal career; Stevenson didn't. Stevenson attended the university at about the same time as J. M. Barrie, whom he would on occasion divert from the lecture theatre to the tavern, and also Arthur Conan Doyle, another Edinburgh native who studied medicine – the Conan Doyle pub on York Place is near his birthplace. One of Doyle's professors was Joseph Bell, a surgeon who was to become an inspiration for Sherlock Holmes, as Doyle admits in his *Memories and Adventures*: 'I thought of my old teacher Joe Bell, of his eagle face, of his curious ways, of his eerie trick of spotting details. If he were a detective he would surely reduce this fascinating but unorganised business to something nearer to an exact science.'

Evidence of Edinburgh's illustrious history of medical research can be found at the Surgeons' Hall Museum on Nicolson Street, which has been open to the public since 1832. Like a walk-in textbook, the hall contains case after case of specimens: organs, limbs, skeletons attacked by every conceivable disease and deformity. These are preserved in solution, in jars and containers which have often sat unopened for nearly 200 years. The exhibition is sober and well lit, with none of the theatrics of a chamber of horrors, but to examine each seemingly alien object is simultaneously to intrude upon the deepest privacy of unknown men, women and children, and to feel a strong sense of one's own fragility. It's a haunting experience. The poet and essayist Kathleen Jamie writes frankly and thoughtfully about the Surgeons' Hall in her 2005 book *Findings*: 'Each of the bays on the main floor of the Playfair Hall is given to a particular body part or type of ailment. Thus the specimens taken from cancerous breasts oppose, as though in a shy dance, those from cancerous testicles.' Later on, she conjures a startling image: 'Many of the specimens are beautiful. One of the earliest is what looks like bracket fungus, but is actually a fine slice of kidney into which the then preservator has introduced mercury. Silver threads of mercury fan through the tissue, illustrating its blood vessels. It is quite lovely; one could wear it as a brooch.' Jamie's intense scrutiny and lyricism testify to the beauty as well as the macabre qualities of this unique museum of the human body.

Beyond the City Centre

Edinburgh's Old and New Towns might be full of history and literary heritage, but other parts of the city have their own distinctive identities and histories too. Leith, Edinburgh's port and until 1920 a separate town, lies to the north-east of the New Town and is reached via Leith Walk. This road is more infamous than famous. In the 1870s Robert Louis Stevenson was sufficiently familiar with the Walk's prostitutes that they knew him by the nickname 'Velvet Coat', on account of his dapper appearance. In Ian Rankin's *Fleshmarket Close* the parents of a missing teenager harass the women working the streets here in the hope of obtaining information about their daughter's whereabouts.

Two of Edinburgh's most successful modern writers have lived in and around Leith. Before her literary career took off, J. K. Rowling lived in a flat just off Leith Walk. As a trainee teacher she taught at the local high school, Leith Academy. Irvine Welsh, author of *Trainspotting*, was born in Leith. Written in a phonetic rendering of working-class speech, *Trainspotting* follows the exploits of a group of heroin addicts, petty criminals and chancers living in this part of the city. Their Edinburgh seems to be a different world from the city Welsh has called 'shortbread Disneyland', but the author is capable of surprising sensitivity not only in his characterisation of Renton, Begbie, Spud and the rest, but also in his depiction of the run-down, deprived areas of the city that they inhabit. In a chapter titled

'Trainspotting at Leith Central Station', Renton and Begbie share a poignant moment while urinating in this derelict train station:

> We go fir a pish in the auld Central Station at the Fit ay the Walk, now a barren, desolate hangar, which is soon tae be demolished and replaced by a supermarket and swimming centre. Somehow, that makes us sad, even though ah wis eywis too young tae mind ay trains ever being there.
>
> – Some size ay a station this wis. Git a train tae anywhair fae here, at one time, or so they sais, ah sais, watchin ma steaming pish splash oantae the cauld stane.

As Welsh notes, Leith Central Station has now been redeveloped. This is the case with many of the places mentioned in the novel, and Leith itself is regenerating rapidly, with fashionable restaurants, bars and apartments lining its harbour front. These days *Trainspotting*'s characters would doubtless be priced out and herded to estates elsewhere in the city.

To the south-west of the Old Town, in a neighbourhood of golf courses, parks and playing fields, sits Napier University's grand, mansion-like Craiglockhart Hydropathic building. During the First World War this was a hospital where soldiers were treated for physical and nervous conditions. In July 1917, the influential war poet Siegfried Sassoon was sent here, primarily to avoid a court martial for his public opposition to the war. He used his time here to write *Counter-Attack*, his most important collection of poems. The hospital magazine, the *Hydra*, published some of these poems under the editorship of another poet, Wilfred Owen, who had been admitted to Craiglockhart a month before Sassoon. Owen had been influenced by Sassoon's poetry and was inspired by his encounters with him at Craiglockhart as he worked out how his own, Romantically inclined, poetry might better reflect the experience of trench warfare. Owen was to return to the front line a few months later and was killed on 4 November 1918, a week before the

Armistice. The first book of Owen's poems was published in 1920, with an introduction by Sassoon. Craiglockhart and its patients, including Sassoon and Owen, are brought to life in Pat Barker's 1998 *The Regeneration Trilogy*, which tells the story of the Great War as seen through the eyes of William Rivers, Craiglockhart's psychologist.

Edinburgh can justifiably claim to be Scotland's literary capital city. As we shall see, however, other regions of Scotland have their own dynamic literary cultures and have inspired a diverse range of writers. Edinburgh's Enlightenment heyday was a demonstration of the power of the intellect, but other parts of the country can make strong appeals to the heart.

❧ 3 ❧

SOUTHERN SCOTLAND

Poets and Adventurers

The majority of Scotland's population lives in the Central Belt, the lowland region that runs across the narrow 'waist' of Scotland, about a third of the way up from the border. The cities of Edinburgh, Glasgow and Dundee dominate the trade and industry of the Central Belt. To the south lies the Southern Uplands, the range of hills that forms a barrier between the Central Belt and the country's borderlands. Between the thirteenth and seventeenth centuries this region was the stronghold of the Border Reivers, the cross-border raiding parties that specialised in kidnapping and cattle rustling. Although only a few miles' drive from major cities, these hills feel as remote as anywhere in Britain, and their appeal to writers and travellers is often based on the sense of rugged isolation. Around the coasts and in the valley of the River Tweed are towns and villages that cherish their own distinctive identities and traditions, such as the Common Ridings, the annual displays of horsemanship that take place in many Border towns, dating back to the time of the Reivers. Although this region is sometimes overlooked by travellers drawn to the better-publicised Romantic grandeur of the Highlands and Islands, the Borders have a great deal of beauty and charm to offer and make a rewarding trip in their own right.

East Lothian

East of Edinburgh the Firth of Forth rapidly broadens, and on a hazy day, when the Fife shore is hidden, it's easy to look across this wide estuary and think you're looking out into the North Sea. Whales and dolphins are regularly sighted in the Firth and seabirds and seals congregate in large numbers on the Firth's coasts and islands. At the mouth of the Firth, just before its southern coast turns down towards England, is the small and picturesque town of North Berwick. Two miles out to sea from here is the Bass Rock. A volcanic plug rising steeply for over 100 metres, in summer it's populated by over 150,000 gannets and is described by Sir David Attenborough as one of the wildlife wonders of the world. It's a metropolis of birds, and with so many nesting on the cliffs it's little surprise that it is visibly stained with guano: on a sunny day the Bass Rock is a luminous apparition, gleaming above the water.

The Bass Rock is uninhabited, but ruins of a chapel and fortifications remain. Its high cliffs and isolation make it a natural stronghold, so it's no wonder it's been used as a prison, notably for Presbyterian Covenanters in the seventeenth century. It performs this role in Robert Louis Stevenson's *Catriona* too: the enemies of Stevenson's hero David Balfour want to prevent him giving evidence at a trial, and so he is captured and bundled into a boat at night. Afraid that he is being sold into slavery (as nearly happened in the novel's prequel, *Kidnapped*), David's fears are only slightly assuaged by the sublime sight of the Bass:

> It is just the one crag of rock, as everybody knows, but great enough to carve a city from. [. . .] With the growing of the dawn I could see it clearer and clearer; the straight crags painted with sea-birds' droppings like a morning frost, the sloping top of it green with grass, the clan of white geese that cried about the sides, and the black, broken buildings of the prison sitting close on the sea's edge.

3 The Bass Rock, white with gannets and their guano

The Bass was a familiar landmark to Stevenson, who spent childhood holidays in North Berwick. He belonged to an engineering dynasty: his grandfather, father and uncles were all famous lighthouse engineers. As a result, Stevenson knew the islands and skerries of the east coast well, and three years after he died, his cousin David was commissioned to design the Bass Rock lighthouse, first lit in 1902.

In sight of the Bass Rock and just to the east of North Berwick is Tantallon Castle, a spectacular clifftop fortress. Its red sandstone walls block off the headland, with cliffs on three sides adding to the fortifications. Although a semi-ruin, it's one of the best examples of a fourteenth-century Scottish castle, and evidence of the highly disputed nature of this stretch of coast, fought over for centuries by the Scots and English. The castle was built by the first Earl of Douglas, the nephew of one of Robert the Bruce's most powerful commanders. In around 1474 his descendant Gavin Douglas, provost of St Giles' Cathedral, was born here. Tantallon was breached by Oliver Cromwell's forces in 1651 and after this it

4 Tantallon Castle, birthplace of poet Gavin Douglas

fell into disrepair. In *Catriona*, set almost exactly a century after this, David Balfour is led past here on his way to the Bass and by moonlight sees 'the three huge towers and broken battlements of Tantallon, that old chief place of the Red Douglases'.

Ten miles south is the town of Dunbar. Lying midway between Edinburgh and the English border, it has been besieged and invaded numerous times over the centuries. A formidable castle, now ruined, guards its harbour. More recently Dunbar has faced an invasion of a more modest sort. John Muir, the conservationist who played a major role in the foundation of America's national parks, was born in Dunbar in 1838 and emigrated with his parents when he was 11. Muir's books on the spiritual and physical rewards of nature, including *My First Summer in the Sierra* (1911) and *The Yosemite* (1912), have been read by millions and inspired such devotion that admirers have sought out the house at 128 High Street, Dunbar, where he was born. There is a possibly apocryphal story of the woman who lived at number 128 several years ago, who opened her door one day to find an elderly Japanese man kneeling in prayer on her doorstep. Pilgrimages such as this were doubtless a source of incredulity and mirth to Dunbar's inhabitants, since for much of the twentieth century Muir (a household name in America, where there is a Muir Glacier, a Mount Muir and a John Muir Day) was almost forgotten in the country of his birth. Muir is no longer ignored in Scotland: his Dunbar house is now a museum and the John Muir Country Park lies to the west of the town. The John Muir Trust in Scotland was established in 1983 with the remit of conserving the country's wild places. Although Muir left at a young age, the literature and culture of Scotland stayed with him and played a formative role in his ideas about the appreciation of nature. As a boy he would smuggle Walter Scott's novels past his stern father, who disapproved of his son reading secular literature, and many years later Muir carried a volume of Burns's poems in his rucksack on his celebrated expeditions.

Rosslyn

As you head south from the centre of Edinburgh the city soon gives way to farmland and rolling hills. Nestled above the wooded valley of the River Esk is Rosslyn Chapel, built in the fifteenth century and still used as a place of worship. Although its flying buttresses and high ceilings resemble those of a great medieval cathedral, Rosslyn is tiny: 21 metres long and 13 metres tall. Like all the best Gothic buildings, it is a monument to the prolonged diligence of countless unnamed craftsmen. Almost every surface inside the chapel is ornately carved and the subjects depicted include Biblical scenes, folk mythology and courtly imagery. Knights on horseback share wall space with farmers' wives; a bound Lucifer hangs upside-down in a pose long used as a Masonic symbol; a hanging boss represents the nativity but the pagan figure of the Green Man can also be found in cornices. There is nonetheless a Scottish flavour:

among the many carvings of angels playing musical instruments is one that shows the Lord being praised with bagpipes.

When William and Dorothy Wordsworth visited Rosslyn Chapel in 1803 it wasn't the immensely popular attraction that it is today. Dorothy records in her *Recollections of a Tour Made in Scotland* that it is 'kept locked up, and so preserved from the injuries it might otherwise receive from idle boys'. Once inside, she was captivated by carvings of 'leaves and flowers, so delicately wrought'. The chapel was in poor condition at this time and many of its features were covered by real foliage too: 'three or four leaves of a small fern, resembling that which we call adder's tongue, grew round a cluster of [the carved leaves] at the top of a pillar and the natural product and the artificial were so intermingled that at first it was not easy to distinguish the living plant from the other.' William Wordsworth returned on two subsequent occasions, once sheltering in the chapel during the storm that inspired his sonnet with the unimaginative title 'Composed in Roslin Chapel during a Storm'. The poem begins with a wonderfully melancholic declaration about the neglected building: 'The wind is now thy organist!'

The chapel has been restored and attracts tens of thousands of visitors every year. The turning point came when Queen Victoria visited in 1842 and expressed her desire that it be preserved for the benefit of the nation. An equally important visitor, around the turn of the millennium, was the thriller writer Dan Brown, whose novel *The Da Vinci Code*, published in 2003, became a worldwide bestseller and brought Rosslyn to a whole new audience. Brown's hero, Robert Langdon, accompanied by French police officer Sophie Neveu, finds himself in a frenetic search for the Holy Grail. Accused of murder and caught up in a power struggle between secret societies trying to uncover and suppress information about the grail, Langdon and Neveu follow the clues left by a deceased Louvre curator who had knowledge of the grail's whereabouts. The trail eventually leads to Rosslyn Chapel, nicknamed 'the Cathedral of Codes' in the book because of the many symbols, acronyms and mystical images found on its walls. According to Brown's narrator, it lies on the same longitudinal line as Glastonbury (not true) and King Arthur's Avalon (enjoyably spurious). It's easy to see why Rosslyn was an appealing location for Brown. Its eclectic and frequently Masonic or pagan iconography blend seamlessly into his story of Grail myths, secret societies and Catholic cover-ups. The success of *The Da Vinci Code* has brought more sightseers to the chapel than ever before, many of whom are keen to solve the mysteries that may or may not be contained in its symbols. As well as the Holy Grail, visitors have also sought the remains of Elvis Presley here, and there are rumours of a UFO hidden in a vault.

About a mile east of Rosslyn Chapel is Hawthornden Castle, perched on the opposite bank of the River Esk. Now a retreat for writers, in the seventeenth century it was the home of William Drummond of Hawthornden. Drummond was an urbane and celebrated poet, a polymath and a bibliophile. He wrote elegant verse (he was given the moniker the 'Scottish Petrarch') but he also designed and patented 16 different weapons of war, including battering rams and a machine gun. In 1618 Drummond welcomed a famous literary guest to Hawthornden Castle – Ben Jonson. Since Shakespeare's death two years earlier Jonson had been England's leading playwright, but in the summer of 1618 he left the London literary scene behind in order to walk to Scotland. It's uncertain why Jonson undertook this 400-mile expedition, although there is some evidence that it was for a bet. Certainly this hike was no mean feat for a man who was 46 (average life expectancy at the time was about 35) and who weighed nearly 130 kilos. Jonson stayed with Drummond at Hawthornden, and the two writers talked a great deal: Jonson's biographer Ian Donaldson notes that their conversation covered subjects including Jonson's family and personal history, opinions about other writers, sexual encounters and religion. Drummond took notes of these discussions, which now form the basis for biographical accounts of Jonson, and these notes include Jonson's notorious declaration that 'Shakespeare wanted [i.e. lacked] art'. The relationship between host and guest seems to have been fairly fractious. Drummond wrote of Jonson: 'He is a great lover and praiser of himself, a contemner and scorner of others, given rather to lose a friend than a jest, jealous of every word and action of those about him (especially after drink, which is one of the elements in which he liveth).' Jonson never came to stay again.

The Borders

Half an hour's drive south of Rosslyn is Peebles, the first town of any size on the River Tweed. Downstream of here are the heartlands of the Scottish Borders, the cluster of towns including Galashiels, Selkirk, Hawick, Melrose, Jedburgh and finally Kelso, which is little more than a cannonball's flight from the English border. Most of the Borders towns retain their agricultural identity but Peebles has a different feel. Its heyday was in the nineteenth century as a homeopathic resort, and its handsome Victorian hotel buildings and grey stone high street remain popular with tourists. In the centre of Peebles are three white buildings that seem to have been transported from Edinburgh's Royal Mile, adorned as they are with turrets and towers and a hotpotch of other features. This is the Chambers Institution, gifted to the people of the town by the publisher William Chambers (famous for encyclopedias and dictionaries). The institution houses the county museum and also the John Buchan Story, a museum celebrating the colourful life and work of the influential thriller writer.

The son of a Presbyterian minister, Buchan grew up in Glasgow, was educated at the universities of Glasgow and Oxford, and enjoyed prolific and successful careers in politics, journalism and colonial administration. Although work took him to Africa and Canada (where he was appointed governor general), throughout his life he retained a love of the Scottish Borders, where he had spent childhood holidays. When he was ennobled in 1935 he chose the title Lord Tweedsmuir. He published scores of books, including a biography of Sir Walter Scott, as well as his famous thriller, *The Thirty-Nine Steps*, in which the Borders plays a starring role (although Alfred Hitchcock's film adaptation shifts the action north to the Highlands). Set on the eve of the First World War, *The Thirty-Nine Steps* is very much of its time. Buchan's hero, Richard Hannay, has recently returned to London from working in Rhodesia and unwittingly becomes embroiled in a plot to provoke a Europe-wide conflict. Forced to go into hiding, he looks at a map and decides upon Galloway in the western Borders, as 'it was the nearest wild part of Scotland'. What follows is a pursuit over the Southern Uplands in which a colonial gentleman is put through his paces, exercising his 'veldcraft' in 'a great wide moorland place, gleaming with lochs, with high blue hills showing northwards'. With classic British fortitude, Hannay relishes his adventure despite being followed by the henchmen of war-mongers: 'I chose a ridge which made an angle with the one I was on, and so would soon put a deep glen between me and my enemies. The exercise had warmed my blood, and I was beginning to enjoy myself amazingly. As I went I breakfasted on the dusty remains of the ginger biscuits.'

Hannay keeps mainly to the high ground south and west of Peebles, around the upper reaches of the Tweed and the Galloway hills. When the jolly game of cat-and-mouse is over, the novel's action moves south to Kent as Hannay races to prevent a German spy in possession of Britain's military secrets from escaping to the Continent. Buchan's fast-paced romp is reminiscent of the cross-country travels of Stevenson's *Kidnapped* and *Catriona* and influenced later Scottish espionage writers, including Ian Fleming. Like *The Da Vinci Code*, it brings adventure and international conspiracy to this quiet part of Scotland. Leading west from Peebles there is now a trail called the John Buchan Way, which runs for 13 miles across hills and glens, allowing walkers the chance to experience the landscape of Hannay's escapades.

Dan Brown and John Buchan both turned to southern Scotland as a location for adventure, quest and mystery. But long before the thriller genre was invented, the Borders were a setting popular with those keen to enthral audiences with tales of war, betrayal, tragedy and the supernatural: these storytellers were the singers of the Border ballads. The ballads were composed to be sung, and many of their composers were peasant women. They weren't the products of single authors but evolved over time in a process like Chinese whispers: ballads were learned by listening and repeating, so additions and embellishments were not just inevitable but positively encouraged. Most ballads are stories, folk tales in which disturbing, violent or supernatural events are narrated with disarming frankness. 'The Four Maries' starts with adultery in the court of Mary Queen of Scots, and tells of the lady-in-waiting who murders her resulting child:

> She's tyed it in her apron
> And she's thrown it in the sea:
> Says, 'Sink ye, swim ye, bonny wee babe!
> You'll ne'er get mair o me'.

Another ballad, 'The Twa Corbies' ('The Two Crows'), is a haunting poem in which these birds divvy up their next meal, a slain knight, with one crow sitting on his white collar-bone while the other pecks out his 'bonny blue eyes'.

Some of the ballads can be traced to the medieval period, but in the seventeenth and eighteenth centuries people began to write them down and compile collections of them. Walter Scott, James Hogg and Robert Burns all took part in this process, often adding their own embellishments or borrowing ballad stories for their own 'original' works. A similar process was taking place in Germany at about the same time with some correspondents of Scott, the Brothers Grimm, who compiled, and to some extent rewrote, German folk tales. The directness, power, rhythm and downright weirdness of the ballads continue to inspire writers, and among those who have been influenced by them are Washington Irving (who met and discussed ballads with Scott), Jorge Luis Borges (an avowed lover of British oral culture) and the contemporary poets Kathleen Jamie, David Harsent and Seamus Heaney. Along with Aberdeenshire, the Borders is the Scottish region most strongly associated with balladeering, and the name 'Border ballads' became the umbrella term for this body of literature.

The people and landscape of the Borders feature prominently in the narratives of the ballads, including in 'Thomas Rhymer', a famous ballad that may have been a source for John Keats's poem 'La Belle Dame Sans Merci'. The ballad tells the story of a real historical figure, the thirteenth-century Thomas of Erceldoune (the present-day Earlston, near Melrose), who was a poet and gained a reputation as a prophet. In the ballad Thomas is resting on a grassy bank between Melrose and the nearby Eildon Hills when he sees the Queen of Elfland 'Come riding down by the Eildon Tree'. The Queen takes Thomas back with her to her enchanted realm to serve her for seven years. At the end of one version of the ballad Thomas is clothed in the garb of Elfland:

> He has gotten a coat of the even cloth,
> And a pair of shoes of velvet green,
> And till seven years were gone and past
> True Thomas on earth was never seen.

Tales of crossing over to a supernatural realm are common in the Border ballads. With its landscape of dark old woods and fields that have been tilled for centuries, its ancient standing stones and ruined abbeys, it's easy to imagine magical and mysterious goings-on. Thomas's Eildon Tree no longer exists, if it ever did, but on a footpath crossing the Eildon Hills between the villages of Melrose and Newtown St Boswells is the Rhymer's Stone. Resembling a gravestone and sited at an excellent viewpoint of the surrounding countryside, the stone supposedly marks the site of the Eildon Tree where Thomas had his vision. Sadly, when the Melrose Literary Society erected the stone in 1929 they didn't plant a tree at the location as well.

Walter Scott, plagued by ill health as a child, was sent to live at his grandparents' farm at Sandyknowe, within view of the Eildon Hills, in the hope that the country air would cure his ailments. It was here that he fell in love with the ballads that his grandmother and a favourite aunt told him. As early as 1792 Scott started collecting the ballads he heard on his yearly visits to the region and in 1802 he published the resulting compilation, *Minstrelsy of the Scottish Border*. As well as traditional ballads, Scott's *Minstrelsy* included popular eighteenth-century versions of older works. These include 'The Flowers of the Forest', a Scots-language lament for the dead of the Battle of Flodden in 1513. The version Scott included remains the most well known today and was written by Jean Elliot, a noblewoman from the village of Minto, between Hawick and Jedburgh. The song's refrain compares the fallen soldiers to forest flowers which have withered away, leaving a hauntingly quiet landscape.

Even more than the Border ballads, Scott fell in love with the Borders themselves. In 1799 he was appointed sheriff-depute of the Borders district of Selkirkshire and was able to use this job as a reason for travelling the area in search of ballads as well as ideas for his own fiction. In 1811, flush with the earnings from his hugely successful poetry (those were different times for professional poets!), he bought a small, dilapidated farm on the banks of the Tweed not far west of Melrose. His vision for this new home was worthy of one of his historical romances: he renamed the farm Abbotsford, a nod to the medieval monks who would have crossed here en route to Melrose Abbey. Grand extensions were soon underway that would make Abbotsford the envy of Britain's landed gentry, and by 1825 Scott had extended the estate tenfold by buying neighbouring farms; his holdings included Rhymer's Glen, where Thomas crossed into Elfland. Abbotsford was the pioneering example of the Scottish

Baronial style of architecture, a Romantic imitation of medieval Gothic castles, and inspired buildings such as Balmoral Castle, Queen Victoria's Highland retreat.

Today Abbotsford is open to the public, and exploring it is a unique experience. The library and study are packed with Scott's 9,000 books, but also on display is his extensive collection of historical memorabilia: Mary Queen of Scots' crucifix; a lock of Napoleon's hair; a piece of fruitcake from the Battle of Culloden. Needless to say, some of this collection is of dubious authenticity. Scott constructed an armoury in which to display his alarmingly large assortment of swords, shields, guns and suits of armour. Abbotsford is a shrine to literature, Scottish history and Scott's own conception of medieval Britain, but it's also a house of contrasts, as Scott admitted when he described it as his 'flibbertigibbet of a house'. The elaborate ceiling of the library is an imitation of Rosslyn Chapel, but the adjoining drawing room is decorated with exquisite hand-painted Chinese wallpaper that depicts flowers, birds and pastoral Chinese scenes. From the outside Abbotsford is equally eccentric, adorned with thistle-topped turrets and the crow-stepped gables that were particularly fashionable in nineteenth-century Scotland. Built into an external wall is another idiosyncratic ornament: the door that once kept convicts in and rioters out of Edinburgh's Old Tolbooth Prison (breached, of course, in Scott's *The Heart of Midlothian*). Abbotsford's grounds are tranquil and more reassuringly conventional than the house, with a lush walled garden and a lawn sloping gently down to the Tweed.

Scott's fortunes changed drastically when the financial crash of 1825 left him with debts that in modern values amounted to almost £9 million. He was forced to sell his Edinburgh home but couldn't countenance losing Abbotsford. He tried literally to write himself out of debt: over the next seven years he wrote furiously and published many novels, including the commercially successful *Woodstock*. But tragedy clung to Scott. In 1832 he suffered a series of strokes and died at Abbotsford, overlooking his beloved River Tweed.

In his pomp, Scott entertained many distinguished visitors at Abbotsford. He was a genial and charismatic host, and guests were known to dine to the accompaniment of bagpipes on the terrace outside. But even before he achieved fame as a writer, Scott enjoyed meeting literary visitors. In September 1803 William and Dorothy Wordsworth, coming to the end of their Scottish tour, arrived in the Borders and spent several days in his company. At this time Scott was sheriff of Selkirkshire and yet to publish any of his poetry or fiction. He seems to have relished playing the part of tour guide to the famous poet, accompanying the Wordsworths to Melrose, Jedburgh and other places in the Borders. On more than one occasion he read from his work in progress, *The Lay of the Last Minstrel*. Scott's connections to Jedburgh aren't all positive, however; in 1831 he made a hustings appearance in favour of the local Tory parliamentary candidate and was heckled by a posse of radical Hawick weavers. They stoned his carriage as it passed, shouting 'Burke Sir Walter', a reference to the method of suffocation used by the Edinburgh-based murderers Burke and Hare. Scott was evidently haunted by this reception, and a year later on his deathbed repeated the phrase 'Burke Sir Walter' deliriously to himself.

Jedburgh is an attractive market town, situated only ten miles from the English border and surrounded by fields and woods. As a frontier town it was often subject to cross-border raids. Mary Queen of Scots stayed in a fortified house here in 1566 (now open to visitors), and Jedburgh Abbey, founded in 1138, had to be rebuilt several times. In 1780 the pioneering female scientist Mary Somerville (after whom Somerville College, Oxford, is named) was born here in the same manse, or minister's house, in which the Wordsworths were later to be entertained by Mary's clergyman uncle. Dorothy Wordsworth was quite taken with the town, which she described as 'exceedingly beautiful on its low eminence'. She and her brother stayed at a lodging house near the abbey and were captivated by their hostess, an elderly woman of 'overflowing gaiety and strength' who looked after her deaf and infirm husband. William commemorated them in his poem 'The Matron of Jedburgh and her Husband':

> The joyous Woman is the Mate
> Of him in that forlorn estate;
> He breathes a subterranean damp;
> But bright as Vesper shines her lamp.

Even in a region famed for its ruined abbeys, Jedburgh's is one of the most spectacular. On either side of the nave rise three levels of arcade arches which are still impressively intact, although the roof is long gone. The abbey is in an elevated position and, seen from below, the sandstone pillars pointing upwards are something like the ribcage of a carcass, with light passing freely through the whole structure. On her visit to the abbey, Dorothy was horrified to see women using the gravestones in the grounds for their laundry, laying their linen on flat table-tombstones and 'batter[ing] as hard as they could with a wooden roller, a substitute for a mangle'.

Perhaps because of these irreverent locals, Dorothy wasn't especially impressed by Jedburgh Abbey. She was, however, full of praise for the more ornate and extensive Melrose Abbey, founded in 1136, which she had visited two days earlier. Melrose sits in the Tweed Valley below the slopes of the Eildon Hills and is a picturesque small town that remains an appealing location for visitors. Renowned for rugby and salmon fishing, and boasting some good independent bookshops, pubs and hotels, the town has a strong local identity and a welcoming atmosphere. The Wordsworths were given a tour of the Melrose Abbey ruins by Scott, as Dorothy records:

> He was here on his own ground, for he is familiar with all that is known of the authentic history of Melrose and the popular tales connected with it. He pointed out many pieces of beautiful sculpture in obscure corners which would have escaped our notice.

The Abbey has been built of a pale red stone; that part which was first erected of a very durable kind, the sculptured flowers and leaves and other minute ornaments being as perfect in many places as when first wrought.

For the Wordsworths, the journey through the Borders took a Gothic turn when they visited another abbey, at Dryburgh:

We rang a bell at the gate, and, instead of a porter, an old woman came to open it [. . .] the poor creature herself was a figure fit to frighten a child, – bowed almost double, having a hooked nose and overhanging eyebrows, a complexion stained brown with smoke, and a cap that might have been worn for months and never washed.

Despite appearances, the old woman turned out to be a knowledge-able guide, 'sedulous in pointing out the curiosities, which, I doubt not, she had a firm belief were not to be surpassed in England or Scotland'. Scott didn't accompany the Wordsworths on this visit but he did have a personal connection with Dryburgh Abbey: the land it stands on belonged to his great-grandfather. When he died in 1832 Scott was buried here in St Mary's Aisle, beside his wife.

Dumfries and Galloway

The high fells, secluded valleys and stretches of dense forest in the Borders seem to have been tailor-made as hiding places for the Reivers and their stolen English cattle. To the west of Selkirk is Ettrick, a quiet rural district with an impressive literary pedigree. James Hogg, author of *The Private Memoirs and Confessions of a Justified Sinner*, was born at a farm here, and his birthplace is marked by a bold, white, six-metre monument near the Loch of the Lowes on a stunningly rugged section of the A708 that links Selkirk and Moffat. A prolific writer in several genres, Hogg's agricultural background was both a blessing and a curse in the snobbish Edinburgh literary scene of the early nineteenth century. He had success as a novelist, poet and satirist, but never shook off the nickname of the 'Ettrick Shepherd', a term which was used as a way of belittling his supposed lack of urban sophistication.

In 1801 Hogg introduced his mother Margaret Laidlaw to Walter Scott, who was at that time collecting ballads for his *Minstrelsy*. According to her son, Margaret was 'a living miscellany of old songs', but she wasn't afraid of upbraiding the magpie Scott for printing some of her repertoire and, to her mind, disenchanting the ballads of their oral power. Hogg quotes his mother in his *Anecdotes of Scott* as saying: 'they were made for singing an' no for printing; but ye hae broken the charm now, an' they'll never be sung mair.' This story is also reported by a distant descendant of Margaret's brother, the contemporary Canadian short-story writer and Nobel Prize-winner Alice Munro, in her 2006 book *The View from Castle Rock*. The opening story of this collection is closer to memoir than fiction and includes a description of the time she spent in Ettrick and Selkirk researching the history of her family, who emigrated to Canada in 1818. When she arrives, her reaction is refreshingly honest and self-critical – her first impression is something of a damp squib:

> [T]he valley disappointed me the first time I saw it. Places are apt to do that when you've set them up in your imagination [. . .] I was struck with a feeling familiar, I suppose, to many people whose long history goes back to a country far away from the place where they grew up. I was a naïve North American, in spite of my stored knowledge. Past and present lumped together here made a reality that was commonplace and yet disturbing beyond anything I had imagined.

The title of this story is 'No Advantages', a reference to the 1799 Statistical Report of Scotland, quoted by Munro as an epigraph, in which the minister of Ettrick parish intones that 'This parish has no advantages.' Munro, however, is drawn by her own ancestry and by the broader cultural history of the place. As well as referring to Hogg and Scott, she records a rumour that William Wallace, guerrilla hero of the Wars of Independence, hid from the English in the Ettrick Valley. She also claims that Michael Scott, a thirteenth-century polymath whose reputation for sorcery earned him a place in the eighth circle of Hell in Dante's *Inferno*, lived in Ettrick. The mythical wizard Merlin was also said to have been 'hunted down and murdered' by shepherds in Ettrick Forest. Munro's subject is mythology, and how the real and imagined figures of the past have been mythologised. Lesser-known historical figures that earn a place in her story include an ancestor who, it was claimed, had visions of the fairy folk (we're still in ballad country, after all), and a local Calvinist minister preaching sin and damnation to the local people.

South of Ettrick is the village of Langholm, not far from Britain's elopement capital, Gretna Green. The Wordsworths stayed in Langholm soon after parting from Walter Scott, and Dorothy, no doubt fed up with rural hotels of dubious quality, remarked wryly that: 'the inn [was] neat and comfortable – exceedingly clean: I could hardly believe we were still in Scotland.' More recent visitors to the village are welcomed by a road sign that proudly declares: 'Here comes Langholm, birthplace of Hugh MacDiarmid'. On a hillside overlooking the village a sculpture of a giant metal book is also dedicated to MacDiarmid.

Born Christopher Murray Grieve in 1892, MacDiarmid was the outspoken catalyst of the Scottish Renaissance of the early twentieth century. Writing in Scots and English under the pseudonym Hugh MacDiarmid, he argued tirelessly and not without self-contradiction for an independent, communist Scotland and was a founder of the National Party of Scotland. His political claims about the distinctiveness of Scottish culture and the principles by which an independent Scotland might diverge from the rest of the United Kingdom are perhaps best demonstrated in his poetry rather than his prose. His output was voluminous, but at its best MacDiarmid's poetry reinvigorates the Scots language by making it do things it had never done before, tackling the modern world of Freud and Einstein rather than being the vehicle for sentimental and nostalgic pastoral verse about glens and heroes of the past. For some critics his work was forbiddingly modernist, colliding images and ideas in a similar way to Ezra Pound or James Joyce. But his short Scots poems can also be hauntingly beautiful, in particular in their evocations of the natural world, and MacDiarmid skilfully deploys Scots words that don't always have an exact equivalent in English: in 'The Eemis Stane' ('The Wobbly Stone') the world seems to quiver in the cold of a harvest night, and the speaker's memories fall 'like a yowdendrift' ('like a snowdrift'). Another poem, 'The Watergaw', compares the 'broken rainbow' of the title to the 'last wild look' of someone on their deathbed. Such sensitivity belies the pugnacious nature of MacDiarmid's public persona, which gained him fame (or notoriety) in Scotland and possibly led to his neglect among poetry readers from outside Scotland.

MacDiarmid waxed lyrical about his Langholm childhood, and its influence on his verse can be seen in his 1943 autobiography *Lucky Poet*, although his account also contains bawdy stories of his youth that made him a divisive figure in his hometown. *Lucky Poet* nevertheless paints Langholm as a pastoral idyll overflowing with:

> a bountifulness so inexhaustible that it has supplied all my subsequent poetry with a tremendous wealth of sensuous satisfaction, a teeming gratitude of reminiscence, and that I have still an immense reservoir to draw upon. My earliest impressions are of an almost tropical luxuriance of nature – of great forests, of honey-scented hills, and moorlands infinitely rich in little-appreciated beauties of flowering, of animal and insect life, of strange and subtle relationships of water and light.

The hills and moors around Langholm are a rich environment, and the numerous footpaths around the village lead to open hills and woodlands where sightings of wildlife such as hen harriers and lapwings can be as awe-inspiring as the panoramas of the surrounding landscape.

After the Second World War MacDiarmid came to be seen as the elder statesman of Scottish letters, a friend and champion to younger poets such as Norman MacCaig and (for a time) Ian Hamilton Finlay. From 1951 until his death in 1978 he lived with his wife Valda in Brownsbank Cottage, near Biggar, about 20 miles west of Peebles. Here he was visited by many fellow poets, including Seamus Heaney, Allen Ginsberg and the Russian Yevgeny Yevtushenko. The cottage is now run as a museum and also hosts writing residencies.

Far to the south of Biggar, where the wide estuary of the Solway Firth marks the border between Scotland and England, and the flattening landscape gives way to the gleaming of sunlight on tidal mudflats, a minor road winds through the tiny rural parish of Ruthwell on the way from Gretna to Dumfries. Those driving through here might assume there's little reason to stop, but if you pull over at the tidy if unspectacular whitewashed church you can see what no less an authority than Nikolaus Pevsner described as one of the marvels of medieval Europe.

The wonder hidden in this secluded corner of Scotland is the Ruthwell Cross, a five-metre-high Anglo-Saxon monument thought to date from the eighth century. Its stone sides are carved with patterns and Biblical scenes, including the crucifixion and the anointing of Jesus's feet – the immaculate sweeping lines of the latter image give it the appearance of a twentieth-century 'primitivist' sculpture. Around these carvings are phrases from the poem known today as *The Dream of the Rood*, written in Anglo-Saxon runes. Although the runes can't be dated with absolute certainty, they constitute one of the oldest surviving 'texts' in English poetry. These inscribed phrases are probably quotations from a longer work which was doing the rounds at the time, rather than a complete poem in their own right, but they stand alone perfectly well. The word 'rood' means cross, and the poem tells the story of Christ's crucifixion but from a rather unique perspective – that of the cross itself. The stone cross at Ruthwell is, as it were, speaking to us directly.

There's a great deal of mystery surrounding the Ruthwell Cross. Why was it made and for whom? Was it the creation of local craftsmen? Did it attract visitors from far and wide? Should it be regarded as an example of religious devotional art or as a monument to the power of the person who commissioned it? Or was it, like a Renaissance painting, a bit of both? Stylistically, it has similarities with crosses in Northumbria, Ravenna in Italy and Byzantium, so perhaps it should be considered as part of European, rather than local, culture. The runic inscriptions of *The Dream of the Rood* present the crucifixion in a way that could be readily understood within the framework of Anglo-Saxon culture: Christ is cast in the role of a heroic military leader, more dragon-slaying Beowulf than meek, suffering servant. My modern English translation is an attempt to capture the physical immediacy of the original poem:

> The stripped young hero (Almighty God himself!)
> was strong, unyielding. Willingly he climbed
> the towering gallows tree; he was brave before all men.

> I, the cross, raised up this great king,
> heaven's overlord: I didn't dare bend an inch.
> They mocked us both. I was bespattered
> with all the blood that streamed forth.

> Christ on the cross. From far afield the people came
> to this noble prince – I saw it all.

> I ached with sorrows, I was run through with arrows.
> They lowered him down, shattered, and stood by his head.
> They just stood there looking at him.

Standing in front of a monument like the Ruthwell Cross is a humbling experience. Imagine it positioned on its own in the landscape, outdoors, and imagine that the landscape bore far fewer signs of human cultivation than it does today. The cross starts to take on the presence of a declaration, of medieval Christians claiming this land for their God in a similar way to Neil Armstrong planting a flag on the moon to claim it for humanity (or, at least, America). It would surely have had an aura that impressed those at the time and, although it's been ravaged by the centuries, broken into pieces by Protestant iconoclasts and then restored in the nineteenth century, some of that aura remains with the Ruthwell Cross today.

Just under a mile to the west of Ruthwell, a few paces from a marked lay-by, is Brow Well. This is a natural spring, paved round and now of little use: a sign warns that the water is unsuitable for drinking. In the eighteenth century, however, this well gained repute with the people of nearby Dumfries for its healing qualities, and the most famous patient directed here was Robert Burns. In July 1796 Burns's doctor, in a desperate attempt to find a cure for the ailing poet, prescribed drinking from Brow and wading daily in the cold waters of the Solway Firth, where the patient was required to stand immersed up to his armpits. Burns seems to have had a heart condition at the time, and this bathing almost certainly killed him. He was buried in the kirkyard of St Michael's Church, Dumfries, within a month of beginning this 'treatment'.

Burns had spent the last five years in Dumfries, some of this time in a pretty red sandstone house in Millbrae Vennell, later renamed Burns Street. The Globe Inn, Burns's favourite haunt, remains popular today and proudly declares its literary connection. Burns's grave was visited by the Wordsworths in 1803 and William wrote another imaginatively titled poem, 'At the Grave of Burns'. In 1815 Burns was reinterred in a more elaborate mausoleum, which was visited by John Keats in 1818. Keats wrote to his brother that the mausoleum was 'not very much to my taste', and his poem 'On Visiting the Tomb of Burns' shares the ambivalent tone that Alice Munro would later use in describing her first impressions of Ettrick. Addressing Burns, Keats admits his negative feelings about the 'cold beauty' of the place and his poem ends with typical Keatsian melodrama:

> I have oft honoured thee. Great shadow, hide
> Thy face – I sin against thy native skies.

A more enchanted visitor to the south-west corner of Scotland was the crime writer Dorothy L. Sayers. In 1928 she and her husband stayed in the Anwoth Hotel in the Galloway village of Gatehouse of Fleet (now the Ship Inn, a welcoming hotel and pub that works to keep the Sayers flame burning bright). From 1929 they rented a studio in the High Street, Kirkcudbright, a few miles away at the mouth of the River Dee. Sayers's 1931 novel *The Five Red Herrings* is set in this district and her meticulous attention to detail (including accurate train timetables to Glasgow and Carlisle) brings the time and place to life. It is dedicated to the Anwoth Hotel's Joe Dignam, the 'kindliest of landlords'. In the book, Sayers's famous detective, the endearingly named Lord Peter Wimsey, is holidaying in Galloway and becomes embroiled in a murder investigation that involves a forged painting – this evidence implicates one of the many artists living and working in Kirkcudbright and Gatehouse. With six suspects, the question is who is guilty and who are the red herrings of the title? In a wonderfully jovial opening paragraph, Sayers offers a description of the area that (almost) holds true to this day:

If one lives in Galloway, one either fishes or paints. 'Either' is perhaps misleading, for most of the painters are fishers also in their spare time. To be neither of these things is considered odd and almost eccentric. Fish is the standard topic of conversion in the pub and the post-office, in the garage and the street [. . .] Weather, which in other parts of the Kingdom is gauged by the standards of the farmer, the gardener, and the week-ender, is considered in Galloway in terms of fish and paint.

About a century before Sayers holidayed in Galloway, another visitor, the American essayist Ralph Waldo Emerson, travelled to the Uplands north of Dumfries in search of a remote farm called Craigenputtock. He was intent upon delivering a letter to its famous resident, Thomas Carlyle, whose books and essays Emerson admired immensely. Carlyle's wife Jane had inherited the farmhouse and they moved there in 1828, partly for the sake of scholarly seclusion and partly because of a lack of money. This move was against Jane's better judgement and she displayed her characteristic acerbic wit when she told her husband: 'You and I keeping house at Craigenputtock! I would as soon think of building myself a nest on the Bass Rock.' Writing in his *Reminiscences* about life at Craigenputtock, Carlyle, in return, recalled Jane's 'beautiful thrift' as a housekeeper – a compliment that manages to be both incredibly condescending and stereotypically Scottish. In his 1856 book *English Traits*, Emerson – not the only visiting writer to conflate England and the United Kingdom – writes about meeting his literary hero and, perhaps carried away by the uncompromising landscape around the farm, proceeds to describe Carlyle himself in almost geographical terms: 'I found the house amid desolate heathery hills, where the lonely scholar nourished his mighty heart. [. . .] He was tall and gaunt, with a cliff-like brow, self-possessed, and holding his extraordinary powers of conversation in easy command; clinging to his northern accent with evident relish.'

Emerson aside, visitors to the farm were few, although letters arrived from all over the world. Carlyle, never one to play down his friendship with Germany's great Romantic poet, once commented, 'it is so strange to see "Craigenputtock" written in Goethe's hand.' Goethe may have been replying to an earlier letter in which Carlyle loftily explains his residence at the farm: 'I came hither purely for this one reason: that I might not have to write for bread, might not be tempted to tell lies for money.' In 1834 Thomas and Jane moved to Chelsea.

For a present-day book-lover no trip to the south-west of Scotland is complete without spending some time in the small coastal town of Wigtown. Awarded the status of 'Scotland's National Book Town' in 1998, making it the Scottish equivalent of Hay-on-Wye, it's home to around 20 new and second-hand bookshops catering to almost every taste. The oldest of these is the Book Shop, Scotland's largest second-hand bookseller with over 100,000 items and more than a mile of shelves. Look out for its dazzling display of orange Penguin paperbacks. It's easy to lose days at a time in Wigtown's bookshops (and indeed to incur the wrath of your bank manager), but if flesh-and-blood authors are your thing then head there in autumn for the Wigtown Book Festival, one of Scotland's major literary events which attracts a host of famous writers, many of whom will be found eagerly browsing the shops after their readings.

☙ 4 ☙

GLASGOW AND WEST CENTRAL SCOTLAND

No Mean City?

Glasgow, wrote the Scottish novelist Lewis Grassic Gibbon in 1934, 'is one of the few places in Scotland which defy personification'. In contrast to Edinburgh, which has long been the legal, political and cultural centre of the country, most of Glasgow's literary history is relatively recent, dating back little further than the Industrial Revolution. Once a small university and cathedral town, from the eighteenth century onwards it rapidly expanded to become a major industrial centre: by 1913 a fifth of the world's shipping was built on Glasgow's River Clyde. Growth in industry led to a population explosion, from an estimated 40,000 in 1780 to over a million by the early twentieth century. Novels set before this expansion, such as James Hogg's *The Private Memoirs and Confessions of a Justified Sinner*, make illuminating reading when it comes to exploring Glasgow. Hogg's seventeenth-century 'sinner', Robert Wringhim, walks through 'the field and wood of Finnieston', an idyll conducive to peaceful contemplation. By Hogg's own lifetime, the early nineteenth century, this was an area of docks and warehouses; today it's been transformed again, into a neighbourhood of trendy bars and concert venues.

The great wealth of the city's traders and industrialists can be seen in the magnificent architecture of the city centre – a particularly opulent example is the City Chambers, opened in 1888, which boasts the world's largest solid marble staircase. Glasgow was one of the chief beneficiaries of the 1707 Act of Union, which gave its businessmen access to England's colonial trade in tobacco. Daniel Defoe, visiting Glasgow at the start of the eighteenth century, wrote in *A Tour Through the Whole Island of Great Britain* that it was 'the cleanest and beautifullest, and best built city in Britain, London excepted'. But two centuries later, after the Industrial Revolution had brought mass industry to the city, Karel Čapek, who so admired 1920s Edinburgh, consigned Glasgow to a short postscript in his *Letters from England* and found very little to praise:

> O Glasgow, city without beauty, city of noise and commerce, city of factories and wharves, harbour for wares of all kinds. What am I to say about you? Is there then any beauty in factories, docks and warehouses, cranes in the harbour, towers of steel-works, flocks of gasometers, clattering cartloads of goods, tall chimneys and thunderous steam-hammers, structures of girders and iron, buoys in the water and mountains of coal?

The contrast between Defoe's and Čapek's descriptions gives a sense of how much the city changed, but it was the appalling social conditions brought about by rapid urbanisation that horrified twentieth-century writers, politicians and social reformers. In *Scottish Scene* Lewis Grassic Gibbon goes on to describe notorious Glasgow slums such as the Gorbals as 'waste jungles of stench and disease and hopelessness'. The deindustrialisation of the second half of the twentieth century caused further upheaval, and its effects continue to be seen to this day. An unsurprising result of this is that a great deal of the twentieth- and twenty-first-century fiction and poetry about Glasgow engages with issues of class, poverty, social justice and radical politics. Despite Čapek's reservations, many writers also find beauty in this urban landscape.

Today Glasgow is a city on the rise again, in part because of a renewed sense of confidence that comes from its flourishing arts, music and literary scenes. To judge by its world-class orchestras and alternative rock bands, its Turner Prize-winning artists, its film-makers and its award-winning poets, playwrights and novelists, it's not only one of the coolest places in Britain but also one of the most culturally dynamic cities in Europe. It's increasingly recognised as a top destination for city breaks. But Glasgow's cultural renaissance is relatively recent, and for decades the city's literary reputation was grounded in accounts of its gritty underworld.

One of the main literary contributions to Glasgow's negative image was the 1935 novel *No Mean City*, written by Alexander McArthur, an unemployed Gorbals baker, with input by journalist H. Kingsley Long. The novel follows the rise of a Gorbals gangster, Johnnie Stark, who is known in the slum as 'Razor King' because of the damage he inflicts on rivals with his weapons of choice. Razor King's greatest triumphs come in pitched battles fought with blades and broken bottles on Glasgow Green, the large park to the east of the city centre. At times *No Mean City* feels like a 1930s American gangster noir, with its narrative of the rise and fall of an underworld figure. At other times it has a documentary tone as it educates the wider world about social conditions in the Gorbals. *No Mean City* was a sensation, selling about a million copies, although its depiction of working-class Glasgow as amoral and unremittingly violent had its critics: the city's bookshops and libraries refused to stock it. No doubt many baulked at the characters' heavy drinking – red wine laced with raw spirits is Razor King's tipple of choice. But the Gorbals, let alone Glasgow as a whole, can't simply be boiled down to the image of a tough, mean city. The city excels in confounding expectation. On the edge of the Gorbals, south of the River Clyde and within walking distance of the city centre, is one of Scotland's best theatres, the Citizens, founded in 1943 by writers keen to enrich Glasgow's cultural life. And more recently Glasgow has reclaimed the phrase 'no mean city' – with tongue firmly in cheek – as the name of one of its many music festivals.

If there was a word that could summarise Glasgow it would probably be 'gallus'. Gallus is a Scots word meaning boldness, daring, rascallish impudence. It also has connotations of self-confidence, especially the self-confidence of the underdog who refuses to be put in his place. Increasingly it's a word used to describe something stylish and, as Scots dictionaries will tell you, it's used more commonly as a term of approval in Glasgow than in Edinburgh, its great rival.

City Centres

The streets of Glasgow's central precinct are laid out in a grid, and even lifelong Glaswegians can find this confusing: with so many parallel roads it's easy forget which one is which. Three streets, however, dominate the bustling retail and commercial life of the city centre. These are Sauchiehall Street, Buchanan Street and Argyle Street, which all connect and can be followed in a vaguely z-shaped meander that begins near the West End and passes close to George Square, Merchant Square and other important Glasgow landmarks. When walking these streets, look up. The neoclassical architecture is often ridiculously grand: the columns are crowned with the bulging torsos of Greek gods; cornices are embellished in every conceivable way. On the roof of an old fish market pigeons roost between the stone hooves of a hippocampus, the mythical horse with dragon wings and the tail of a fish. Allegorical figures of commerce, navigation and wealth look down on revellers entering the Corinthian, once a bank but now one of the city's most popular nightspots.

George Square is, arguably, the centre of Glasgow. The site of choice for political rallies and New Year celebrations, its role in the civic life of the city is probably as pronounced today as it's ever been. Among the numerous plinths and statues dotted about the square are memorials to Sir Walter Scott and Robert Burns. But modern-day civic centres can only tell you so much about a city, and to get to know Glasgow well it's crucial to venture beyond George Square. A minute's walk to the west of the square is the pedestrianised Buchanan Street, Scotland's high-street shopping Mecca. The view downhill from the elevated north end of the street, where there's a statue of Scotland's inaugural first minister, Donald Dewar, is one of the best in the city: crowds ebb and flow between the shops and arcades, overlooked by elegant façades; on the horizon green hills break the sense of urban sprawl. In Christopher Brookmyre's comic crime novel *The Sacred Art of Stealing*, published in 2003, Buchanan Street stars as the scene of a surreal, 'Dadaist' bank robbery in which gunmen perform a choreographed dance as they attempt to get away. Such a scene wouldn't look out of place amid the buskers and bag-laden shoppers navigating this hectic street.

Sauchiehall Street leads west from the top of Buchanan Street. Today Sauchiehall Street is one of the busiest Glasgow streets but, despite its present-day central location and its assortment of shops, restaurants and nightclubs, it was developed in the early nineteenth century as a quiet and leafy area on the edge of the city. 'Sauchiehall' means 'willow grove' in Scots. The Willow Tea Rooms on Sauchiehall Street is a café that appealed to the area's chattering classes at the turn of the twentieth century and was designed in its entirety, from exterior walls to cutlery, by Charles Rennie Mackintosh.

One of the best evocations of life in this part of town at the dawn of the twentieth century is Catherine Carswell's *Open the Door!* Carswell was born in Glasgow in 1879 and studied English at the University of Glasgow. An early champion of D. H. Lawrence, they exchanged manuscripts of *Open the Door!* and *Women in Love*, and his positive feedback encouraged her to seek publication. Set in Glasgow, Italy and London, *Open the Door!* follows a young woman named Joanna Bannerman as she seeks independence, leaving behind her strict evangelical upbringing and travelling in Europe. Joanna and her sister Georgie grow up in a townhouse on the hill overlooking

Sauchiehall Street. The girls enjoy the excitement of the city's grand occasions: 'three times they had hung out great flags over the sills for Royal Processions. Once Georgie was quite certain that Queen Victoria driving up Sauchiehall Street, had waved her hand in special acknowledgement to their high window.' Joanna's is a sheltered childhood, and she is described as 'a fugitive from the realities surrounding her town existence'. She spends much of her time in the city's affluent West End, a few minutes' walk from her home. Carswell's descriptions of the elegant terraces, parks and bridges over the quiet River Kelvin are a world away from the 'no mean city' image of Glasgow, but are no less accurate. As Joanna walks in the West End with a lover, the prose has a Lawrentian lushness:

[T]hey paused, leaning on the parapet of the high-hung bridge, and they gazed down into the wooded bed where the river was only betrayed from time to time by a snaky gleam. To their right rose a sheer escarpment of stone, and towering yet higher behind it, tier upon tier of flats full of windows seemed in the darkness to be a dense forest screen hung unevenly with barred, many-coloured lanterns. To their left ran the low crescent of shops, like a necklace of gold and brilliants curved in a velvet case.

A pivotal moment in Joanna's development comes when she enrols at the Glasgow School of Art, situated on Renfrew Street, parallel to and uphill from Sauchiehall Street. Today the School of Art is one of Britain's best; its alumni include leading contemporary artists Martin Boyce and David Shrigley. The actors Robbie Coltrane and Peter Capaldi also studied here, as did Scotland's recent makar, or poet laureate, Liz Lochhead. The school's main building, designed by Charles Rennie Mackintosh and completed in 1909, was one of the world's greatest art nouveau buildings, an eclectic warren of galleries and classrooms crammed full of Mackintosh's elaborate geometric and floral motifs, which ornamented wooden fixtures, tiles and ironwork. The library in particular, a thicket of unique wooden furniture and bookcases, was a marvel. In 2014 disaster struck when the building was seriously damaged by fire; restoration to its former glory will take several years.

Another accomplished graduate of the School of Art is Alasdair Gray. Gray is a painter and author, and his murals adorn several iconic buildings in the West End. He's best known, however, for *Lanark*, a sprawling novel that encompasses social realist *Bildungsroman*, science fiction and a bleak, post-industrial form of magical realism. *Lanark*'s experimental construction – its four sections are ordered three, one, two, four, while an epilogue lists plagiarisms embedded in the narrative – led to it being hailed as a post-modern or even 'post-post-modern' classic. The middle sections of *Lanark* are a semi-autobiographical account of a young muralist called Duncan Thaw, who grows up in a council flat in Glasgow's East End before attending the School of Art. In the novel the institution isn't particularly dynamic and Thaw, like Gray an eccentric and independent-minded artist, finds himself at odds with his drawing tutor. During an exercise she scolds him:

'Hold the pencil lightly; don't grip it like a spanner. That shell is a simple, delicate, rather lovely thing. Your drawing is like the diagram of a machine.'

'But surely, Miss Mackenzie, the shell only seems delicate and simple because it's smaller than we are. To the fish inside it was a suit of armour, a house, a moving fortress.'

Thaw's future career is fraught with similar misunderstandings as he strives to make viewers understand and appreciate his art. *Lanark* splices the story of Thaw growing up in postwar Glasgow with scenes set in the futuristic Unthank, an alternative-reality Glasgow on which the sun never shines. In this parallel Glasgow the hapless Thaw is reincarnated as a character called Lanark and becomes embroiled in Unthank's arcane politics. The political centre of Unthank is a dystopian parody of Glasgow Cathedral.

Unthank Cathedral is described as a squat building blackened by soot, a 'sturdy Gothic ark' filled with war memorials and torn regimental flags. In *Lanark* it isn't used for ecclesiastical purposes, but serves as council headquarters.

If you've read *Lanark* it's hard to visit the real Glasgow Cathedral, which was begun in the twelfth century, without seeing it through the lens of Gray's fiction. This was the focal point of medieval Glasgow, and today it sits about a mile and a half to the east of the School of Art. It is indeed squat, by the standards of Gothic cathedrals, and on a gloomy day its dark stone walls lend it a brooding presence. Inside there are regimental colours and tributes to fallen soldiers. The interior is dim and atmospheric rather than bright and airy, but the cathedral's stained-glass windows are indisputably resplendent. Before the Reformation this was a popular place of pilgrimage because its crypt is said to house the remains of St Kentigern, also known as St

5 Glasgow Cathedral, heart of the 'dear green place'

Mungo, the founder and patron saint of Glasgow. The building is best approached from the city centre along Cathedral Street: its spire and green copper roof loom over the surrounding buildings, some of which are among Glasgow's oldest. Nearby is the imposing stone façade of the Royal Infirmary, another soot-blackened, forbidding building; behind rises the Necropolis, Glasgow's city of the dead.

Built on a wooded hill, the Necropolis is a graveyard of haunting solitudes and ostentatious monuments. The city's wealthy merchants and politicians commissioned Scotland's leading architects – including Charles Rennie Mackintosh and Alexander 'Greek' Thomson – to design their tombs. The Necropolis covers 15 hectares and provides a sanctuary for a rich array of wildlife, including a herd of roe deer. In pride of place at the top of the hill is a column with a four-metre statue of John Knox, Scotland's Reformation firebrand. In her 2002 crime novel *The Cutting Room*, set in a seedy Glasgow underworld of pornographers, pimps and people smugglers, Louise Welsh neatly captures the history of the Necropolis, emphasising its more grisly

6 The Necropolis

qualities in true hard-boiled style. Her protagonist, a promiscuous auctioneer called Rilke, passes the graveyard on his way to visit a mysterious client who is being treated at the infirmary, and pays his own disrespectful tribute to the city's Protestant heritage:

> A shadow horizon of half-tumbled monuments and mausoleums formed the backdrop to the Royal Infirmary. The Necropolis. Glasgow's first 'hygienic cemetery', established in the early nineteenth century, designed to avoid the spread of cholera and a slippage of corpses from ill-dug graves, which had become a city scandal. A convenient stroll across the Bridge of Sighs from the hospital. John Knox pointed down at us sinners from his high vantage point on the hill, 'next only to God'. I gave him a V sign and steered the van into the hospital courtyard.

The Necropolis has grandeur, but Rilke's ambivalence is shared by many Glaswegians. Its graves, stone angels and statues of the dead are a somewhat macabre sight for patients lying in the infirmary's wards.

A few streets south of Glasgow Cathedral, past the concert halls, boutiques and stylish restaurants of the Merchant City district, is another of the city's oldest remaining buildings. This is the Tolbooth Steeple, built in 1625–6 at Glasgow Cross, the junction of the Trongate, Gallowgate and Saltmarket, at the eastern end of Argyle Street. The steeple is all that remains of the city's Tolbooth: the old council chambers, courthouse and jail. Over 30 metres tall, it stands incongruously in the middle of the road. Much of William McIlvanney's *Laidlaw*, the 1977 novel that is often viewed as the beginning of the Scottish crime genre known as 'tartan noir', takes place in the backstreets, windowless pubs and run-down housing estates near Glasgow Cross. The titular detective is Glasgow's answer to Raymond Chandler's jaded detective Philip Marlowe. A 'systematically' heavy drinker, Laidlaw keeps volumes of 'Kierkegaard, Camus and Unamuno' in his desk drawer, and their philosophy informs his melancholy but wry observations on the city's psyche. At Glasgow Cross Laidlaw and his partner, an idealistic young officer, read the Latin inscription on the Tolbooth, '*nemo me impune lacessit*'. Laidlaw translates into English and Scots: '"No one assaults me with impunity," Laidlaw said. "Wha daur meddle wi me? [. . .] That's a wee message carved on the heart of Glasgow. Visitors are advised not to be cheeky."'

Glasgow Cross is a corner of town now known for its drinking dens, discount stores and amusement arcades. But the Trongate and Gallowgate, which converge at Glasgow Cross, were once Glasgow's city centre and these streets swarmed with shoppers and trams. Dorothy Wordsworth described the Trongate as 'very picturesque' and was amazed at the large shops and fashionable coffee rooms in this part of town. Samuel Taylor Coleridge, travelling with the Wordsworths, was less in awe, and one of the few Glasgow entries in his notebook is a rather sneering account of an 'asthmatic town crier, a ludicrous combination'. A few years after their visit John Keats found himself in a fracas with a drunk man and wrote to a friend, 'I was obliged to mention the words Officer and Police before he would desist.'

The East End

In 1803 Coleridge and the Wordsworths stayed together at the Saracen Head, an inn to the east of Glasgow Cross on the Gallowgate. It still exists and is one of several pubs that claim to be Glasgow's oldest. In a city of gastropubs with vegan brunch menus, the 'Sarry Heid' is an uncompromising east Glasgow bar of the old school, only opening its doors when the proprietor decides – on weekends and for Celtic football matches mostly. What these cosmopolitan upstarts don't have, however, is the Saracen Head's literary pedigree. As well as Coleridge and the Wordsworths, both Robert Burns and the theologian John Wesley, co-founder of Methodism, stayed here. At the end of their Hebridean journey,

Samuel Johnson and James Boswell returned to the Saracen Head, and their drinking companions on that occasion may have included their friend, the economist Adam Smith. Smith and Johnson seem to have had a fairly feisty relationship: the story's still told that at the end of a heavy night's drinking in the Saracen Head, Smith was forcibly ejected for calling the great man of letters a 'son of a bitch'.

Were he alive today Adam Smith would probably think twice about calling anyone in an East End pub a 'son of a bitch'. Nowhere in Glasgow does the motto *nemo me impune lacessit* ring more true than in the city's eastern neighbourhoods. In McIlvanney's *Laidlaw*, the detectives enter a bar in the Calton district, not far beyond the Saracen Head. They immediately feel the tension that comes from 'knowing at once that you were in the presence of a lot of physical pride, a crowd of it, so that you sensed the need to move carefully, in case you bumped an ego. This room was the resort of men who hadn't much beyond a sense of themselves and weren't inclined to have that sense diminished.' McIlvanney's Glasgow can be a tough place, but it's also the most gregarious of cities. Laidlaw comments that he loves Glasgow because 'It's not a city, it's a twenty-four hour cabaret.' Laidlaw's observation is as true today as it was in the 1970s. If you're visiting Glasgow for the first time and ask a stranger for directions, beware – a dozen others will probably stop to help, and their thoroughly partial advice as to the best attractions to visit will keep you detained for some time.

Directly across the road from the Saracen Head are two other Glasgow landmarks, the Barras Market and the Barrowland Ballroom. 'Barras' is short for the 'barrows' which were formerly used by traders at this street market. The Ballroom is a legendary music venue with a sprung dance floor that has bounced to Britain's biggest bands, many of whom have named it their favourite venue: its no-frills grunginess attracts the most passionate crowds. Jackie Kay features the Barrowland Ballroom in *Trumpet*, her 1998 novel about a transgender jazz trumpeter gigging in London and Glasgow, and her description captures the venue's pulsating atmosphere: 'We dance at the Barrowland way into the early hours. The atmosphere, jumping. The dance style, gallus. There is no tomorrow. There is just the minute, the second, the dip. The heat and the sweat. That feeling of being your body.'

The Barras Market is beloved by the city's many bargain-hunters, and a must for travellers keen to experience a resolutely down-to-earth taste of Glasgow. The stalls sell everything from vegetables to bootleg CDs. Laptops and cigarettes are cheap and of equally dubious provenance. Many visitors happily part with their cash just to hear the rapid-fire banter of the hawkers milling through crowds, always with half an eye out for a passing police officer. In Louise Welsh's *The Cutting Room* Rilke rubs shoulders with these traders in Glasgow's dingier auction rooms: they leave 'long-faced relatives to freeze at the stall' while they rummage through the wares being put under the hammer.

Glasgow's name comes from the Gaelic *Glaschu*, which is usually translated as 'dear green place'. In *The Dear Green Place*, Archie Hind's 1966 novel about a struggling Glasgow writer, the protagonist Mat remembers how his parents came to the Barras 'every third week' as newly-weds in the 1920s, searching for cheap household goods:

> It was in this famous street market that they picked up [. . .] screwdrivers, a plane, chisels, pliers for odd jobs round the house, huge earthenware plates that were still in use, the egg cups of turned wood that had all disappeared, the same miniature grandfather clock that had ticked in accompaniment to Mat's thoughts as he sat up years later reading and writing.

Towards the start of the book Mat, who wants to pen the best-ever Glasgow novel, is writing a history of the city from its origins as a verdant ecclesiastical centre on a river with 'grey mossy slopes and thymy banks' to its mid-twentieth-century existence 'at the heart of the industrial world'. Perhaps surprisingly, *The Dear Green Place* feels more European than British, a moody, existentialist meditation on the city. It's possible to imagine Mat walking the overcast streets of Paris, Vienna or Prague, talking aloud to himself as he wrestles with self-doubt and searches for literary inspiration.

The etymology of Glasgow is still apt – the city has about 90 parks. Glasgow Green is one of the largest and is situated just to the south of the Barras on the banks of the Clyde. It's the oldest park in the city, established by King James II in 1450. Over the years it's been used for grazing, laundering, drying fishing nets and, more recently, for music and sports events, including the 2014 Commonwealth Games. In Jessie Kesson's 1958 novel *The White Bird Passes*, gypsies hold markets here. Nearby is the former Templeton's Carpet Factory, an exuberant industrial building whose crenellations, mosaic-patterned walls and lancet windows are modelled on the Doge's Palace in Venice. Appropriately enough, Hind's *The Dear Green Place* contains a stirring, if ambivalent, evocation of the Green and the river flowing past it. Mat, still struggling to write his great Glasgow novel, skives off from his office job to wander the city, his thoughts a mixture of love and disdain for his hometown:

> He turned up past the gates of the Glasgow Green to the parapet of the bridge from where he could see the old Clyde, the colour of a back court puddle, winding in through the Green towards the centre of the city. [. . .] The park looked grey like a plucked fowl with its stark leafless trees. He leaned on the smooth granite parapet of the bridge easing the weight on his legs. Glasgow! Gles Chu! The dear green place!

The West End

While Archie Hind treats the greenery of Glasgow Green with a fairly heavy dose of irony, the same scepticism can't be directed towards Kelvingrove Park, which extends for 35 leafy hectares on either bank of the River Kelvin in the heart of Glasgow's West End. This beautiful park is in the city's university quarter, and the nearby streets are lined with boutiques, bistros and bookshops. Rising above it to the east is the handsome sweep of Park Circus, location of some of Glasgow's most desirable residences; to the west, on the brow of Gilmorehill, is the striking profile of the University of Glasgow. The university is the second-largest Gothic Revival building in Britain after the Palace of Westminster. Its sandstone turrets and bell tower are the unmistakable focal point on the local skyline. Joanna Bannerman walks through Kelvingrove Park on her way to Italian classes in Catherine Carswell's *Open the Door!* and is enraptured by her surroundings:

> [I]t came upon her that she was walking amid beauty [. . .] Church-spires – St Jude's among them – and tall houses, mysterious at their bases, rose triumphantly through the sullied lower air to the serenely brooding blue above, where they seemed suspended. And away to the left on its hill, dominating the park, the Gothic University stood high and black and alien against the sky.

7 The University of Glasgow from Kelvingrove Park

Joanna's route to Kelvingrove Park from the city centre would have taken her along Sauchiehall Street, which now passes over the M8 motorway that bisects this part of the city. It passes close to the Mitchell Library, one of Europe's largest public reference libraries, and home to extensive collections of literature about Glasgow; its grand façade, crowned with a distinctive green copper dome and a statue of Minerva, Roman goddess of wisdom, overlooks the motorway. This western part of Sauchiehall Street is very different from the bustling eastern stretch with its array of shops and nightclubs. Instead it feels almost – whisper it – like part of Edinburgh's New Town, a broad, straight road lined with townhouses and stately hotels. Glimpses of gardens become more frequent, and the name 'willow grove' seems suddenly more credible.

Just before Sauchiehall Street meets the edge of Kelvingrove Park it crosses Claremont Street, and at the end of this street is the Henry Wood Hall, a former church which was the home of the Royal Scottish National Orchestra for over 30 years. A classic Victorian parish church with a slender spire and Gothic stained-glass windows, it was converted into a concert hall and rehearsal space in 1979. This is the setting for the climactic concert in Bernard MacLaverty's *Grace Notes*, published in 1997. The novel follows Catherine McKenna, a young composer from small-town Northern Ireland, as she prepares for the biggest concert of her life: the world premiere of her orchestral piece *Vernicle*. Catherine is Roman Catholic and her composition is guaranteed to shock her family because it incorporates Lambeg drums – the booming percussion used by Protestant marching bands. On the night of the concert, the final scene in the novel, she is understandably nervous, convinced that her bold creation will appal the audience. In *Vernicle*'s opening movement the Lambegs intrude on the melody played by the strings: 'Suddenly everything is cut short by the entrance of the Lambegs. It is almost like machine-gun fire. A short burst – enough to kill and maim. Silence. It's the kind of silence induced by a slap in the face or the roarings of a drunk.' As

Vernicle goes on, the drumming becomes increasingly integrated into the sound of the orchestra: 'The whole church reverberates. The Lambegs have been stripped of their bigotry and have become pure sound. The black sea withdraws. So too the trappings of the church – they have nothing to do with belief and exist as colour and form. It is infectious. On this accumulating wave the drumming has a fierce joy about it.'

MacLaverty's descriptions of the music are spellbinding, leaving the reader wishing that *Vernicle* really existed and could be heard live. *Grace Notes* goes beyond music, however, and is a moving meditation on community and creativity. Despite her obvious talent, Catherine struggles to justify working as a composer – a full-time occupation with next to no salary, in a male-dominated industry – and at the same time her life changes dramatically with the birth of her daughter. Much of the novel is set in Glasgow, where Catherine studies and composes, and here she fights to maintain her commitment to an artistic life.

Sauchiehall Street meets Kelvingrove Park at a junction overlooked by another of Glasgow's iconic Victorian buildings, the Kelvingrove Art Gallery and Museum. The gallery is housed in a sprawling red sandstone building in the baroque style, studded with towers and turrets and modelled on the pilgrimage church of Santiago de Compostela. It's an irrefutably gallus tribute to the original, a brash apparition rising from the wooded park. Its permanent collection is suitably eclectic: paintings by Rembrandt and Salvador Dali sit alongside an extensive display of work by the 'Glasgow Boys', a group of late nineteenth-century artists influenced by Whistler. But the Kelvingrove is about far more than paintings. Its arrangement encourages you to expect the unexpected: a Second World War Spitfire flies over the head of a giraffe; bees from a working hive rub shoulders (or wings) with Ancient Egyptian mummies. There are daily recitals on the gallery's pipe organ. Everything is imaginatively juxtaposed in what Archie Hind describes as a 'huge mad Victorian megalomaniac art gallery'.

The University of Glasgow is the focal point of the West End's cultural life, and many writers from Scotland and beyond have connections to the university. Alasdair Gray and Louise Welsh both studied and taught here and other alumni include crime writers Christopher Brookmyre and Denise Mina, poets Robert Crawford and Tom Leonard, and novelists William Boyd, Janice Galloway, William McIlvanney, Zoë Strachan and Alan Warner. Perhaps the most acclaimed writers with connections to the university, however, are Edwin Morgan and James Kelman.

Morgan, who died in 2010 at the age of 90, was one of Scotland's favourite poets, appointed the first makar, or laureate, of Glasgow in 1999, and the first national makar in 2004. Highly versatile, he wrote everything from sonnets to concrete poetry, an experimental form employing unusual typographical arrangements. He belonged to that rare breed of poet equally respected by his peers and by the wider public, including the poetry-averse. He wrote a poem for the opening of the Scottish Parliament building in 2004 and collaborated with musicians, including the Scottish rock band Idlewild.

Morgan had a long and prestigious career as an academic at the University of Glasgow and, apart from six years in the Second World War, spent his entire life in Glasgow. His poetry is concerned with a diverse range of topics, from mythology to science fiction, and from sexuality to urban planning. But, as the title of one of his collections, *From Glasgow to Saturn*, suggests, it's the city of his birth which provided the subject matter for much of his work. At times Morgan's Glasgow is full of colour and energy, but he is particularly drawn to the city's darker side, to dingy corners, deprivation and violence. In one of his 1973 sequence of 'Glasgow Sonnets', a crooked landlord offers a family of seven the rental of two rooms in a tenement block due for demolition. Morgan often finds tenderness and fugitive beauty in the city: another sonnet quotes a gang's graffiti tag, painted on a wall, and compares it to a prayer.

Glasgow has the third-oldest underground metro railway in the world. It opened in 1896 and is one of the world's smallest, too, consisting of just one loop of 15 stations. In the early 1980s Morgan was commissioned to write poster poems for display in the Glasgow Underground to celebrate its modernisation. The impish poems he produced were rejected as unsuitable by the transport executive. They all have an animal theme: in 'The Budgie' a bird lives in the tunnels, riding along on train roofs and eating scraps left by a friendly guard. 'The Cat' is a busker, dancing and playing harmonica on platforms. 'The Giraffe', always hunched over, lives on a diet of discarded tickets, chips, cigarette ends and ring-pulls. The transport executive felt that these poems contradicted their no-smoking, no-litter policies, and might confuse passengers because there were no longer guards on the trains. The final straw for them, however, was the fourth poem, 'The Piranhas', a piece of horror-movie tomfoolery in which Morgan imagines that on each train there's one seat with a hole in it, and underneath a tank of hungry piranhas. This poem has sadly never been displayed on a subway train, but Morgan's 'The Loch Ness Monster Song', written entirely in the monster's gobbledegook 'language', was one of London's Poems on the Underground.

James Kelman is a very different writer to Morgan, and it might be slightly misleading to introduce him in a discussion of the university. As an unpublished writer Kelman, along with others including Alasdair Gray and Liz Lochhead, attended a writers' group run by lecturer Philip Hobsbaum, who taught at Glasgow from 1966. More recently, Kelman has taught creative writing at the university. But although his fiction is mostly set in Glasgow, his characters – a bus conductor, an unemployed ex-convict, a child on a council estate – rarely venture into the university's cloistered courtyards. Kelman is a disarming writer, absolutely committed to writing in the language of working-class Glaswegians and capable of showing warmth and humanity in lives that at first glance might appear unremittingly tough. His work contains little description of the city where his characters live; instead they worry about relationships, cigarettes and the claustrophobia of poverty.

Kelman's *How Late It Was, How Late* was the controversial winner of the 1994 Booker Prize. The book tells the story of Sammy, who at the start of the novel is arrested and beaten up by the police. He loses his sight, probably as a result of this beating, and we follow him as he meets doctors, benefits agents and old drinking buddies, struggling to find his way from place to place. Little else of note happens – the appeal of the novel is everything that goes on in Sammy's head, a furiously foul-mouthed, but also lyrical and moving, stream of consciousness. Kelman is a meticulous writer and Sammy's story is as word-perfect as it is profound. The opening scene finds Sammy waking up half-drunk against some railings, confused and consumed by self-loathing:

> Ye wake in a corner and stay there hoping yer body will disappear, the thoughts smothering ye; these thoughts; but ye want to remember and face up to things, just something keeps ye from doing it, why can ye no do it; the words filling yer head: then the other words; there's something wrong; there's something far far wrong; ye're no a good man, ye're just no a good man. Edging back into awareness, of where ye are: here, slumped in a corner, with these thoughts filling ye.

Kelman's novel divided the Booker judges. One member of the panel, Rabbi Julia Neuberger, threatened to resign if Kelman won, and told the media that the book was 'crap'. Simon Jenkins, writing in *The Times*, thought that awarding the prize to Kelman was an act of 'literary vandalism'. Other columnists decried the number of swear words in the book (several thousand). In his acceptance speech Kelman responded that: 'My culture and my language have the right to exist, and no one has the authority to dismiss that.' Kelman was the first Scot to win the Booker but the spat that ensued diverted attention away from his literary skill and towards questions such as how much swearing is 'acceptable' in a novel.

The University of Glasgow and the Kelvingrove Gallery are the two most prominent institutions in the West End, but for book-lovers there are plenty of hidden gems, too. Off a small thoroughfare called Otago Street are two of the best second-hand bookshops in the city, Thistle Books and Voltaire & Rousseau. The shops could hardly be more different. Thistle is hidden down an alleyway about halfway along the street, accessed through an archway in a row of sandstone buildings. Inside, it has the atmosphere of an Aladdin's cave, albeit a very tidy one. As well as an outstanding assortment of sheet music, there's a large selection of fiction and poetry, including shelves of signed first editions and rare books. Ask for anything in stock and it will be found for you instantly. On the other hand Voltaire & Rousseau, situated on Otago Lane, is a dishevelled monument to clutter, in the best possible sense. Books are piled everywhere, often making the shelf-lined walls inaccessible. There are library ladders, but the rungs of these have also been swamped by volumes on every subject imaginable, from car manuals to Byzantine archaeology. The bookseller is just about discernible behind a counter covered by precarious towers of paperbacks. Every few minutes there's a sound like a distant landslide as a brave customer pulls a low-lying Edith Sitwell from a pile of old textbooks. Both Thistle and Voltaire & Rousseau, in their very different ways, are gold mines. Bargains abound, and the counterpoint of order and chaos is to be savoured as you depart with armfuls of purchases.

To the north and west of the university is Byres Road, the focal point of the West End's eating, drinking, shopping and promenading culture. Alasdair Gray's most famous Glasgow mural can be found in Òran Mór, a bar, restaurant and nightclub on the corner of Byres Road and Great Western Road. This is another converted church and has a neon slipped halo looped around its spire. *Òran mór* is Gaelic for 'big song' or, more poetically, 'great melody of life'. As well as hosting a tremendously popular lunchtime play series, 'A Play, a Pie & a Pint', Òran Mór is one of the city's leading comedy and music venues. Its main auditorium is in the sanctuary of the old church, and the ceiling is a sight to behold, decorated with Gray's huge mural. In *Lanark*, Duncan Thaw's church mural is an ambitious representation of the six days of creation. Gray's Òran Mór mural is even more dizzying: it's cosmic in scale, its background the deep blue of an evening sky, lit up with constellations, astrological figures and fundamental questions such as 'what are we?' and 'where are we going?' It's a confident, thought-provoking piece of humanist art, infused with a hint of surrealism and psychedelia. If William Blake rather than Michelangelo had been commissioned to paint the Sistine Chapel, the result would probably be something like this.

Clydeside

In Catherine Carswell's *Open the Door!* Joanna can hear the pounding machinery of the city's shipyards on the Clyde as she walks through Kelvingrove Park. Today the enormous Finnieston Crane, which lifted steam locomotives onto international cargo ships, is one of the few pieces of machinery remaining on the riverbank and it stands as an elegiac monument to the city's industrial past. Stretches of the riverside have been regenerated: the latest addition to the cluster of concert halls and exhibition centres here is the Riverside Museum, a jaggedy piece of modern civic architecture by the internationally acclaimed Zaha Hadid, built on the site of a former shipyard at the confluence of the Clyde and the Kelvin. According to Hadid, the building resembles a wave and is a reference to Glasgow's shipbuilding heritage, but seen from the water the façade looks more like the graph on a cardiac monitor, rising and falling as if to indicate that a once-derelict area is coming back to life.

'The Clyde made Glasgow and Glasgow made the Clyde', goes one of the city's many sentimental proverbs, quoted by the aspiring novelist Mat in Archie Hind's *The Dear Green Place*. When many of Clydeside's factories and shipyards closed in the twentieth century, they left a void both in terms of jobs and in terms of Glasgow's sense of itself. One of the most devastating portraits of the effects of this decline is Ross Raisin's 2011 novel *Waterline*. The protagonist is Mick Little, a shipbuilder from Govan, an area of Glasgow on the south bank of the river. The novel opens on the day of his wife's funeral; she was killed by asbestosis, contracted whilst washing Mick's work clothes. Mick is harrowed by guilt and grief but is unable to express these emotions in front of his family and friends. Longing for anonymity, he travels to London, finding work as a dishwasher at a hellish airport hotel. When he loses that job, he ends up sleeping rough, far away from his family and his home. While much of the novel traces Mick's attempts to survive in London, his troubles begin in the city of his birth, where many communities that existed in symbiosis with shipyards struggle to find a new role. Near the start of the book Raisin describes two apprentices heading along an otherwise deserted street towards the yard where they work, and contrasts the scene with the crowds that formerly walked this route before a shift began:

> The noise of boots on the road, the hooter about to sound up the way and signal the start of work. The occasional wife in a tenement window in her nightdress, watching her man off, and him finding his way into his own team, grouping up as they move on – riveters, caulkers, blacksmiths, the welders clear and visible in their spotted hats and their leathers, boilermakers, platers – the whole black squad marching on up the road. And at the back, the apprentices, pishing about.
>
> A different story the now. Two lads in blue overalls walking through the empty streets like a pair of convicts who've just survived the end of the world.

Mick, like many a Govan shipyard worker, is a devout follower of the local football team, Glasgow Rangers. Rangers and their arch-rivals Celtic inspire an unparalleled level of support in Scotland, often playing in front of crowds of well over 50,000. Glasgow is a football-mad city. The slightest bit of gossip to do with these teams inspires endless bar-room discussion. Matches between the two foes are not for the faint-hearted: they are invariably furious affairs, on and off the pitch, and the sporting rivalry is sometimes marred by sectarianism. The huge popularity of football in Glasgow has had its critics, including the politically outspoken poet Hugh MacDiarmid, who was concerned that an obsession with sport distracted people from revolutionary politics and questions of cultural identity. In his 1935 poem 'Glasgow, 1960' MacDiarmid imagined the crowds of the future streaming towards Rangers' Ibrox Stadium to hear a debate about 'la loi de l'effort converti', a literary theory about creativity and the imagination. Later in the poem copies of a newspaper bearing the headline 'Turkish Poet's Abstruse New Song' are snapped up by readers eager to find out more. Glasgow has certainly had a cultural renaissance since MacDiarmid wrote this poem and, as its literature shows, it's a dynamic and increasingly confident modern city. But for better or worse, literary debates are yet to lure crowds of 50,000, and newspaper owners haven't discovered the mass-market appeal of poetry in translation.

Renfrewshire and Inverclyde

Downstream from Glasgow in the districts of Renfrewshire and Inverclyde is a series of towns which, like Glasgow, were once heavily reliant on shipbuilding and other heavy industry. These include Greenock, Port Glasgow and, a few miles inland, Paisley, a town formerly known for its textile industry. These towns have suffered more than most from deindustrialisation. Regeneration projects have gathered pace in recent years, and these towns have much to celebrate, not least a literary heritage that includes a rich seam of poetry.

Two of the best poets to have come from Greenock are John Davidson and W. S. Graham. Both were influenced by the vocabulary of industry: reading their work, you can almost hear the riveters' hammers clanging and smell the smoke and tar of the quayside. Davidson was born in nearby Barrhead in 1857 and spent his childhood in Greenock. He was a poetic innovator and incorporated modern scientific ideas into his verse; his experiments gained posthumous admirers among the modernist poets, but he was plagued by debt and depression, and committed suicide in 1909. His long poem 'A Ballad in Blank Verse' is about a young poet growing up in Greenock and captures the bustling atmosphere of industrial Greenock:

> [...] this grey town
> That pipes the morning up before the lark
> With shrieking steam, and from a hundred stalks
> Lacquers the sooty sky; where hammers clang
> On iron hulls, and cranes in harbours creak
> Rattle and swing, whole cargoes on their necks.

W. S. Graham, like Davidson, struggled to make a living as a poet. Born in 1918, he trained as a draughtsman and structural engineer before moving to Cornwall in 1944, where he scraped by with the financial and practical support of friends, including Harold Pinter. There's a plaque outside his birthplace at 1 Hope Street; in some of his poems he puns on the 'hope' of his childhood address. Graham was an exemplary craftsman, ceaselessly experimenting and wrestling with language. His first editor at Faber was T. S. Eliot, who praised the technical skill and emotional depth of his work, but for much of his career he existed in obscurity. Between his two groundbreaking books of poetry, *The Nightfishing* in 1955 and *Malcolm Mooney's Land* in 1970, he fell off the literary scene's radar to such an extent that his publisher, Faber and Faber, thought that he had died. Only after his actual death in 1986 did his reputation really take off, and Graham is cited by many contemporary poets and critics as one of the most innovative and influential twentieth-century British poets.

The urban and rural landscapes of Graham's youth haunt his poetry. 'Greenock at Night I Find You' describes the 'long rope-working / Hide and seeking rivetting town' of his childhood, where at night the 'welding lights in the shipyards' glow like blue flowers. In 'Loch Thom', Graham writes of returning to this quiet reservoir on moorland about two miles south of Greenock. A narrow track leads to the loch, a wind-roughened stretch of water surrounded by low hills. In the poem Graham hears the melancholy cries of curlews, echoing across

> The heather-edges of the water held
> Between the hills a boyhood's walk
> Up from Greenock.

There are no fields, only grouse moors leading down to the water, and in the shallows he imagines minnows like 'iron-filings' swimming by. The loch is literally and figuratively colder than he remembered, bringing back memories of his dead father and mother. His return to a beloved childhood place is a harsh reminder of the struggles and disappointments of his adult life, and the poem ends with the crowing call of grouse on the moorland, sounding as if they're telling him to 'GO BACK, GO BACK' and not return again.

Port Glasgow, the town just to the east of Greenock, has its own poetic alumnus, James Thomson. Thomson was born in 1834 and is best remembered for his long and nightmarish poem *The City of the Dreadful Night*, in which a speaker explores a dark, nameless city filled with all the worst aspects of Victorian Britain. Thomson spent most of his life in London, but it's easy to see smoky Glasgow, with its polluted river, in his descriptions of an urban hell:

A river girds the city west and south,
  The main north channel of a broad lagoon,
Regurging with the salt tides from the mouth;
  Waste marshes shine and glister to the moon
[. . .] Myriads of habitants are ever sleeping,
  Or dead, or fled from nameless pestilence!

Thomson lays it on thick, and there is little in his poem to lighten the mood, but his hallucinatory vision expressed the sense of doom with which many of his contemporaries regarded the sprawling and impoverished industrial cities of the nineteenth century.

Paisley's main contribution to Scottish poetry is Robert Tannahill, a weaver inspired by the example of Robert Burns, who was publishing poems to great acclaim when Tannahill was a boy. Whereas Burns managed to thrive under the condescending label of 'heaven-taught ploughman', Tannahill remained in obscurity, was unable to wring a living out of poetry and eventually drowned himself in Paisley Canal aged 35. Too late, his work gained appreciation after his death, and his face is carved on the Scott Monument in Edinburgh, alongside other Scottish writers. Perhaps the most fitting tribute that has been paid to Tannahill is by the contemporary poet Douglas Dunn, who grew up in the village of Inchinnan, not far from Paisley. In 'Tannahill', a poem in his 1981 collection *St Kilda's Parliament*, Dunn imagines the earlier poet combining his work and his vocation, weaving lines of poetry together as he sings his 'common heart'.

Lanarkshire

To the south-east of Glasgow is Lanarkshire, a region that combines former mining and industrial towns with some of the best farming country in Scotland. It can feel like a relief to explore the lush fruit farms of the Clyde Valley or gaze, as Coleridge and the Wordsworths did, upon the wispy ribbons of the Falls of Clyde, a series of waterfalls near the mill village of New Lanark. New Lanark was founded in 1786 and run with an emphasis on the welfare and education of the tenant-employees: it's now a popular tourist attraction and one of Scotland's five UNESCO World Heritage sites.

Fifteen miles east of New Lanark, among upland farms, lies one of Scotland's hidden cultural treasures. This is Little Sparta, the garden designed by poet and artist Ian Hamilton Finlay and his wife Sue. Its name is a play on Edinburgh's nickname, the 'Athens of the North'. Finlay died in 2006 and Little Sparta is now run by a trust and open three afternoons a week in the summer. Few will stumble across the garden by accident – about a mile west of the tiny village of Dunsyre on the quiet road from Newbigging there's a small car park, seemingly located in the middle of nowhere. From here visitors must walk for about half a mile up a rough track to reach the three hectares of Little Sparta.

The garden is itself a work of art. When Finlay moved here in 1966 it was a tumbledown farm. Over the next four decades he transformed it into a unique garden, divided into areas landscaped in various styles, from a woodland of shaded groves and narrow paths to the open vistas of an 'English parkland'. There's a working allotment and also a rugged wild garden, complete with artificial loch. The best way to explore the garden is without a plan, wandering through its glades and over its lawns, savouring the contrasting atmosphere of each section. Following the garden's paths is an adventure through the 'glooms and solitudes' that Finlay wrote were intrinsic to its design.

Little Sparta is as meticulously designed as any sculpture, but it's also crammed with individual works: sculptures in wood, stone and metal, and poems inscribed on every conceivable surface, including benches, bridges, obelisks and stiles. These inscriptions are often forbiddingly intellectual. There are quotations written in several languages, references to the French Revolution and pre-Socratic philosophy abound, and a good working knowledge of Latin,

Classical mythology and art history are needed to untangle Finlay's complex allusions. The themes of conflict, revolution and social order are explored in bird tables shaped like aircraft carriers and a watering can painted with the dates of the revolutionary leader Maximilien Robespierre. Finlay's own poems feature heavily.

Little Sparta can probably stake a claim to be the world's most erudite garden, but it also contains a lot of humour. Two fibreglass tortoises half-covered by a border have 'Panzer Leader' written on their shells, a reference to the German tank battalions of the Second World War. An avenue enclosed by hedgerows is called Huff Lane and its benches, inscribed with poems about solitude, offer a place for the brooding gardener or visitor to sit and sulk. Whether its cultural references leave you stimulated or perplexed (and trying to find method in the high-culture madness is part of the fun), Little Sparta is intended as a retreat in which to contemplate. Finlay was a writer as well as a garden designer, but the words in his garden are never didactic. Little Sparta asks you to make of it what you will.

Ayrshire

In some ways Ayrshire feels like a halfway house between the factories and ports of Clydeside and the rugged countryside of the Scottish Borders. Its northern towns include Kilmarnock and Ardrossan, hubs for textile and manufacturing industries until the late twentieth century, and vast quantities of coal were dug from nearby pits. Ayrshire's landscape isn't all chimneys and collieries, though. As you travel south through the region it becomes increasingly rural, and its southern limit is near the Galloway Forest Park, 300 square miles of wooded uplands that are so free of light pollution that the forest was awarded the status of Britain's first 'Dark Sky Park' in 2009. The 84 miles of the Ayrshire coast boast long sandy beaches, rocky shores and golf links, and towns like Largs, Troon and Ayr are Scotland's answer to the English seaside resort: shrines to ice cream, fish and chips, and paddling in the sea with your trousers rolled up.

Most of all, Ayrshire is Burns country. Tracing all the places in Ayrshire that have Burns connections would take a whole book. Although the influences on his poetry were far from parochial, Burns's work is firmly rooted in the communities of rural Ayrshire. Scotland's most famous poet was born in Alloway in 1759. At that time it was a hamlet with a mill; today it's a suburb of Ayr and the centre of an extensive Burns heritage industry. Although the poet's connections to other places in Ayrshire, including Ayr, Irvine and the village of Mauchline, are extensive, this guide will focus on the one Burns location that every literary tourist should visit – Alloway.

Burns's first childhood home was a neat, two-roomed thatched cottage built by his father, William, who was a gardener and tenant farmer. William did everything in his limited means to ensure his son had a good education and although Robert had to help his father with agricultural work he wasn't a 'heaven-taught ploughman' whose poetic abilities sprang from divine inspiration. The Alloway cottage was sold to the Incorporation of Shoemakers of Ayr by Burns's father, and these owners leased it as an alehouse. Within a few years of Burns's death the house was attracting pilgrims keen to see where the poet had been born. One of these was John Keats, who hoped to channel the inspiration of the place into a poem, but was unimpressed with the boozy surroundings and the drunken landlord. In a letter to a friend, John Hamilton Reynolds, he wrote:

> We went to the Cottage and took some Whiskey – I wrote a sonnet for the mere sake of writing some lines under the roof – they are so bad I cannot transcribe them – The Man at the Cottage was a great Bore with his Anecdotes – I hate the rascal – his Life consists in fuz, fuzzy, fuzziest – He drinks glasses five for the Quarter and twelve for the hour, – he is a mahogany faced old Jackass who knew Burns – He ought to be kicked for having spoken to him.

Visitors continued to flock to Alloway to see the Burns Monument, erected in 1823. A lofty neoclassical structure with nine columns representing the nine muses of Greek mythology, the monument is the focal point of the Burns Memorial Gardens. By the start of the twentieth century Burns's Cottage had been bought by the trust that erected the monument, and it was converted back into the kind of house that Burns had lived in: animals in one room and people in the other. Although the poet only lived here for a few years as a child, this building more than any other has become the emblem of his humble rural background, fetishised to such an extent that in 1911 the Burns Club in Atlanta, Georgia, constructed a replica in which to hold their meetings. Today the Alloway cottage is the centrepiece of the Robert Burns Birthplace Museum complex, which also includes a stylish modern museum building housing interactive exhibits. The museum boasts the world's most significant collection of items relating to Burns, including thousands of manuscripts and artefacts such as his pistols (inscribed with his initials and carried by him when he worked as an exciseman) and a copy of his *Poems, Chiefly in the Scottish Dialect* with a dedication to his illegitimate daughter Elizabeth. The museum is a much more family-friendly and engaging place than the alehouse Keats visited.

Across the road from the Memorial Gardens a medieval arched bridge crosses the River Doon as it meanders through woods to the south of Alloway. Known as the Brig o' Doon, this is the scene of the supernatural climax to Burns's masterpiece, the narrative poem 'Tam o' Shanter'. The poem, a staple at Burns Suppers and recital competitions, displays all of Burns's poetic skill. Some sections of the poem are written in robust vernacular Scots – 'She tauld thee weel thou was a skellum' – but these drift into lines of elegant English:

> But pleasures are like poppies spread,
> You seize the flow'r, its bloom is shed [. . .]
> Or like the rainbow's lovely form
> Evanishing amid the storm.

At the beginning of the poem, the character of Tam o' Shanter is described as having spent a market day in Ayr getting thoroughly drunk and flirting with a landlady while his wife Kate waits at home, 'Nursing her wrath to keep it warm'. The hour comes for Tam to ride home on his mare, Meg. It's a foul, stormy night: lightning flashes and thunder booms as Tam and Meg approach the Auld Kirk of Alloway, with its haunted graveyard. This church was a ruin by Burns's time, and remains in a state of atmospheric decay today. Its gravestones are carved with skeletons and images of items like ploughs, depicting the deceased's occupation. It's also where Burns's parents are buried.

The drunken Tam, looking into the graveyard, witnesses a terrifying sight: warlocks and witches dancing furiously to tunes played by the Devil himself. Satan's instrument of choice is, of course, a shrieking bagpipe. Around the dancers coffins stand upright and open, displaying their corpses. Murder weapons, dripping with blood, lie around. Even for readers unaccustomed to Burns's Scots there's a real energy to his lines:

> As Tammie glowr'd, amaz'd, and curious,
> The mirth and fun grew fast and furious;
> The piper loud and louder blew;
> The dancers quick and quicker flew;
> They reel'd, they set, they cross'd, they cleekit [linked arms].
> Till ilka carlin swat and reekit [each witch sweated and stank].

Tam's eyes are drawn to Nannie, a scantily clad witch twirling and leaping in the dance, so provocative that even Satan is aroused as he blares away on the pipes. As the witch dances her dress rides up and eventually Tam can contain his lust no longer, bellowing out his congratulations to the clothing. Immediately the dancing stops. Like a swarm of bees the entire devilish assembly chases after Tam, who with his mare has set off at top speed for the Brig o' Doon. Nannie leads the pursuit, but Tam races for the keystone of the

8 *The Brig o' Doon, Alloway, scene of the supernatural climax of Burns's 'Tam o' Shanter'*

bridge, knowing that witches can't cross running water. Just as the mare reaches the summit of the arch, Nannie lunges and grabs her by the tail. Tam and Meg escape, but at the cost of the horse's tail, left hanging in the witch's hand.

Burns overshadows all other writers in the area, but if he'd never existed Ayrshire would be known as a hotbed of fiction. Among the earliest Ayrshire novelists to find international fame was John Galt, the son of an Irvine sea captain and author of some of the first novels to critique Britain's corrupt nineteenth-century politics. More recently, Janice Galloway's experimental tour de force *The Trick is to Keep Breathing*, published in 1989, is set in Irvine. Its protagonist is Joy Stone, a drama teacher trying to cope with the death of her married lover. She suffers from depression and an eating disorder, and struggles to get help from a health service staffed by condescending male doctors using depersonalised, institutional language. Galloway's narrative is fragmented and mimics Joy's sense of being trapped: sentences seem to flow over the edge of the page and some sections read like a drama script in which Joy speaks like an actor unable to influence her role.

Inland from Ayr is Ochiltree, where in 1869 another influential Scottish writer, George Douglas Brown, was born. Brown gave a fictionalised account of Ochiltree in *The House with the Green Shutters*, a dark novel about a bullying father and his intelligent but weak son, living in a judgemental and petty small town. The son, John Gourlay, leaves for university convinced of his intellectual superiority. While there he discovers whisky rather than philosophy and upon his return his arrogance leads to his ruin. Brown's novel was published in 1901 at a time when almost all novels about Scottish rural life were highly sentimental. Brown railed against this genre, known as 'kailyard' fiction after the Scots word for a cabbage patch, and in *The House with the Green Shutters* he undermines its cosy stereotypes with a novel culminating in scenes approaching Greek tragedy in the depths of their violence and misery. The book was well received and its author compared to Balzac, Flaubert and Robert Louis Stevenson, but Brown, troubled by ill health, died a year later, depriving Scotland of one of its most promising young writers. Given his poor health it's perhaps appropriate that the house where he was born, 90 Main Street, is now the Green Shutters Pharmacy.

Andrew O'Hagan deals with the themes of masculinity and its role in the labour movement in his powerful novel *Our Fathers*, first published in 1999. His protagonist Jamie Bawn is a thirty-something engineer responsible for the demolition of tower blocks. He returns to Saltcoats, the Ayrshire town where he grew up, in order to spend time with his ailing grandfather, Hugh. They have hardly spoken in years: Hugh, known to his former colleagues in Glasgow and Ayrshire as 'Mr Housing', was the driving force behind the 1960s boom in high-rise construction, motivated by the conviction that the need for modern social housing justified building blocks of flats as tall as possible, in as short a timeframe as possible, for as little money as possible. Jamie reflects on the Saltcoats he grew up in, a landscape of postwar expansion, of fields transformed into streets of council flats, of borstals and dog food factories. O'Hagan is sensitive to the optimism that accompanied his grandfather's futuristic buildings, which stood 'Proud like a Soviet gymnast'. He admits that when they were built people were impressed: 'A thing of wonder, they stretch to the skies, and can seem for a time great catacombs of effort. They stand for how others had wanted to live, for the future they saw, and for hopes now abandoned.'

The tower blocks in *Our Fathers* represent a battle between deprivation and hope. They may have failed their purpose, but they were Hugh Bawn's attempt to haul Glasgow and the west of Scotland into the modern world. In reality, as in the novel, many of these buildings have now been demolished and substantial regeneration projects are under way. The skyline of post-industrial Scotland is changing dramatically, but its cultural self-confidence is stronger than ever.

5

THE TROSSACHS, ARGYLL
AND THE
WESTERN HIGHLANDS

Tourists and Outlaws

Travelling North from Glasgow

When Robert Burns wrote 'My Heart's in the Highlands', where exactly was he thinking of? People use the term 'Highlands' to refer to such a large proportion of Scotland that it's almost too vague to be useful, applied to pretty much any mountainous or sparsely populated area north of the Central Belt. The sudden change from the flat and fertile land between Glasgow and Edinburgh to the mountains and valleys of the southern Highlands occurs at what is termed the Highland Boundary Fault Line, the site of tectonic collisions that happened about 500 million years ago, and that raised up many of Scotland's mountains. The fault line runs diagonally across the country, from the island of Arran in the west to Aberdeenshire in the north-east. There are few official markers of this fault line but, travelling north from the Central Belt, it's impossible not to notice the change in scenery. Steep mountain slopes covered in heather or scree replace the rolling farmland. Waterfalls become more frequent, gushing down rocks a few metres from the road. Long stretches of water – Scotland's extensive network of lochs – glisten in the glens. Sea lochs make fjord-like incursions into the coast, and large settlements are few and far between. The sensation that you're suddenly in the Highlands starts a mere 20 miles north of Glasgow, at the southern end of Loch Lomond.

For hundreds of years, the hills on the Highland Boundary were a frontier, and territories to the north of them were largely under the control of clans who had varying degrees of loyalty to the monarchy in Edinburgh and, later, in London. There was mutual suspicion between the relatively prosperous inhabitants of the lowlands, who spoke English or Scots, and their Gaelic-speaking clannish neighbours. After the failed Jacobite risings of 1715 and 1745, which many clans supported, the autonomy enjoyed by clan chiefs was curtailed by the British government. Laws were passed forbidding Highlanders from carrying weapons and prohibiting aspects of Highland culture, including the wearing of tartan. In the 1720s and 1730s General George Wade built hundreds of miles of road, allowing troops access to mountainous regions that had previously been beyond the authority of the state. A sign of the success of Wade's road-building is that Scotland's main north–south arteries still generally follow the routes of his roads.

But in the nineteenth century something changed: the Highlands stopped being seen as a lawless and uncultivable wasteland and instead the idea that it was a desirable destination for tourism took hold. One of the main factors in this change was Sir Walter Scott, whose poems and novels set in the Highlands introduced a wide readership to the stirring beauty of Scotland's lochs and mountains. Travellers flocked to Loch Lomond and the Trossachs, keen to see sublime landscapes and experience the remnants of a different culture. This movement has never really stopped: tourism is one of the main industries of the Highlands today, drawing people from all over the world.

As you leave Glasgow, heading north on the A82 to Loch Lomond, Fort William and beyond, the last hurrah of the industrial Central Belt is the cluster of small towns in the Vale of Leven, which includes Renton, founded in 1762 by Jane Smollett, whose family were major landowners in the area. Her brother was the writer Tobias, whose epistolary novel, *The Expedition of Humphry Clinker*, follows a group of Welsh tourists travelling in England and Scotland. One of his characters observes that 'people at the other end of the island know as little of Scotland as of Japan.' *Humphry Clinker* was published in 1771, the year of Smollett's death, and his cousin James Smollett had an ostentatious memorial erected to him on Renton Main Street. A Tuscan column on a tall plinth, it dwarfs the twentieth-century war memorial beside it. The plinth includes an extensive Latin inscription, which was being drafted in 1773 when James Boswell and Samuel Johnson stayed with the Smollett family on the homeward leg of their journey to the Hebrides. In his *Journal of a Tour to the Hebrides* Boswell records that Dr Johnson, upon being shown the draft of the Latin inscription, 'sat down with an ardent and liberal earnestness to revise it, and greatly improved it by several additions and variations'.

Whether or not Johnson's contribution improved the text is open to debate. Thirty years later, Dorothy Wordsworth recorded in her *Journal of a Tour of Scotland* that: 'There is a long Latin inscription, which Coleridge translated for my benefit. The Latin is miserably bad – as Coleridge said, such as poor Dr Smollett, who was an excellent scholar, would have been ashamed of.'

After Renton the Central Belt is soon left behind. Steep hills rise on either side of Loch Lomond, the largest freshwater lake in Britain. The road west from the foot of the loch leads into Argyll, whose wooded peninsulas are carved by sea lochs. Five miles west of Loch Lomond, on the banks of the smaller Gare Loch, is the town of Helensburgh. In 1928 Cecil Day-Lewis, the poet, translator, and father of actor Daniel, took up the post of English teacher at the town's Larchfield Academy. Day-Lewis described Helensburgh as the 'Wimbledon of the North'. Although the two places have diverged in nature somewhat since the late 1920s, Helensburgh's attractions include the fine Charles Rennie Mackintosh-designed

Hill House, a mansion now open to the public. When he left Helensburgh two years later, Day-Lewis recommended another young poet, W. H. Auden, as his replacement at Larchfield. While he taught there, Auden's career as a poet took off, with his *Poems* published by Faber and Faber in 1930; his 'The Watchers' refers to the melancholy stillness of the lochside town at night.

The road north from Helensburgh follows Gare Loch and the predictably elongated Loch Long before rejoining the main road into Argyll at Arrochar. Turning west, the road climbs over the shoulder of the hills nicknamed the 'Arrochar Alps'. When soldiers constructed a military road here in the eighteenth century, they marked the highest point of the pass into Argyll with a stone inscribed 'Rest and Be Thankful', an instruction which weary travellers needed little encouragement to follow. John Keats passed this way on his walking tour of 1818, labouring under a misapprehension which he was happy to transform into an anecdote in his letters to friends: 'At the top of the glen my itinerary mentioned a place called "Rest and Be Thankful" nine miles off; now we had set out without breakfast, intending to take our meal there, when, horror and starvation! "Rest and Be Thankful" was not an Inn, but a stone seat!' Keats wouldn't be quite so disappointed today: a humble but welcome catering van trades in the lay-by and picnic area here. On a clear day this is a beautiful place to pull over and watch the shadows of clouds float over the slopes of Glen Croe. The old military road and the modern A83 snake up towards you; behind lurk the opaque waters of Loch Restil, a sliver of water overlooked by crags.

In Iain Banks's 1992 novel *The Crow Road*, student Prentice McHoan has a close encounter with a 'kamikaze deer' on this stretch of road, a not-infrequent experience in the Highlands, where the deer population is so large that culls are permitted. More than one farmhouse freezer has been filled with cuts from a road-killed deer, but Prentice's reflexes save both animal and driver from a grisly fate:

One moment the road ahead was clear in the headlights, next second Wha! Something dark brown looking big as a horse with huge antlers like some twisted aerial array came belting out of the forest across the road and leapt the downhill crash barrier. I slammed the brakes on, nearly locking the wheels. The beast disappeared into the darkness and the car swept through the single cloud of steamy breath it had left behind.

Loch Lomond

Jules Verne, the famed French author of *Around the World in Eighty Days* and *Twenty Thousand Leagues under the Sea*, loved Scotland and even claimed Scottish ancestry. He set three of his lesser-known novels in the country. The earliest of these is a fictionalised account of his own travels in Scotland in 1859, a work that lay forgotten for well over a century before being rediscovered and published in France in 1989. In 1992, Janice Valls-Russell's English translation, titled *Backwards to Britain*, was released. Verne's impressions of Scotland are narrated by a character named Jacques Lavaret, who travels with a friend from Edinburgh to Glasgow and then on to the Trossachs, visiting landmarks such as Arthur's Seat, Glasgow Cathedral and the Necropolis. Jacques, like Verne, is passionately excited about being in Scotland, to the extent that he even waxes lyrical about a steam-operated sausage machine in a Glasgow butcher's window: '"What a people," Jacques exclaimed. "What genius to apply steam to *charcuterie*! No wonder the British are the masters of the world!"' Upon reaching Loch Lomond, the two travellers sail from Balloch, on the southern shore, and Jacques can't help being reminded of 'his favourite novels', including Walter Scott's *Rob Roy*, and anyone seeking similarities between Verne's writing and that of Scott will find them in this description of the loch:

9 Loch Lomond, with its rugged northern shores in the background

The first, overwhelming impression of Loch Lomond is of countless delightful islands of every shape and size imaginable. The *Prince Albert* weaved its way between them, skirting their rugged outlines and revealing a myriad different countrysides: here a fertile plain, there a solitary glen, elsewhere a forbidding ravine bristling with age-old rocks. Ancient legends clung to every shore, and the history of this land is written in these gigantic characters of islands and mountains.

The large area of Loch Lomond, and its position on the Highland Boundary Fault, mean that it feels less like a single body of water than like a series of interconnected lochs with changing characteristics. At its southern end it's broad and surrounded by fields and parkland. As Verne points out, there are numerous islands, some of which are inhabited and many of which can be visited on boat trips. The south of Loch Lomond is busy with yachts and jet skis; on a sunny day the villages and pubs on its shores are filled with Glaswegians escaping the city.

The northern half of the loch is very different. About a third of the way up it narrows, and slopes rise on either side for almost 1,000 metres to form the mountains of Ben Lomond and Ben Vorlich. Lochside fields give way to wooded crags and banks of ferns. There are fewer pleasure boats on the water. On the eastern bank the road ends altogether at the hamlet of Rowardennan and only a rough footpath continues northwards to another settlement, Inversnaid. In Walter Scott's *Rob Roy*, the rough country to the east of Loch Lomond is the territory of the eponymous outlaw, a real historical figure whom Scott describes as a Robin Hood character, a 'kind and gentle robber'. Rob Roy MacGregor lived in the early eighteenth century and was both a cattle drover and, latterly, a cattle thief who earned a living by rustling. He's the presiding spirit, but not really the hero, of Scott's novel. Instead much of the action follows Frank Osbaldistone, a young Englishman caught up in intrigue involving Jacobites.

Such was the popularity of Scott's Highland romance that countless tourists sought out its landscapes for themselves. 'We ought to traverse the district novel in hand,' says one Victorian guidebook of 'Rob Roy's country', searching for locations such as 'the precise spot where Francis Osbaldistone for a moment pressed the flushed cheek of Diana Vernon'. In the summer of 1817, the year before the novel was published, Scott came here himself, visiting 'Rob Roy's Cave', not far from Inversnaid. The cave is one of countless landmarks in the area associated with Rob, an indication of his reputation as a folk hero. It's allegedly one of his hideouts, though there might be little truth in this – it's really just a cleft in a pile of boulders, and for visitors today the solitude of the location is more rewarding than the cave itself. Scott himself may have been disappointed by the cave, as he didn't even mention it in his novel. For those seeking the real Rob Roy, a good place to start is Balquhidder, a quiet village an hour's drive north of Aberfoyle, at the eastern end of Loch Voil. Rob Roy farmed at Balquhidder and his grave lies in the village church.

For hikers on the West Highland Way, the 100-mile footpath from Glasgow to Fort William, Inversnaid is something of an oasis, the only natural stopping point on the lochside on the rough path north from Rowardennan, and the site of a hotel and a cosy bunkhouse. In 1881 a young Jesuit priest based in Glasgow, Gerard Manley Hopkins, stopped briefly at Inversnaid. Hopkins found life in the big city oppressive and came north with a yearning for wilderness. His poem 'Inversnaid', with his distinctive rhythmical stresses, is a brilliant evocation of the sounds, colours and movements of the waterfall at the edge of this hamlet where Arklet Water cascades into Loch Lomond:

> This darksome burn, horseback brown,
> His rollrock highroad roaring down,
> In coop and in comb the fleece of his foam
> Flutes and low to the lake falls home.
>
> [. . .]
>
> What would the world be, once bereft
> Of wet and wilderness? Let them be left,
> O let them be left, wilderness and wet;
> Long live the weeds and the wilderness yet.

Today a bridge crosses in front of the waterfall, affording spectacular views. Inversnaid itself is difficult to reach – visitors must either walk here from Rowardennan, navigate a long and twisting road from Aberfoyle or take a ferry from Tarbet on the western shore. As a proto-environmentalist Hopkins would be pleased that Inversnaid now lies within Loch Lomond and the Trossachs National Park, which was established in 2002.

Loch Katrine and the Trossachs

The Trossachs is the region to the east of Loch Lomond. Its secluded lochs and hills were the haunts of Rob Roy, and it's easy to imagine the outlaw disappearing into its woods and glens to perplex his pursuers. The meaning of the name 'Trossachs' is highly disputed. In the early nineteenth century Patrick Graham, a minister at Aberfoyle in the heart of the region, suggested that 'Trossachs' came from the Gaelic for 'the rough and bristled territory'. As an etymology this is dubious and the good reverend might have plucked this Gaelic origin out of thin Highland air, but nevertheless it's a perfect description of the landscape, as many craggy peaks rise between the lochs and glens crisscrossing the area.

From Inversnaid it's five miles due east to Stronachlachar on the shore of Loch Katrine. In the summer the steamship *Sir Walter Scott* stops here on its east–west cruises of the loch. Like Loch Lomond, Loch Katrine is a place of contrasts: its eastern reaches are easily accessible by car, with a large car park and a busy restaurant. The shores are heavily wooded and the boat weaves past thicketed islets. Beyond Stronachlachar in the west, the scenery is wilder. Here the loch is bordered by moorland and the occasional isolated farmhouse emphasises rather than reduces the sense of remoteness. Dorothy Wordsworth, sailing from west to east, was enraptured by the forested eastern slopes and the mountains rising above the glade: 'It was an entire solitude; and all that we beheld was the perfection of loveliness and beauty [. . .] no thought of dreariness or desolation found entrance here; yet nothing was to be seen but water, wood, rocks, and heather, and bare mountains above.'

Travelling to Loch Katrine was a serious undertaking in 1803, and the Wordsworths were in the vanguard of tourists to the region. Loch Katrine's real tourist boom came after the publication of Walter Scott's long poem *The Lady of the Lake* in 1810. In the poem three knights vie for the affections of Ellen Douglas, a modest maiden, and these competing relationships are set against the backdrop of conflict between King James V of Scotland and the Highland clans in the sixteenth century. The poem was a sensation, selling 25,000 copies in eight months. Readers fell in love with Ellen and also with Loch Katrine, where she lives in a castle on one of the loch's small islands. Hotels were built nearby to accommodate the many tourists who wanted to visit 'Ellen's Isle', a tiny islet on the loch that quickly became associated with Scott's heroine. Scott's writing has a picturesque quality and his description endows Loch Katrine with a luxuriant abundance that must have convinced his readership that he had in fact discovered the Garden of Eden:

> The wild rose, eglantine, and broom
> Wasted around their rich perfume;
> The birch-trees wept in fragrant balm;
> The aspens slept beneath the calm;
> The silver light, with quivering glance,
> Played on the water's still expanse;
> Wild were the heart whose passion's sway
> Could rage beneath the sober ray!

In the 1850s, a few decades after the Scott-inspired tourist boom began, the rapidly expanding city of Glasgow was in desperate need of a clean water supply. Surveyors found that Loch Katrine, about 35 miles to the north, was both clean and large enough to supply the city. A series of pipes and reservoirs was constructed and the loch still supplies Glasgow with fresh water today. This feat of engineering was celebrated by William McGonagall, the gloriously inept Victorian poet whose verse is so clumsy that, despite his protestations of seriousness, it's always been treasured as comedy. McGonagall's 'Loch Katrine' combines hydrology with recognition of the loch's popularity with tourists:

> And as I gaze upon it, let me pause and think,
> How many people in Glasgow of its water drink,

That's conveyed to them in pipes from its placid lake,
And are glad to get its water their thirst to slake.

Then away to Loch Katrine in the summer time,
And feast on its scenery most lovely and sublime;
There's no other scene can surpass in fair Scotland,
It's surrounded by mountains and trees most grand.

Among the more articulate visitors to the region was John Ruskin, the Victorian art critic and social reformer. In 1853 he and his wife Effie stayed about three miles east of Loch Katrine in the leafy village of Brig o' Turk. They were accompanied on this holiday by the Pre-Raphaelite painter John Everett Millais. Millais's portrait of Ruskin standing by a waterfall in nearby Glen Finglas is one of his most celebrated works, but the significance of the holiday for all three goes far beyond art. The Ruskins' marriage was never consummated, and a year after this holiday it was annulled on the grounds of Ruskin's impotence. Whether this was the truth, or merely an excuse to safeguard Effie's reputation, has been the subject of biographers and gossips ever since. The holiday arrangements are worthy of a Victorian melodrama: at the same time as John and Effie's marriage was on the rocks, Millais and Effie were enjoying a suspiciously close relationship. Did the two conduct a holiday affair under Ruskin's nose? Did Ruskin engineer the whole thing in the hope that an act of infidelity would give him reason to separate from his wife? Or was he consciously setting her up with someone who loved her, as he did not? Whatever the truth, Effie and Millais married soon after the annulment and were together until Millais's death in 1896.

Ruskin was a great admirer of Walter Scott's novels and as he posed for Millais's portrait at the Glen Finglas waterfall his mind may have turned to another Trossachs waterfall, the Falls of Ledard, which Scott thought such a perfect location that he used it in two separate novels. The Ledard Burn gushes down from the shoulder of Ben Venue, the mountain to the south east of Loch Katrine, just before the stream flows into Loch Ard. The winding lochside road from Aberfoyle passes here and a footpath follows the Ledard Burn uphill from near the Forest Hills Hotel. In *Waverley*, the English soldier Edward Waverley travels to the Highlands and is persuaded to join the Jacobite cause by a charismatic clan chief, Fergus MacIvor, and his sister Flora MacIvor. The tipping point in his conversion to Jacobitism comes when Flora uses the scenery as well as her own beauty to convince Waverley that his heart, as a poet might say, is in the Highlands:

> After a broken cataract of about twenty feet, the stream was received in a large natural basin, filled to the brim with water, which, where the bubbles of the fall subsided, was so exquisitely clear, that, although it was of great depth, the eye could discern each pebble at the bottom [. . .] Here, like one of those lovely forms which decorate the landscapes of Claude, Waverley found Flora gazing on the water-fall. Two paces farther back stood Cathleen [Flora's servant], holding a small Scottish harp, the use of which had been taught to Flora by Rory Dall, one of the last harpers of the Western Highlands.

To Waverley's eyes, Flora just happens to be sitting here like a figure in a painting, about to play her traditional harp and sing a ballad about an ancient battle. How could the poetically inclined young man resist? The location is well chosen: the mist rising on the wooded slopes around Loch Ard, and the countless waterfalls rumbling down the glens, are certainly romantic sights. In his notes to accompany *Waverley*, Scott argues that the Falls of Ledard is 'one of the most exquisite cascades it is possible to behold'. Frank Osbaldistone, the hero of Scott's novel *Rob Roy*, agrees. He stops here with Rob Roy and his followers on the way to the banks of Loch Lomond and shares a rustic meal with Rob and his wife, the ferocious Helen MacGregor. They eat near where the Ledard Burn's 'dusky stream' cascades downhill and is 'received in a beautiful stone basin, almost as regular as if hewn by a sculptor'.

Scott was an inveterate collector of all things Scottish: among the paraphernalia in his collection at Abbotsford was an item reputed to be Rob Roy's sporran. Rob Roy's son Robin, an outlaw eventually hanged at Edinburgh's Grassmarket, is briefly mentioned in Scott's novel and also enjoys a convivial afterlife in Robert Louis Stevenson's *Kidnapped*. Despite his thuggish notoriety, Robin meets his match when Stevenson's heroes, David Balfour and Alan Breck Stewart, stop in Balquhidder. Robin and Alan, recalling historical clan feuds, are on the point of drawing swords and fighting to the death when a comically Scottish alternative, a piping contest, is suggested. The bagpipes are passed back and forth until Alan concedes: 'I am not fit to blow in the same kingdom with ye. Body of me! Ye have mair music in your sporran than I have in my head!'

From Dál Riata to Oban

If travelling in the Trossachs invokes the Highlands' nineteenth-century writers, then a journey through Argyll, the region on the west of Loch Lomond, where Scotland's coast gradually succumbs to the Atlantic, takes you back much further in time. Modern-day Argyll corresponds roughly with the ancient maritime kingdom of Dál Riata (or Dalriada), which in the sixth and seventh centuries stretched from the Isle of Skye to Ireland. The knobbly hill of Dunadd, near Kilmartin, was crowned by a hill fort that may have been the capital of this kingdom, and at its summit you can see the 'footprint' in stone used as part of the ceremony to inaugurate kings. In medieval Scotland, and indeed until the construction of eighteenth-century military roads, coastal areas were far more accessible than the forested, mountainous inland areas. Places we now think of as remote were often ideally situated on nautical highways of trade, communication and religion. Along the Argyll coast are chapels and crosses that indicate the significance of Christianity in western Scotland. Even earlier signs of religious life can be seen in the form of the Neolithic, Bronze Age and Iron Age standing stones and burial cairns that remain part of the Argyll landscape. A glance at a map will reveal the positions of dozens of stones cut with cup-and-ring marks, engravings made about 5,000 years ago for unknown purposes. Kilmartin's fascinating museum, dedicated to prehistoric Scotland, is situated in the heart of this landscape – Kilmartin Glen alone has over 800 prehistoric and early historic sites and there's a burial cairn a few steps away from the museum.

Towards the north of Argyll is Oban, the largest west coast town between Helensburgh and Fort William and a major port for those travelling to and from Scotland's Inner Hebrides. In the nineteenth century Oban became a stopping place for tourists doing a 'grand tour' of Scotland; today it's proud to call itself the 'seafood capital of Scotland'. Despite some serious competition, it's fair to say it merits the title, with numerous stalls and restaurants selling the freshly landed fruits of the Atlantic. Virginia Woolf compared Oban to the seaside resort of Ramsgate in Kent, but it's less a destination in itself than a pleasant pause on the way to the Hebrides. Among the islands that can be reached by ferry from Oban are Mull, Coll, Tiree, Barra and South Uist. In his 1865 travel book *A Summer in Skye*, Scottish poet Alexander Smith captured the seasonal, thoroughfare nature of Oban, and his description would be recognised by anyone today who has had to hurry from their guest house to the ferry terminal:

A more hurried, nervous, frenzied place than Oban, during the summer and autumn months, it is difficult to conceive. People seldom stay there above a night. The old familiar faces are the resident population. The tourist no more thinks of spending a week in Oban than he thinks of spending a week in a railway station. When he arrives his first question is after a bedroom; his second, as to the hour at which the steamer from the south is expected.

It's a little harsh to compare Oban to a railway station, not least because of its stunning location. It sits in a horseshoe-shaped bay, sheltered by Kerrera, a quiet island with a population of about 30 people. Wooded and heather-clad slopes surround it, and its shorefront boasts handsome hotels and a neo-Gothic cathedral as well as the more functional ferry port. On a hill above the town centre is Oban's most idiosyncratic landmark: a two-tiered granite coliseum, about 200 metres in circumference, known as McCaig's Tower. Part vanity project and part philanthropic attempt to keep local stonemasons supplied with work, it was commissioned by a banker called John Stuart McCaig in 1897; when he died in 1902 construction halted and never resumed. It's a peaceful stop in a busy town and, needless to say, there are magnificent views of Kerrera and the waters of the Firth of Lorn from here. Seen from the deck of a departing ferry, it's one of the most bizarre follies in Scotland.

There's a touch of absurdity to McCaig's Tower, but Oban is a town that can handle a dose of the surreal. No one makes this

10 Oban, crowned by McCaig's Tower

point better than contemporary writer Alan Warner, who has written six novels set in a fictionalised version of the town known as the Port. The earliest of these is *Morvern Callar*, published in 1995, which follows a young woman from the Port whose novelist boyfriend has killed himself upon completion of his first book. The imperturbable Morvern tells no one about the death, buries the body on a hillside, publishes the novel under her own name and uses her boyfriend's savings to take her best friend on a clubbing holiday in the Mediterranean. Morvern's Oban, like her Ibiza, is a hedonistic place, populated by eccentric characters known by nicknames such as Tequila Sheila, Ramraider (the town driving instructor) and the Argonaut (a drug-addled canoeist). The prose is heavily stylised, capturing Morvern's quirky way of speaking. As she describes dealing with her boyfriend's corpse, the prose is by turns lyrical, brutal and darkly comic:

> Nighttimeness was in the little village beyond the power station at the far end of the pass [. . .] there was dark except from the two skylights up in the rafters, moonlight was showing in two rectangles across the baby house slates of the village. Milky light on the mountain-side where the pylons came down made it real [. . .] I got Him under the ladder leaving a long smear down the corridor.

In his books Warner views the Highland landscape from an unusual angle. He doesn't seek to write lyrically about beautiful scenery: power stations and ferry terminals are as common as rugged mountaintops in his work. His Highland characters would make poor holiday neighbours. In his 2002 novel *The Man Who Walks*, a one-eyed, mentally deranged ex-hippie, suspected of stealing money from a pub, is pursued across the Highlands by his boorish, disreputable nephew. The uncle, known only as The Man Who Walks, stores cannabis resin behind his false eye, always travels by foot, and falls over at any change of gradient on the road.

Oban to the Mull of Kintyre

From Oban to the Mull of Kintyre, the southernmost point of Argyll, is about 100 miles. It's the sort of journey that could take days if you stopped at every viewpoint, standing stone and seafood restaurant. To the south-east of Oban, the elegant Loch Fyne slices into mainland Scotland. This large sea loch is known for its oyster bar at Clachan, at the head of the loch, and for Inveraray, seat of the dukes of Argyll. Inveraray is a curious place with a formally planned layout that is part quaint and part imposingly rigid. A row of whitewashed cottages overlooking the loch includes a holiday cottage which was the birthplace of Neil Munro, a popular Scottish writer of the early twentieth century; Munro's comic novel *The Vital Spark* follows the oddball crew of a steamboat. But in Inveraray, all roads lead to the jail and courthouse from which the dukes administered justice. In the eighteenth century the chiefs of Clan Campbell, holders of the Duchy of Argyll, were among the most powerful families in Scotland and the Hanoverian Crown's staunchest supporters. In Robert Louis Stevenson's *Kidnapped*, set just after the 1745 rising, the Jacobite Alan Breck Stewart can hardly mention their name without appending a curse to it.

Further south is Kintyre, the most remote of Argyll's peninsulas. The fishing village of Tarbert sits at the north of this stretch of land. Tarbert is the setting for *Gillespie*, the 1914 novel by John MacDougall Hay, a Church of Scotland minister who grew up in the village while it was prospering from a boom in the herring trade. *Gillespie* is a dark tale of greed and tragedy whose protagonist, a merchant called Gillespie Strang, seeks to dominate this small community. This novel is not unlike George Douglas Brown's *The House with the Green Shutters*, in its wholly unsentimental depictions of rural life and its narrative of the downfall of an over-proud family. Hay is a master of memorable details, from the conger eel writhing its way out of a drowned corpse to the banter of sharp-tongued fishwives. The novel made Hay's name and was praised by Thomas Hardy, himself no slouch when it came to shattering cosy illusions about rural life. Another reviewer thought it a Scottish equivalent of Herman Melville's *Moby Dick*, because of its unrelenting, elemental energy. The local tourist information office is unlikely to be so effusive: Brown describes the castle above the village as 'a fortress whose rags yet hang from a height over the harbour'; one of Tarbert's cobbled streets is 'twisted like the precarious lives of its inhabitants'.

A worrying number of Scottish novelists have died young. George MacDougall Hay is no exception: he died in 1919 of tuberculosis, aged 40, having published two novels and a collection of poems. His four-year-old son George Campbell Hay grew up in Tarbert and went on to become one of the leading Gaelic poets of the twentieth century. An advocate of Scottish nationalism, his political beliefs led him to refuse to fight in the Second World War, and in order to escape conscription he went on the run in Argyll between October 1940 and May 1941. Eventually he was caught, imprisoned and forced to enrol in the Royal Army Ordinance Corps. George Campbell Hay's war poetry is among the finest to have been written during the conflict and is characterised by internationalism and deep respect for people of different nations and cultures. His masterpiece is 'Mochtàr is Dùghall', a long poem about a cross-cultural meeting between a North African soldier called Mochtar and a Highland soldier called Dougal. Unusually, Hay wrote poetry in all three of Scotland's languages – English, Gaelic and Scots – and he demonstrates a deft touch in each. In his English-language poem 'To a Loch Fyne Fisherman' he addresses a figure who would have been familiar to him from his Tarbert childhood, but he also may have been alluding to his own independent-minded resistance to the political status quo:

> [Y]ou are your judge and master, your sentence unshaken,
> a man with a boat of his own and a mind to guide her.

Travelling south from Tarbert, the largest settlement of any size in Kintyre is Campbeltown, which can feel as isolated as anywhere in the Highlands despite being further south than Berwick-upon-Tweed. It takes over three hours to drive to Glasgow from here, though flights also run from Glasgow to nearby Machrihanish. The landscape of southern Kintyre is gently undulating, with fields clustering round the coastal townships and the rounded hills topped by heather. North of Campbeltown is a small village called Carradale, where writer Naomi Mitchison lived from the Second World War until her death in 1999 at the age of 101. Mitchison was prolific, writing over 90 books, including historical fiction, political ethics and memoirs. She was campaigner for women's rights as well as a socialist (she visited the Soviet Union in 1932 as part of a Fabian Society group), and she was even appointed honorary mother by a tribe in Botswana.

Among You Taking Notes is an edited version of Mitchison's wartime diary, written as part of the Mass Observation project, and is a vivid record of her rural life at that time. It's a fascinating record, not least because of the way it lurches from agricultural labour to revolutionary politics, via references to *Finnegans Wake* and the work of the Forestry Commission. Mitchison was a member of the Haldane dynasty of scientists and intellectuals, and her erudition and literary eloquence shine through in unexpected places:

In the afternoon we got the sheep into the tank and began shearing. I did seventeen. Several had the beginnings of maggots. Very horrid. We rubbed on dip and then removed the dead maggots with knife blades. There were a lot of ticks too. But the fleeces were lovely inside, a bit warm and rough. When the sheep were half sheared they looked like ideas coming into words. I kept on thinking about that and about Spencer's picture, and the new images for my book and whether anyone would want real wool after the war.

If you stand on the rocky shoreline at Carradale and look out to sea, you're actually looking east towards the Scottish mainland. Perhaps fortunately, the towns of Irvine and Saltcoats, which are roughly level with Carradale on the Ayrshire coast, are completely obscured by the mountainous Isle of Arran. For many decades Arran and the nearby islands of Bute and Great Cumbrae were the favourite holiday destinations of Glaswegians, close enough to be reached after a day's work, yet psychologically 'elsewhere' because they can only be reached by ferry. Arran is by far the largest and is divided by the same Highland Boundary Fault Line that marks the transition from the lowlands around Glasgow to the lochs and glens and hills of the Trossachs. On Arran, as on the mainland, the fault line gives the landscape a split personality: flat and fertile in the south, rocky and mountainous in the north. The contrasting terrains, along with the presence of a whisky distillery, herds of red deer and no fewer than seven golf courses, mean that Arran is known as 'Scotland in miniature'. A twelfth-century Gaelic poem praised the island's natural beauty: the spectacular ridges leading to Goat Fell, its highest peak; the quiet woodlands where stags spar and flowers carpet the forest floor; and the rivers which have always provided excellent fishing. Although there are more camper vans now than there were when the unknown twelfth-century bard sat down with his or her goose quill, parchment and oak gall ink, the island's appeal is undiminished.

For much of the twentieth century the lure of Arran and its neighbouring islands was irresistible for families during the July public holiday known as the Glasgow Fair fortnight. Thousands boarded steamers sailing from the Clyde and Ayrshire coast. Their journeys to myriad island arcadias are collectively known by the Glaswegian phrase 'going doon the watter' (down the water). In his 1958 novel *The Changeling*, Robin Jenkins celebrates and satirises this holidaymaking. An idealistic teacher named Charlie Forbes resolves to take one of his pupils, an intelligent but deceitful boy from a Glasgow slum, with him on his annual retreat 'doon the watter' to Towellan (a fictional place). He hopes to give his pupil Tom a taste of a better life and naively assumes that a coastal holiday will inspire the boy to work his way out of poverty. Charlie's wife and children are suspicious of the guarded and seemingly insolent Tom, and as the holiday progresses the tension between husband and wife reaches breaking point. Meanwhile Tom, treated with kindness for the first time in his life, has to find a way to reconcile this brief interlude with the rest of his tough life. At the start of the trip, Charlie's enthusiasm is palpable and he considers the commentary he should give Tom from the deck of the ferry, as they watch the mountains of Arran loom on the skyline:

> 'Here it is,' he should have been able to cry, 'our heritage, Tom, yours and mine, because we are Scottish; and what we see now is only the promise of vaster riches. In no other country in the world, not even in fabled Greece, is there loveliness so various and so inspiring in so small a space. Here is the antidote to Donaldson's Court [Tom's slum home]; here is the guarantee of that splendid and courageous manhood to which every Scots boy is entitled by birth.'

Charlie doesn't give this rousing speech, however, and admits to himself that it's probably a 'lot of guff'. Jenkins's novel has a subversive, socialist note to it, and even at an early stage Charlie's patronising, if well-meaning, social experiment seems doomed to failure.

The Road North from Loch Lomond

The West Highland Line, which links Glasgow with the harbour village of Mallaig via Fort William, is one of the most spectacular railway journeys in the world. After following the banks of the Clyde and the western shore of Loch Lomond, the landscape becomes one of exposed moorland and open vistas. Alan Warner's

2012 novel *The Deadman's Pedal*, an account of an Oban teenager learning to be a train driver in the West Highlands, provides a unique insider's perspective on rail journeys in this region; Warner himself worked for British Rail before becoming a full-time writer. As the train crosses Rannoch Moor it passes the isolated stations of Rannoch and Corrour – platforms that appear to be in the middle of nowhere, with little or no road access. In Danny Boyle's 1996 film adaptation of *Trainspotting*, Renton and his friends take a trip to Corrour Station in order to experience the great outdoors: the image of the city boys drinking vodka and lager on the moor is unforgettable.

Whether travelling by road or rail, one of the grandest and most recognisable landmarks between Loch Lomond and Rannoch Moor is Ben Dorain, a steep grassy cone that rises to over 1,000 metres above sea level. Ben Dorain is a couple of miles from Tyndrum, and there are impressive views of it from the road once you round the bend just north of the village. The West Highland Line curves

11 Ben Dorain: Duncan Ban Macintyre lived in the valley to the right of the mountain

round its lower slopes. The best way to get to know the mountain, however, is by climbing it – a challenging but rewarding hike on a path that avoids the precipitous road-facing slopes. One man who was intimately acquainted with the mountain was Duncan Ban Macintyre, whose long eighteenth-century poem 'In Praise of Ben Dorain' has been considered by generations of critics to be one of the greatest works in Gaelic literature. Macintyre worked as a deer stalker and lived at Ais an t-Sìthein, a sheltered steading on the eastern side of Ben Dorain that now lies in ruins. 'In Praise of Ben Dorain' is a virtuosic poem, richly descriptive, ecologically sensitive and unencumbered by the ponderous meditations that saturate mountain poems by Romantics such as Wordsworth and Shelley. Much of the poem is concerned with Ben Dorain's flora and fauna, especially its population of deer, whose diet of primrose and tormentil is carefully recorded. Amazingly, Macintyre constructed the poem in a style that imitates the pibroch, an elaborate form of bagpipe music. Like a pibroch, it opens with a statement of its overriding theme, which is developed with increasingly complex embellishments as it progresses. In Gaelic, Macintyre's poem has a dense pattern of rhyme and rhythm that adds to this musical sensuousness, and in my translation I've attempted to retain something of the majesty of the original:

> Above all other mountains reigns
> The venerable Ben Dorain.
> Of all the hills I've ever seen,
>> She's my most beautiful Ben.
>
> Sweeping moorland over here –
> The land a storehouse filled with deer.
> And here – the gleaming mountain heights.
>> I savour all these sights.

[. . .]

> Now the white-rumped herd is running
> And the hunters are pursuing.
> Oh, what a graceful gathering!
>   Deer sniff the wind and flee.

In the late 1760s Macintyre was compelled to leave his home beside Ben Dorain because the land was to be let for sheep-farming. He moved to Edinburgh, where he lived until his death in 1812. As well as a memorial in the city's Greyfriars Kirkyard, a monument in his memory was built by public subscription in 1859 above Dalmally, on the road between Tyndrum and Oban.

North of Ben Dorain is the hamlet of Bridge of Orchy, whose hotel offers a taste of luxury before the road passes Loch Tulla and climbs to Rannoch Moor. Some visitors describe the moor, roughly 130 square kilometres of tussocks, peat bogs, lochs and heather, as a bleak wasteland. This is how it appears in Stevenson's *Kidnapped*. The second half of the novel has the kind of plot that would later come to define American road movies, with David Balfour and Alan Breck Stewart arguing and bickering their way across the country, meeting a host of colourful characters, all the while pursued by soldiers who wrongly believe David and Alan are guilty of a political assassination. But unlike the Cadillac-driving stars of the movies, they travel on foot and must avoid roads and bridges which are guarded by troops. Rannoch Moor is a logical part of their covert route, but for David it offers a daunting prospect:

The mist rose and died away, and showed us that country lying as waste as the sea; only the moorfowl and the pee-wees [lapwings] crying upon it, and far over to the east, a herd of deer, moving like dots. Much of it was red with heather; much of the rest broken up with bogs and hags and peaty pools; some had been burnt black in a heath fire; and in another place there was quite a forest of dead firs, standing like skeletons. A wearier looking desert man never saw; but at least it was clear of troops, which was our point.

Were David to cross the moor now, he might view it in a less negative light. Apart from the construction of the road and railway, the moor has seen little human development and is a wilderness in the most positive meaning of the word. For this reason hiking across it (on an old military road, now part of the West Highland Way) is an almost otherworldly experience. On a still day the moor's initially austere beauty gives way to an awareness of its rich biodiversity. A modern visitor, unlike on-the-run David Balfour, can take the time to appreciate the buzzards shrieking overhead, the stags bellowing on distant hills, and, most ominously, swarms of midges hovering over the marshes.

Glencoe and Ben Nevis

Rannoch Moor is a stunning place, but just to the north is the landscape that encapsulates the history and terrain of the Highlands more than any other – Glencoe. Mountains rise on both sides to

12 Buachaille Etive Mor, the forbidding peak at the entrance to Glencoe

form imposing ridges, leading Dorothy Wordsworth in her journal to invoke John Milton's description of Satan in *Paradise Lost*: 'his stature reached the sky'. Crags and cliff-faces look down on the road and somehow feel threatening even to the driver passing through. Room-sized boulders – left here by glaciers receding at the end of the last ice age – are strewn on hillsides and the valley floor. Pockets of woodland cling to the few sheltered spots. Once you pass the Kings House Hotel, one of the country's oldest inns, visited by the Wordsworths in 1803, the land is stark and empty, often eerily quiet.

But Highland glens aren't merely striking scenery, a giant adventure playground for the many hikers, climbers and skiers that come to Glencoe year-round. In many places in the north of Scotland the emptiness of the landscape is partly a result of the Highland Clearances, a process that lasted about 100 years in the eighteenth and nineteenth centuries by which many thousands of Highlanders were evicted from their ancestral homes as landowners sought to maximise profit through sheep-farming and deer-stalking. Many Highlanders emigrated, in particular to Canada, the United States, New Zealand and Australia. Others, including Duncan Ban Macintyre, settled in the burgeoning towns and cities of the Central Belt. Although similar upheavals took place in many rural societies, the Clearances have an especially prominent place in Scotland's historical imagination, and the social and ecological effects of changing land use in the Highlands are still seen today. The Glencoe area, like many of the glens and straths (broad valleys) in the Highlands, experienced its share of evictions during the Clearances. However, Glencoe's notoriety largely rests on an earlier injustice which came to be known as the Glencoe Massacre.

In the late seventeenth century, the supporters of King William perceived that the Highlands had to be brought under greater military control. William had been installed as king in 1689 following the 'Glorious Revolution' which saw the abdication of the unpopular James II (James VII of Scotland); he ruled as joint sovereign with his wife Mary II, James's daughter. After an abortive Jacobite attempt to regain the British throne for James II later that year, a new Highland garrison, Fort William, was established. In 1691, fearing continued rebellion because many of the clans supported the Jacobite cause, William's most powerful Scottish supporters proposed that all Highland clan chiefs should be made to swear an oath of allegiance. One of these chiefs was Alasdair MacIain, head of the Glencoe MacDonald clan. MacIain set out in terrible weather to take the oath at Fort William on 31 December, a day before the deadline, only to be told that he was in the wrong place. With time running out he had to travel to Inveraray, 60 miles away. He arrived too late, and it wasn't until 6 January that he swore allegiance to William. Because of his lateness MacIain was promptly singled out for punishment as an example to other Highland chiefs. Orders were given for two regiments belonging to Archibald Campbell, the Earl of Argyll, to 'put all to the sword under seventy'.

Under the command of another Campbell, Captain Robert Campbell of Glenlyon, the soldiers marched to Glencoe and on 1 February took up lodging with the 500 or 600 MacDonalds who lived there. For almost a fortnight they enjoyed the hospitality of the MacDonalds who, adhering to Highland custom, were generous in providing food, drink and accommodation. Then, in the middle of the night of 12 February, they burst into the bedroom of the clan chief and shot him. At least 38 other men, women and children were slaughtered, and many more who fled then perished in a blizzard.

When news of the massacre reached the public there was uproar, and people were particularly shocked by the betrayal of hospitality involved. Few visiting writers can resist dwelling on the glen's bloody past. In his 1950 *Autobiography*, Bertrand Russell describes Glencoe as 'a gloomy valley [. . .] as dark and dreadful as if the massacre had just taken place'. T. S. Eliot, in the melancholy poem 'Rannoch, by Glencoe', dwells on the landscape's history of conflict, pride and the labyrinthine motives of its 'confused wrong'.

The popular historian John Prebble's 1966 book *Glencoe* remains one of the most engaging accounts of the massacre, but the events surrounding it are also brought to life in Susan Fletcher's novel *Witch Light*, published in 2010.

Witch Light tells the story of the massacre through the eyes of Corrag, a young woman hounded out of her home in the north of England after being accused of witchcraft. She travels north and eventually finds refuge with the MacDonalds of Glencoe. More attuned to the natural world than to other people, her descriptions of Rannoch and Glencoe are mesmerising: 'Some called it *a dark place* – like there was no goodness to be found inside those hills. But I know there was goodness. [. . .] The hills were very black, like they were shapes cut out of cloth, and the cloth was dark-blue, starry sky.' Although an outsider, Corrag feels at home in Glencoe and thinks of it as 'an open hand that I could lie inside, and it would keep me safe'. Unable to speak Gaelic, she invents her own names for the mountains: 'Ridge Like a Church', 'The Arrowhead'. But her happiness comes to a tragic end when soldiers arrive in the glen. After the massacre, she is apprehended and taken to Inveraray jail. Here she awaits burning at the stake, ostensibly for witchcraft but really in order to suppress her eyewitness account of the massacre. Unknown to the authorities, she narrates her tale to an idealistic pro-Jacobite clergyman keen to make news of the massacre widely known.

After Glencoe it's not far to Fort William, which with a modest population of 10,000 is nevertheless the second-largest settlement in the Highlands, behind Inverness. The town is lauded as Scotland's outdoor sports capital and draws mountain bikers, climbers, hillwalkers and other adventurers from all over the world. Above it is the hulking mass of Ben Nevis, Britain's highest mountain, which rises to 1,344 metres above sea level. From below, it's a lucky visitor who sees the summit, as it's usually brooding in cloud, but a quarter of a million people climb at least part of the way to the top each year.

In 1818 John Keats climbed Ben Nevis, an undertaking which in a letter to his brother he compared to 'mounting 10 Saint Paul's without the convenience of staircases'. Keats delighted in views of some of Britain's highest cliffs which, he wrote, 'turn one giddy if you choose to give way to it'. The summit of Ben Nevis is a relatively flat plateau and Keats notes that the weather seldom stays bright, warm and dry here for long, with clouds shrouding the view even on a good day: 'It was not so cold as I expected – yet cold enough for a glass of whisky now and then – There is not a more fickle thing than the top of a mountain – what would a lady give to change her head-dress as often and with as little trouble!'

The climb was heavy going and is unlikely to have done Keats's fragile health any good. Before setting out on his walking tour of Scotland, his physician had advised him that he 'mustn't go out', and he had been complaining of a sore throat since visiting Mull about a week prior to climbing Ben Nevis. Combined with poor nutrition and long hikes in the rain, the exertion is likely to have been a factor causing the emaciation and feverishness that alarmed an Inverness doctor soon afterwards. Although he recovered from this complaint, his health was never quite the same after his Scottish journey, and he died two and a half years later, in 1821, aged 25. Nevertheless, at the summit of Ben Nevis he had sufficient energy and inspiration to write a sonnet. It suggests that the view from the top led him to dark, rather than uplifting, thoughts:

> [...] all my eye doth meet
> Is mist and crag – not only on this height,
> But in the world of thought and mental might.

✤ 6 ✤

JOURNEYS TO THE HEBRIDES

Setting Sail

On a rainy September morning in 1773 James Boswell and Samuel Johnson set sail from Glenelg for the Isle of Skye. They had spent an uncomfortable night in the village inn, a squalid place with 'bare walls, a variety of bad smells' and 'not a single article' to eat or drink. Boswell had quarrelled with the older, crotchety Johnson, and hasty apologies were needed before they stepped into the boat bound for Armadale, a village on Skye's southern Sleat peninsula. Boswell and Johnson had set off on their journey to the Hebrides keen to 'find simplicity and wildness', and they hoped to witness 'a system of life almost totally different from what we had been accustomed to' in mainland Britain. Along the way they were received by acquaintances and other gentry eager for pearls of wisdom from Dr Johnson. Some of their metropolitan friends had been appalled at the notion of travelling to the Scottish islands: Boswell claims that Voltaire 'looked at me, as if I had talked of going to the North Pole' and asked fearfully if he was required to accompany them.

Despite being an Englishman with a well-documented prejudice against Scotland, Johnson's interest in the Hebrides was piqued by an early Scottish travel book, Martin Martin's *A Description of the Western Islands of Scotland*, published in 1703. Boswell and Johnson's trip took them to the islands of Skye, Raasay, Coll, Mull, Ulva, Inch Kenneth and Iona. Johnson's *A Journey to the Western Islands of*

Scotland and Boswell's *The Journal of a Tour to the Hebrides* now rank alongside Martin's book as the definitive early travellers' accounts of the Hebrides. Johnson's book is an eloquent record of the places they visited, a meditation on the culture, language and religion of the islands, and a thoughtful discussion of how to deal with rural Scotland's poverty and emigration. Boswell's journal, on the other hand, is a revealing record of his companion's foibles and opinions.

The two friends were often waylaid by horrendous weather and they were unable to visit all the islands that they had initially hoped to (a hazard even today, as the elements still cause ferry and flight cancellations). In this chapter we'll follow the course they took through the Hebrides, also known as the Western Isles, but along the way we'll digress and stop at some of the islands they failed to reach. To many mainlanders, the Hebrides have an irresistible allure. There's something special about boarding a ferry and crossing the sea to your destination, a confirmation that you're voyaging to a land that's literally and metaphysically set apart. As you set sail you can leave behind your old life, and for the duration of your journey can pretend you're Robinson Crusoe, contentedly untroubled by the world that lies beyond the island shores. That's the theory, at least, and the motivation behind many writers' visits to the outer reaches of the British archipelago. The novels, poems and travelogues inspired by the Hebrides, whether written by visitors or island natives, offer a fascinating introduction to a diverse and dramatic part of the country and, like Boswell and Johnson's books, often reveal as much about the traveller as they do about the places travelled to.

Skye

Skye is the largest of the Inner Hebrides, lying close to Scotland's west coast, north of Mallaig. It has an irregular shape, all peninsulas and sea lochs; on the map it looks like a battle-scarred lobster, waving its pincers towards Harris and Lewis. The landscape is varied, from the relatively low-lying and lush Sleat to the weird glacial rock formations of Trotternish. Home to two Michelin-starred restaurants, the Talisker whisky distillery and an abundance of wildlife including two species of eagle, it's one of Scotland's must-visit locations. The 'capital', Portree, is situated in a beautiful bay and is the centre of the island's vibrant cultural scene; Skye, along with the Outer Hebrides, is an enclave of the Gaelic language. The area to the south around Armadale, where Boswell and Johnson landed, has ruined castles, hidden beaches and craft shops. It's home to Sabhal Mòr Ostaig, Scotland's Gaelic-medium college and hub of the language's small but dynamic contemporary literary scene. Although it's possible to take the ferry to Skye, most modern visitors opt for the only slightly less romantic option of driving over the graceful arc of the Skye Bridge, completed in 1995.

Apart from a four-day excursion to the nearby island of Raasay, Boswell and Johnson were on Skye for a month, their departure repeatedly postponed because of bad weather. They met a host of local gentry and clergy, and Johnson was happy to dispute the finer points of philosophy and social reform with them. Johnson's first port of call in any house seems to have been its library. Boswell keeps a studious record of his friend's reading matter and gleefully includes Johnson's more rumbustious moments, when he 'toasted Highland beauties with great readiness'. On one occasion a young married woman sat on the doctor's knee and, encouraged by some rowdy companions, put her arms round his neck and kissed him. 'Do it again', said Johnson, 'and let us see who will tire first.'

On another, marginally more sober occasion, they visited the home of Flora MacDonald at Kingsburgh, ten miles north-west of Portree. By 1773 Flora MacDonald was a folk heroine whose role in one of the biggest upheavals in British history had made her a household name. Prince Charles Edward Stuart, the Jacobite claimant to the British throne, better known as Bonnie Prince Charlie, spent several months on the run after his defeat in 1746 at the Battle of Culloden, a kingly price of £30,000 on his head. He was holed up in North Uist, government troops closing in, when a plan was concocted to smuggle him to Skye disguised as Flora's Irish maidservant. The Prince was tall, with a long stride, and didn't wear a maid's gown and petticoat convincingly, but they somehow managed to reach Skye without being apprehended. One of Scotland's most popular folk songs, 'The Skye Boat Song', commemorates this journey. It begins:

> Speed, bonnie boat, like a bird on the wing,
> Onward the sailors cry;
> Carry the lad that's born to be king
> Over the sea to Skye.
>
> Loud the winds cry, loud the waves roar,
> Thunderclaps rend the air.
> Baffled our foes stand by the shore.
> Follow they will not dare.

Flora and the Prince parted at McNab's Inn, Portree (which is still there, now part of the Royal Hotel). Flora was soon arrested and was imprisoned in London for six months. Prince Charles eventually escaped to France and a retirement of 'brandy, gout and syphilis', as contemporary poet Mick Imlah puts it in 'The Lost Leader'. After meeting her in Kingsburgh, Johnson referred to Flora as 'a name that will be mentioned in history, and if courage and fidelity be virtues, mentioned with honour'. He may have been simply flattered, of course, by her calling him 'a young English buck'. While at Kingsburgh Johnson slept in the same bed that Prince Charles had used a quarter of a century earlier.

Johnson thought that some parts of Skye were bleak. He complained that Talisker, a settlement about halfway up the island's west coast, was a place 'from which the gay and the jovial seem utterly excluded'. Even though the thrusting Cuillin Ridge can be seen from many parts of the island, Boswell and Johnson devote little attention to Skye's mountains. Skye is one of the most elevated of the Scottish islands, boasting 12 Munros – mountains over 3,000 feet (914 metres). Skye's Munros are loved and feared in equal measures: the peaks make up the Black Cuillin, a seven-kilometre ridge of black volcanic rock carved into sheer precipices. This range is the closest thing Scotland has to the Alps, though a more evocative comparison might be with the mountains of Mordor in *The Lord of the Rings*. The Cuillin are one of the key symbolic landscapes in the work of twentieth-century Gaelic poet Sorley MacLean.

MacLean was born in 1911 in Raasay, which lies between Skye and mainland Scotland. Much of his poetry is set on these two islands

13 A path leading to the Cuillin Ridge, Skye

and combines appreciation for their landscapes with MacLean's political preoccupations. In the 1930s he was an ardent socialist who treated both the British Empire and Europe's emerging fascism with revulsion. His ambitious long poem *The Cuillin*, begun in 1939 and never fully completed, was intended as a work 'radiating from Skye and the West Highlands to the whole of Europe'. The poem is full of vivid descriptions of the mountain range, including its bird life and geology. Embedded in this landscape poetry are references to Karl Marx, Nazism, nineteenth-century Gaelic poetry and philosophical materialism. The poem is influenced by modernists including Ezra Pound, T. S. Eliot and the Scottish poet Hugh MacDiarmid. It begins with a stirring evocation of Sgurr nan Gillean, MacLean's favourite peak, whose name translates as 'Peak of the Young Men':

> The place above all others for me to be
> is on your high shoulder blades,
> striving with your deep-grey rocky throat,
> wrestling with your notched chest, that surges like a wave.

Standing on the Cuillin Ridge is an unforgettable experience. It's composed entirely of rock, no grass or heather. On a bright day the gabbro, the grey-black volcanic rock that the ridge is made of, shimmers like lead; when clouds obscure the sun it's ominously black. The ridge is about the least human place imaginable, completely uncultivable and uninhabitable, and the paths that traverse it are really just lines of scuffed stones leading along the knife-edge ridge. A comparison with the surface of the moon would be possible if it wasn't for the fact that much of the time there's a dizzying drop of hundreds of metres on at least one side of this so-called 'path'. Writing in his 2007 book *The Wild Places*, Robert Macfarlane records that he came here, to the 'most austere and gothic of all Britain's ranges', hoping to climb the 'Inaccessible Pinnacle', the exposed, fin-shaped peak of Sgurr Dearg. After a hard climb from Loch Coruisk, Macfarlane reaches the foot of the pinnacle and is overcome not only by the exposed drop, but also by a sense of the mountain's unfathomable past:

> [T]his rock had once been fluid, I thought. Aeons ago it had run and dripped and spat. On either side of the Pinnacle, the ground dropped immediately away. I took a few steps up the fin. Suddenly I felt precarious, frightened: balanced on an edge of time as well as of space. All I wanted to do was get back off the ridge [. . .] We had talked of climbing the Pinnacle, had brought ropes to do so. But here, suddenly, there seemed neither point nor possibility to such an act. It would be dangerous, and impertinent.

Another visitor to Skye, less adventurous and ultimately less humbled than MacFarlane, was Virginia Woolf. Her 1927 novel *To the Lighthouse* is set on Skye, although Woolf didn't actually go to the island herself until 1938. The novel is a meditation on childhood, marriage, loss and grief, narrated through the alternating perspectives of members of the Ramsay family, over several years of Skye holidays. The setting is described in luscious prose, but Woolf keeps actual geographical references to a minimum. She spent her own childhood holidays in St Ives, and the Skye of *To the Lighthouse* sounds suspiciously like Cornwall:

> It was September after all, the middle of September, and past six in the evening. So off they strolled down the garden in the usual direction, past the tennis lawn, past the pampas grass, to that break in the thick hedge, guarded by red-hot pokers like brasiers of clear burning coal, between which the blue waters of the bay looked bluer than ever.

When Woolf did eventually visit Skye she stayed in the Flodigarry Hotel, a country house overlooking the north-eastern shores of the island (and still popular today). She went to Dunvegan Castle, seat of the chief of Clan MacLeod, and though it wasn't open to visitors at that time she wasn't deterred – 'the door being open I walked in', as she tells her sister in a letter. What stands out in her letters from Skye, apart from some initial condescension, is her appreciation of the subtle gradations of light and colour on the land, which would doubtless have featured more prominently had *To the Lighthouse* been written after her time on the island:

> Well, here we are in Skye, and it feels like the South Seas – completely remote, surrounded by sea, people speaking Gaelic, no railways, no London papers, hardly any inhabitants [. . .] One should be a painter. As a writer, I feel the beauty, which is almost entirely colour, very subtle, very changeable, running over my pen.

The Islands Near Skye: Raasay, Soay and the Small Isles

Near the start of their Skye sojourn, Boswell and Johnson spent four days on Raasay, which is about level with the middle of Skye's eastern coast, and only a short boat trip away. Here, according to Johnson, they received 'nothing but civility, elegance, and plenty' from the laird and his family. Boswell observes, and indeed partakes in, the Highland custom of imbibing a daily dram of whisky: Gaelic has its own word, *sgailc*, for a morning shot. There was dancing and conviviality in the Raasay household every night, led by the laird, his wife, their three sons and ten daughters. On one occasion Boswell left Johnson behind in order to enjoy a more active exploration of the island. He covered 24 miles of 'very rugged terrain' – virtually the whole of the island, which is 14 miles long and, at its widest, three miles wide. He 'had a Highland dance on the top of Dun Can, the highest mountain in the island', but was determined to hold some energy in reserve so as not to be 'outdone at the nightly ball by our less active friends'.

Raasay is an attractive island, beloved by its relatively small cohort of visitors: Peter Irvine, author of the invaluable guidebook series *Scotland the Best* (latest edition published in 2016) ranks it as the most 'magical' of Scottish islands. Like many of the Hebrides, it's a haven for wildlife, prized in particular by birdwatchers. There's a crumbling, ruined castle and a thirteenth-century chapel. The house that Boswell and Johnson stayed in was rebuilt after a devastating fire in 2009 and is now a comfortable hotel, outdoor activity centre and café.

The population of northern Raasay soared in the nineteenth century as a result of forced evictions from more fertile parts of the island, with sheep replacing people during the local manifestation of the Clearances taking place across the Highlands. Sorley MacLean took the Highland Clearances as his subject in many of his poems, including 'Hallaig', by far his most well-known poem. The township of Hallaig was home to 129 people in 1841, but by 1861 just one shepherd and a labourer lived here. Today the remains of Hallaig's buildings can still be seen: low stone walls gradually collapsing and blending into the grassy sweep of the land. Were it not for its history, it would be easy to call the place beautiful – a sheltered, verdant retreat with views of the mainland. But for those who have read MacLean's poem, Hallaig is a haunting place. The poem, written in 1952, is a surreal vision in which the long-dead inhabitants of Hallaig appear as trees growing near the ruined buildings:

> The men lying on the grass
> at the end of each former home,
> the young women a birch wood,
> their backs straight, their heads bowed.

'Hallaig' is an elusive poem. Its tranquil-seeming mysticism makes it an enchanting elegy for those displaced; it is full of love and, simmering away beneath the surface, heartfelt anger about historical wrongs. MacLean's poem is now literally written into the landscape of Hallaig, engraved on a monument overlooking the remains of the township.

Much smaller than Raasay and harder to get to is Soay, a compact island just to the south of Skye consisting of two scrubby landmasses connected by a slim isthmus. In 1944 the island was bought by Gavin Maxwell, the writer best remembered for *Ring of Bright Water*, his memoir about living with otters. Maxwell set up a basking shark fishery on Soay, hunting these placid, plankton-eating creatures and processing them for liver oil. Basking sharks are the world's second-largest species of fish, growing to up to ten metres in length. In his book *Harpoon at a Venture*, published in 1952, Maxwell records his awe at an early sighting of this magnificent fish:

> At first it was no more than a ripple with a dark centre. The centre became a small triangle, black and shiny, with a slight forward movement, leaving a light wake in the still water. The triangle grew until I was looking at a huge fin, a yard high and as long at the base. It seemed monstrous, this great black sail, the only visible thing upon limitless miles of pallid water. A few seconds later the notched tip of a second fin appeared some twenty feet astern of the first, moving in a leisurely way from side to side.

Despite his admiration for these creatures, Maxwell's commercial fishery led to a serious reduction in the shark population of the west coast of Scotland. *Harpoon at a Venture* is at times a gruesome read, full of gory details about shark butchery, and Soay comes to resemble an island-sized abattoir. However, the shark fishery only ran for three years and in business terms was a fiasco. Today the basking shark is protected in Britain, and a sighting of these creatures is invariably an exciting experience. They cruise along near the surface of the water and, seen from a boat, a full-grown adult shark is easily mistaken for two individuals, such is the distance between its fins. The remains of Maxwell's shark oil factory still stand at Soay's harbour.

To the south of Soay are Rum, Eigg, Canna and Muck, known collectively as the Small Isles. They vary tremendously: Rum is very mountainous, whereas Muck and Canna sit much lower in the water. From the Sgurr, the highest point on Eigg, you can enjoy one of the best views anywhere in the United Kingdom: to the south are the low-lying islands of Coll and Tiree, as well as the Ardnamurchan peninsula, mainland Britain's most westerly point. The ragged and mountainous coastline of Scotland stretches for miles to the east; to the west the chain of the Outer Hebrides is a hazy blur on the horizon. Rum and Skye, with their spectacular peaks, rise up to the north, black ridges slicing into the cloud. Despite a forbidding appearance, the Sgurr is an easy climb, and with luck you might spot an eagle soaring above the crags, or an otter in one of the small lochs on the hill's western slopes.

From the Sgurr of Eigg there's almost a bird's eye view of Muck, smallest of the Small Isles, just to the south. Where Eigg is rocky, dominated by cliffs and elevated tracts of moor and bog, Muck is about as close to a pastoral idyll as it gets in the Hebrides. It measures two miles by one and has a population of just 38 people. It has a farm, a shooting estate, a sandy beach and a plentiful supply of seafood: eating lobster thermidor at the island hotel, looking out over the Atlantic, is one possible definition of paradise. Muck's name comes from the Gaelic word *muc*, meaning pig, although it's possible that this is a contraction of *muc-mhara*, or 'sea-pig', the Gaelic name for the porpoises that frequent Gallanach Bay on the northern shore. Regardless of the etymology, the island's name was cause for embarrassment for the eighteenth-century laird, who met Boswell and Johnson during their stay in Skye. Highland convention dictates that he should be called by the title 'Muck', but he was disinclined to take this name and insisted that he be called 'Isle of Muck', to the travellers' amusement. He had also endeavoured to have the name of the island changed to monk, without success, and presumably lived in fear of being known as 'Lord Muck'.

Coll

During a lull in the bad weather Boswell and Johnson eventually sailed south from Skye towards Mull, hoping that the worst of the autumn storms were behind them. They had given up hope of an extended tour of the Hebrides and had decided that Mull, along with its small neighbours Iona and Inch Kenneth, would suffice. But as they rounded Ardnamurchan Point the wind changed and they found themselves sailing into another violent storm. As the sea grew rough and night fell, Boswell became frightened, though he could in retrospect savour its sublimity: 'I now saw what I never saw before, a prodigious sea, with immense billows coming upon a vessel, so as that it seemed hardly possible to escape. There was something grandly horrible in the sight. I am glad I have seen it once.'

The more experienced sailors on board were even more concerned than Boswell. They resolved to make for Coll: the young laird of Coll was on board and he promised that he could guide them to a safe harbour. As the men wrestled with the sails, Boswell asked how he could help. The laird handed him a rope and told him to hold it tight until he was ordered to pull. He stood at his post in the wind and rain for some time before it dawned on him that this small job was a ruse to 'divert my fear, by employing me, and making me think that I was of use'. All the while Johnson, unaware of the danger, lay on a bed in the cabin with a greyhound beside him to keep him warm.

The friends spent a few unplanned days on Coll. They explored the old ruined castle, rode about the island, argued about literature and drank toasts out of a shell: Johnson water; Boswell whisky. There are no fewer than 23 beaches on Coll, including several magnificent stretches of pale sand which you are virtually guaranteed to have to yourself. Boswell and the laird enjoyed galloping over these wide open spaces and Johnson followed behind on what he calls 'a little Highland steed', a short pony which, Boswell assures his readers, made its corpulent old rider look utterly ridiculous.

While on Coll, Boswell and Johnson may have heard the distinctive 'crex crex' sound made by male corncrakes, a once common bird whose territory is now mainly restricted to outlying islands of Britain. They may have been sufficiently familiar with the bird that they paid it no notice at all – Mrs Beeton, less than a century later, thought of them as a foodstuff and described a recipe for skewer-roasted corncrakes. However, due to mechanised farming they have virtually disappeared from the British Isles and birdwatchers and conservationists come to Coll, to its neighbouring island of Tiree and also to Iona to hear and occasionally catch a glimpse of these elusive birds. In her 2005 essay 'Crex-Crex', from *Findings*, Kathleen Jamie describes joining Coll's nature warden on a study of the island's corncrake population. A poet as well as an essayist, her renderings of the bird's call are both memorable and hilarious: 'like someone grating a nutmeg, perhaps. Or a prisoner working toward his escape with a nailfile', 'a goblin carpenter, sawing away at his little workbench', 'more Tom Waits than Tom Jones'. If you are on Coll when the migrant corncrakes are in residence, you'll almost certainly hear them. Seeing them is a different matter – they're camouflaged, timid, and their calls project in such a way that they always seem to come magically from an empty piece of ground.

Mull, Iona and Surrounding Islands

From Coll, Boswell and Johnson sailed east to Mull. Like Skye, it's a large island with a diverse range of landscapes and attractions, and it's safe to say that modern roads make it far easier to explore than it would have been in 1773. The pretty village of Tobermory sits in a bay at the north of the island, its multicoloured seafront buildings making it the perfect setting for the children's TV programme *Balamory*. At the heart of Mull is Ben More, the only island Munro outside of Skye, a steep and rocky peak. The coastal road that circles the mountain ranks as one of the most scenic in the Hebrides,

14 The wild heart of the Isle of Mull

navigating cliffs and beaches and affording the best views of Staffa, Ulva and Inch Kenneth that can be obtained without setting foot in a boat. Mull hasn't many settlements bigger than a few houses, and its population is less than 3,000, but in the summer months this number soars with tourists heading across the island to Iona or standing in lay-bys with binoculars, hoping to catch sight of sea eagles, golden eagles and otters, the 'big three' according to the island's many wildlife tours.

Boswell and Johnson used Mull as little more than a base for exploring the smaller islands within easy reach of its shores. This was also the case for John Keats, travelling across Mull in 1818 on what was effectively a backpacking holiday. Keats's companion, Charles Brown, caused a stir amongst the islanders, who were amazed by one aspect of his appearance: 'they handle his spectacles as we do a sensitive leaf.' For Boswell and Johnson, and also for Keats, Mull wasn't the appealing travel destination that it is today. The main attractions for all three writers were the islands to the west of Mull, in particular Iona. On the way to Iona, Boswell and Johnson stopped at the islands of Ulva (of which Boswell said 'there was nothing worthy of observation') and Inch Kenneth ('a pretty little island'). These judgements were probably based as much on the condition of the landowners' houses and the quality of the company, as on the islands themselves. Ulva retains a small population today and is easy to visit from Mull: the ferry is summoned from the smaller island by uncovering a red panel that is (in theory) visible from the other side of the sound. Apart from the visit by Boswell and Johnson, Inch Kenneth is most famous as the Hebridean retreat of the Mitford family, who owned it between 1938 and 1966. Unity Mitford, a socialite and devoted admirer of Adolf Hitler, shot herself in an unsuccessful suicide attempt after Britain declared war on Germany. She spent much of her remaining few years on the island before dying in Oban from meningitis caused by the bullet that surgeons had never been able to remove from her head.

Iona is a place of religious pilgrimage, and one of the best known of all the Hebrides. Saint Columba, an Irish priest who is traditionally regarded as the founder of the Scottish church, set up a monastery on Iona in AD 563. The island quickly became Scotland's ecclesiastical capital and thrived for centuries, despite repeated Viking raids. Many historians believe that the beautiful illuminated edition of the four Gospels, the medieval Book of Kells, was begun at Iona in the ninth century before being moved to the Irish monastery from which it takes its name: Kells was founded by Iona monks in AD 807. Now held in the library of Trinity College, Dublin, the book is a resplendent example of medieval art, its pages ornamented with elaborate designs and images. Weird gilded creatures gaze out from the text, and figures on horseback ride between lines of Latin script. The book probably took years to make and was the work of several artists and scribes. The Book of Kells is now regarded as one of Ireland's cultural treasures, and those who aren't lucky enough to see it in the flesh – it is, after all, written on calfskin – can explore it in a less fragile form via the university's website.

Archaeological treasures abound on Iona. There are tall stone crosses, some medieval, some relatively modern. Near the jetty at Baile Mòr, the island's village, stand the ruins of the nunnery built in about the year 1200. Many of Scotland's early kings are buried here, as well as more recent political figures, including the Labour leader John Smith. The Benedictine abbey, still a place of worship today, is by far the largest building that can be seen on the short crossing from Mull. It too was built around 1200 and much of the medieval architecture remains despite alterations and restorations over the centuries. Although it has a fine collection of carved stones and monuments, it's a muted place, less ostentatious than the great Christian cathedrals of the period. Following the Reformation in the sixteenth century, the abbey church fell into a state of disrepair and restoration projects didn't begin in earnest until after the Duke of Argyll, owner of Iona, gifted the island's ecclesiastical buildings to the Church of Scotland in 1899.

Dr Johnson arrived on Iona in style, carried ashore by a team of 'Highlanders' because their boat couldn't get close enough to land for him to keep his feet dry. That night he and Boswell slept in a barn on beds made of hay. In 1773 many of the church buildings were in a state of decay, but nevertheless Johnson's impressions of the island are among the highlights of his *Journey to the Western Islands of Scotland* – he seems to have been quite moved by the presence of so much history:

> We were now treading that illustrious island, which was once the luminary of the Caledonian regions, whence savage clans and roving barbarians derived the benefits of knowledge, and the blessings of religion. To abstract the mind from all local emotion would be impossible, if it were endeavoured, and would be foolish, if it were possible. Whatever withdraws us from the

15 Iona Abbey

power of our senses; whatever makes the past, the distant, or the future predominate over the present, advances us in the dignity of thinking beings [. . .] That man is little to be envied, whose patriotism would not gain force upon the plain of Marathon, or whose piety would not grow warmer among the ruins of Iona.

Were Johnson to visit Iona today he would enjoy greater creature comforts, as the island's economy revolves around the tourists who come seeking history, remoteness or spiritual fulfilment. For those wanting tranquillity, the best places on Iona are probably the perfect beaches of the north and the cove in the south, Port na Curaich, where Columba is said to have first set foot on the island (there's no evidence that Highlanders carried *him* ashore). In its ecclesiastical heyday Iona wasn't really as isolated as it seems today: while providing a quiet location for monastic contemplation, it was well placed to communicate by sea with other parts of Scotland and Western Europe. This interplay of remoteness and connectivity is explored in an anthology, *The Book of Iona*, edited by Robert Crawford and published in 2016.

North of Iona is Staffa, an even smaller island with an almost magical allure. Its cliffs are basalt columns similar to those at Giant's Causeway in Northern Ireland, and its magnificent sea caves have impressed generations of visitors. The German composer Felix Mendelssohn visited Staffa in 1829 and was subsequently inspired to write his *Hebrides Overture*. Staffa must rank as one of the most Romantic (with a capital 'R') islands in Europe. In addition to Mendelssohn, Scott, Wordsworth, Keats and Tennyson came here, with Keats writing that 'for solemnity and grandeur it far surpasses the finest cathedral'. Turner couldn't resist painting Staffa, and later Queen Victoria, a lover of Scotland's stirring landscapes, also admired this celebrated, uninhabited island.

Just beyond the end of the road on the south-western tip of Mull is another small island, far less famous than either Iona or Staffa, called Erraid. It's reached by crossing a sandy beach at low tide, but cut off from Mull when the sea comes in. Robert Louis Stevenson visited Erraid in 1870 while his father Thomas Stevenson supervised the construction of the lighthouse at Dubh Artach, a wave-battered rock 15 miles to the south-west. His most memorable evocation of Erraid is in *Kidnapped*. In the novel David Balfour has been tricked aboard a ship bound for America, where he is to be sold into slavery. Before the ship can cross the Atlantic it runs aground on the Torran Rocks to the south of Mull and sinks. David manages to reach the shore of Erraid. When he explores the island it happens to be high tide and as he can't swim he concludes that he's marooned. For four days he sleeps rough on Erraid, eating raw shellfish, his situation becoming rapidly more desperate:

> [M]y plight on that third morning was truly pitiful. My clothes were beginning to rot; my stockings in particular were quite worn through, so that my shanks were naked; my hands had grown quite soft with the continual soaking; my throat was very sore, my strength had much abated, and my heart so turned against the horrid stuff I was condemned to eat, that the very sight of it came near to sicken me.

When he sees two fishermen sail past, he shouts to them for help, but they call back in Gaelic, laugh, and sail on to Iona. On the next day the boat returns with another man on it who can speak some English. Though he too finds David's predicament ridiculous – marooned on a tidal island – he eventually explains the situation and David crosses the strand to Mull. Today Erraid is a secluded place to explore on a sunny afternoon, and tide tables mean David's fate is easily avoided.

Jura, Islay, Colonsay

After they visited Iona, Boswell and Johnson headed back towards the mainland along the Ross of Mull, the island's long southern peninsula. Like many modern tourists, they regarded it as a thoroughfare to Iona, although the region has a quiet beauty worth savouring in its own right. If they paused on their travels to look out to sea from one of the Ross of Mull's pristine beaches, they would have seen three conical hills dominating the horizon. These are the Paps of Jura.

Jura is one of the wildest of all the Hebrides, clad with heather, rock and bog, and populated mainly by deer: its human population is about 200, while there are an estimated 7,000 red deer. The island's name probably comes from the Old Norse for 'deer island'. The island's single road runs down the east coast, where all of Jura's inhabitants live. The west is uninhabited and can only be reached on foot, a strenuous hike over terrain that Roger Deakin has accurately described as a 'giant mantrap' that 'resists you at every step'. In *Waterlog*, his erudite 1999 memoir about wild swimming in every corner of Britain, Deakin is spoilt for choice as he takes a dip in the many lochs, bays and hillside pools of Jura. He is also determined to swim in the Corryvreckan, the world's third-largest whirlpool, which lurks in the strait between north Jura and the island of Scarba. The Corryvreckan has long enjoyed notoriety amongst sailors and travellers to the isles. Martin Martin of Skye, whose *A Description of the Western Islands of Scotland* inspired Boswell and Johnson's own journey to the Hebrides, says this about the whirlpool:

> The sea begins to boil and ferment with the tide of flood, and resembles the boiling of a pot; and then increases gradually, until it appears in many whirlpools, which form themselves in sort of pyramids, and immediately after spout up as high as the mast of a little vessel, and at the same time make a loud report.

Martin goes on to claim that the gulf takes its name from Brekan, son of one of the kings of Denmark, who was drowned here and 'cast ashore in the north of Jura'. Three centuries after Martin travelled to the Corryvreckan, Roger Deakin wisely had second thoughts about swimming in it, and settled for rather less dangerous swims on the island.

In the more inaccessible parts of Jura it's easy to feel as if you're the last human being on the planet. That's probably how Eric Arthur Blair, known to millions by his pen name George Orwell, must have felt when he moved to Jura in May 1946 to work on his novel *The Last Man in Europe*. He stayed there until the end of 1948, by which time the book, now renamed *Nineteen Eighty-Four*, had been completed. Orwell had long desired to find a quiet spot in the Hebrides in which to write, and when a friend found him the remote farmhouse of Barnhill, at the northern tip of Jura, he leapt at the chance. He was in a bad way, emotionally and physically. His first wife Eileen had died the year before during a routine operation; his sister Marjorie also died immediately prior to his move to Jura. He proposed to at least three women in early 1946, longing for someone to ease his loneliness and help raise his adopted son Richard. Furthermore, his health was poor: while on Jura he was diagnosed with tuberculosis and spent several months in Hairmyres Hospital, East Kilbride, undergoing treatment that produced painful reactions including ulcers and blistered lips. Barnhill was a bad place for a man in his condition to move to. There was no electricity and there were no amenities; even today the house is only accessible by boat or 4x4.

Orwell's stay at Barnhill seems masochistic: a man in poor health removing himself from the world, living in a place where there was enough hardship to fuel the imagination that would create the stifling totalitarianism of *Nineteen Eighty-Four*. Towards the end of the novel the protagonist Winston Smith is imprisoned and tortured by government agents. Beaten and starved, his torturer O'Brien encourages him to look in a mirror, and it's tempting to read something of Orwell's own physical condition, following his treatment, in the reflection Winston looks upon:

> The creature's face seemed to be protruded, because of its bent carriage. A forlorn, jailbird's face with a nobby forehead running back into a bald scalp, a crooked nose, and battered-looking cheekbones [. . .] At a guess he would have said that it was the body of a man of sixty, suffering from some malignant disease.

Nineteen Eighty-Four was Orwell's last novel, a work of such prevailing power that the ideas in it – Big Brother, doublespeak – are familiar even to those who haven't read the book. Barnhill still stands on a headland overlooking the Sound of Jura and is still an austere place to live, despite the addition of a diesel generator for electricity. For those wanting solitude, inspiration or a taste of Orwell's spartan lifestyle, the house is available for rental.

Next to Jura is Islay. The two islands are often regarded as siblings and talked about as a pair, but they could scarcely be more different. While Jura is all mountain, rock and heath, Islay is flatter, more fertile, and has a much larger population: with about 3,500 people it's one of the most populous of the Scottish islands. Islay was the seat of the Lords of the Isles, MacDonald chieftains who ruled over a large extent of the Highlands and the Hebrides at their peak in the fourteenth century; they were powerful enough to have their own separate treaties with England, France and Ireland. The lords held court on an island within an island – a small patch of land on Loch Finlaggan, in Islay's interior. Today Islay's influence comes from being one of the two main centres of Scotland's whisky industry. Islay's whiskies are usually peaty and smoky, with a hint of the sea about them. There are eight distilleries on the island, including Ardbeg, Bowmore, Lagavulin and Laphroaig, and their presence has led to Islay becoming one of the wealthier of the Hebrides.

Between Islay and Mull lies Colonsay. In 1969 John McPhee, a staff writer with the *New Yorker* magazine, came to live for several months on this small Hebridean island, along with his wife and four daughters. McPhee's ancestors had emigrated to the United States from Colonsay; when he passes a graveyard, one islander tells him that 'this place is full of your people'. His daughters enrolled at the island school, boosting the number of pupils to 23, and McPhee devoted himself to studying the island's people, their culture and their everyday lives. The resulting book, originally published as a series of articles, is *The Crofter and the Laird*, a meticulous and incisive portrait of a way of life and of the relationship between Colonsay's tenant crofters and its aristocratic owner, Lord Strathcona. McPhee is acute about the way that gossip travels in a small community. The multiple whisky-fuelled judgements expressed in the pub when the topic turns to someone who isn't there – be it the postman, a crofter, or the perennially unpopular laird – have the tone of a Greek chorus. McPhee's writing is affectionate and it's clear that he has a great deal of respect for the islanders, but he's also honest about the negative aspects of living on an island as small (only eight miles long) as Colonsay:

Colonsay is less like a small town than like a large lifeboat. By a scale of things that begins with cities and runs to hamlets, the island is some distance off the end. The usual frictions, gossip, and intense social espionage that characterise life in a small town are so grandly magnified on Colonsay that they sometimes appear in surprising form, in the way that patches of skin magnified a

hundred diameters may appear to be landscapes of the moon. [. . .]
Everyone is many things to everyone else, and is encountered daily
in a dozen guises.

McPhee and his family embrace island life – he forages for mussels
which he cooks in whisky, he hunts for lobsters in rock pools with
his neighbour, and he listens to an impromptu bagpipe recital. He
also listens to the life stories of crofters who started out as actors, to
likely lads who've just been made redundant from the island estate,
and to the ambitious young minister alluding to Cliff Richard as he
preaches to a congregation of fewer than 20.

The Outer Hebrides

The Outer Hebrides is an island chain lying off Scotland's north-
west coast and stretching for 130 miles, from Lewis in the north
to tiny, wedge-shaped Berneray in the south. Each of the islands
has its own personality and distinctive landscape: Harris with its
knuckly hills; the vast peat bogs of Lewis; North Uist, so drowned
by lochs and pools that it appears to be made of water rather than
land. The western seaboards of many of the islands comprise long
sandy beaches which, were they a few degrees warmer, would attract
millions of visitors. You can walk for miles along the shore with only
a few oystercatchers for company. The dunes and grassland on the
landward side of these beaches is called machair, low fertile plains
which in summer are carpeted with wildflowers. The Outer Hebrides
are the last remaining heartlands of the Gaelic language, and many
of the islands are also strongholds of conservative Christianity:
Lewis, for example, still has a strong enough Sabbatarian culture
that many shops and some public facilities are closed on Sundays.

Lewis and Harris are actually the two parts of a single landmass,
although they are rarely referred to as such. They are by far the
largest and most populous of the Outer Hebrides. A natural barrier

of mountains and moorland divides them, and so for much of their history they were regarded as different islands. Even though a road now links them they retain their separate identities. Natives of the two islands speak different dialects of Gaelic. The terrain of Harris, in the south, is grander and more mountainous, while Lewis's moors, scarred by the cutting of peat for fuel, can at times feel as barren as a lunar landscape. Between the communities of Harris and Lewis there are all the rivalries and mutual suspicions that one expects from two close societies determined to emphasise how separate they are.

Two of the twentieth century's leading Gaelic writers, Iain Crichton Smith and Derick Thomson, grew up on Lewis. They were bilingual and wrote in both Gaelic and English. When asked to reflect on the formative influences on their writing for Maurice Lindsay's 1979 book *As I Remember,* both cited their island childhood as crucial. Smith, who died in 1998, was a diverse writer, publishing poetry as well as essays about Gaelic culture, and his fiction ranges from European-style existentialism to pithy interior monologues. In *As I Remember* he wrote: 'I didn't feel myself as belonging to Scotland. I felt myself as belonging to Lewis.' Until he left for university, he explained, 'I had never been out of the island in my whole life, I had never even seen a train.' Smith's family home was in a small township and as a child his first sight of the town of Stornoway, Lewis's port and commercial centre, was like travelling to a different country – 'could Babylon have been a more lustrous city?'

Derick Thomson also grew up in a rural district before becoming professor of Celtic at the University of Glasgow, as well as a poet and Gaelic-language publisher. He captures the island's sometimes extreme weather as well as the sensation that Lewis is clinging on to Europe from its precarious Atlantic edge:

Lewis is a windy place. It was not difficult to feel that the whole island was in motion, being birled about in the general movement of the planet, and with a definite danger of being blown off, into the sea, into space. In winter gales it had a loud, eerie howl, which one grew to love. My mother used to put a coat over her head and a jacket over mine, and we would go out and stand at the end of the house for a while, in the dark, listening to the wind and enjoying it.

Reminiscences by definition often become nostalgic, and in these accounts Smith and Thomson are more generous to Lewis than they sometimes are in their poetry, which probes the darker sides of island life – rural poverty, stifling religion, ageing populations, petty village squabbles. Another Lewis writer, Kevin MacNeil, delves into the same territory in his novel *The Stornoway Way*, published in 2005. The narrative is supposedly written by 'R Stornoway', a hard-drinking Lewisian keen to undermine every sentimental notion poets and visitors have about the island:

> Anxiety? It isn't just the salt air that makes us thirsty. I've seen how men respond to stress [. . .] The Western Islander's response to our diminishing way of life is that of the oppressed the world over, from Native American to Australasian aborigine: a powerful urge to drink oneself underground.
>
> The sleepy tranquil hills and when O when will ye come back again glens of the Hebrides. Wish you were here? Fuckit, none of this is postcard pretty. Stornoway's the kind of place where the birds are woken by the sound of drunks singing.

Louis MacNeice, the cosmopolitan poet who first made his mark on the 1930s literary scene, wrestled with the romantic preconceptions and the more complex reality of the Hebrides in *I Crossed the Minch*. He made two visits to the Hebrides in the spring and summer of 1937, and his book is a masterpiece of disillusionment. Commissioned to write a book that gets under the skin of the islanders, he finds that his inability to speak Gaelic

16 On a sunny day the dramatic coastline of Lewis can resemble the Mediterranean

makes this impossible, as the islanders are less comfortable or forthcoming in their second language:

> Owing to my ignorance of their language I was unable to become intimate with the lives of the people. This book consequently is a tripper's book written by someone who was disappointed and tantalised by the islands and seduced by them only to be reminded that on that soil he will always be an outsider. I doubt if I shall visit the Western Islands again.

From this introduction onwards, *I Crossed the Minch* is a distinctly odd kind of travel book. MacNeice is lukewarm about the standing stones at Calanais, one of Lewis's most striking attractions for visitors. This monument was erected between 4,500 and 5,000 years ago and, curiously, has the formation of a cross rather than a circle. For MacNeice they are 'all right of their kind'. He admits that he is drawn to bleakness rather than dramatic scenery, and his description of Ness, the northern tip of Lewis, is vivid if not exactly the stuff of tour operators: 'It has no hills, which is a good thing, for a single jutting hill would spoil the magnificent stretch of bogs that go on and on, the colour of grizzly bears or burnt toast.'

More recently the townships in the northern district of Ness, as well as the vast and glorious beach at Uig on the west coast, feature prominently in the Hebridean crime books of Peter May, and it's easy to see how the islands' small communities lend themselves to a British version of Scandinavian crime sagas. Maybe one day bookshop shelves will be heaving with 'Hebri noir'.

MacNeice also travelled to Harris, Scalpay, North Uist, Barra and Vatersay, as well as the Inner Hebrides of Coll and Tiree. On each island he chronicles details of damp hotel beds, poor food, arrogant fellow travellers and long walks in variable weathers, all with a tone that lurches towards boredom. On Barra, one of the southernmost of the islands, he has a memorable encounter with the writer Compton Mackenzie, an inveterate island-hopper and eccentric who had settled there. MacNeice paid Mackenzie the dubious compliment of calling him 'one of the most autobiographic conversationalists whom I have ever met'. He records Mackenzie intoning that the landscape from his window was 'the nearest thing to Greece this end of Europe'.

Mackenzie was born in London but spent large periods of his life island-hopping: going to Capri then to the Channel Islands. After a stint as owner of the Shiants (see below), he settled on Barra from 1933 to 1944. At the time, Barra's population was about 2,000 (it's now half that), consisting almost entirely of Gaelic speakers and, unusually for the Hebrides, Roman Catholics. Mackenzie, who had converted to Catholicism in 1914, was enthralled with Barra and the surrounding islands. He also embraced Scottish nationalism, co-founding the National Party of Scotland. On Barra he built a house called Suidheachan – Gaelic for resting or sitting down – and many writers, politicians, scholars and musicians visited him here. It's not far from Traigh Mhor, another of the Hebrides' majestic beaches, a paradise for shellfish foragers sometimes called the Cockle Strand.

It's also the location of the only airport in the world where scheduled flights land on a beach; at high tide the runways are under water. Mackenzie is buried at Barra's Eoligarry Cemetery which, on a sunny day at least, is about the most peaceful final resting place imaginable.

Mackenzie dedicated his time on Barra to a six-volume Proustian epic, *The Four Winds of Love*. This ambitious work is largely neglected today, but two of Mackenzie's comic novels are still perennially popular: *The Monarch of the Glen*, a Wodehousian farce set on a Highland estate, and *Whisky Galore*, his paean to Barra. It was first published in 1947, not long after he had relocated to Berkshire, and was turned into a popular film by Ealing Studios. *Whisky Galore* is based on a true story. On 4 February 1941 a cargo ship called the SS *Politician* ran aground on a rock near Barra. As the islanders rushed to rescue the crew of the stricken ship, they learned what was in its hold: 264,000 bottles of whisky. Men from the nearby islands, along with seemingly anyone with a boat in the north-west of Scotland, set to work unloading the whisky and secreting it away into every conceivable hiding place. Their caution was justified, as 36 islanders were arrested on suspicion of theft, and 19 men were eventually sent to Inverness Prison for up to two months – a long time to be separated from their bounty.

Mackenzie's novel is set on the islands of Great and Little Todday, thinly veiled portraits of Barra and a small neighbouring island (most people say Little Todday is Eriskay, though Vatersay has also been suggested). The islanders are demoralised – most of Scotland's whisky is being exported to pay for the war, meaning that the Toddays are unwillingly dry islands. Fathers fret that they won't be able to provide drink for their children's weddings. The doctor and the priest are unable to provide their usual level of pastoral care as they can't offer their charges a dram. A young teacher fears to cross his domineering mother, and lacks the resources to acquire Dutch courage. The cargo ship, Christened SS *Cabinet Minister* in the novel, serves as Mackenzie's *deus ex machina*: its abandoned crates of booze present a solution to all the islanders' woes.

Outliers: The Shiants and St Kilda

The Shiant Islands lie about four miles east of Lewis, in the stretch of water between the Outer Hebrides and the mainland called the Minch. They consist of two small islands, dominated by sea cliffs, and several rocks. In 1925 Compton Mackenzie bought the Shiants at auction for £500, having never visited them. He restored an old shepherd's cottage and would occasionally stay there, but in 1937, short of money, he sold the Shiants to a colonel whom he persuaded could use this tiny archipelago (which he once described as 'three specks of black pepper' on the map of Scotland) as a stud for breeding racehorses. Within a year the islands had been sold on to publisher Nigel Nicolson, son of Vita Sackville-West and father of Adam Nicolson, to whom he gifted the Shiants on his twenty-first birthday.

In his book *Sea Room*, from 2001, Adam Nicolson writes about the history, ecology and politics of the Shiants. In particular he gets to know the bird life while he spends time on the islands. About a quarter of a million puffins – roughly 2 per cent of the world's population – breed on the islands, as well as thousands of kittiwakes, fulmars, shags and other seabirds. Nicolson's imaginative writing brings these birds to life on the page: shags are 'scandal and poetry, chaos and individual rage, archaic, ancient beyond any sense of ancientness that other birds might convey'. Compared to them, puffins are 'prep-school boys', innocent and easy to catch. He's also alive to the long human history of the Shiants and the politics of owning them; he doesn't overlook the fact that his ownership creates resentment among the crofters of Lewis, to whom a benevolent laird can seem anathema. Aside from visits by the Nicolsons or a tenant shepherd they are now uninhabited, but these unpromising-looking islands once supported a stable population and were surprisingly fertile:

> For most of their history, the Shiants were not, like some piece
> of Wagnerian stage scenery, lumps of rock in a hostile sea, beside

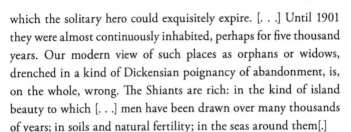

which the solitary hero could exquisitely expire. [. . .] Until 1901 they were almost continuously inhabited, perhaps for five thousand years. Our modern view of such places as orphans or widows, drenched in a kind of Dickensian poignancy of abandonment, is, on the whole, wrong. The Shiants are rich: in the kind of island beauty to which [. . .] men have been drawn over many thousands of years; in soils and natural fertility; in the seas around them[.]

Even more remote than the Shiants is the archipelago of St Kilda. About 50 miles west of Harris the towering sea cliffs of Hirta, at 426 metres the highest in Britain, rise from the Atlantic like a citadel of ancient gods. The only island in St Kilda that supported people, Hirta was continuously inhabited for at least 2,000 years until 1930 when, with a dwindling population that was no longer viable, the 36 remaining residents requested that they be resettled on the mainland. Life on Hirta was never easy and the islanders' diet was largely dependent on seabirds: in 1697 Martin Martin estimated that 180 St Kildans ate 22,600 birds in a year. Puffins were used to flavour porridge; gannets were eaten and their tough necks then fashioned into shoes.

In the nineteenth century Britons became fascinated with their outermost isle, with its fiercely independent islanders and a lifestyle that hadn't changed much in hundreds of years. The first tourist ship called here in 1834, and the impact of exposure to outsiders who brought trade and disease undermined the St Kildans' way of life. Aside from a small military base and a few conservationists (the island has several indigenous sub-species of fauna, and its buildings, like its creatures, are protected), the village on Hirta is inhabited only by ghosts and, fleetingly, by the many modern visitors keen to experience this unique place.

Unsurprisingly, many writers have been drawn to the story of St Kilda's tragic decline. As well as a healthy library of books speculating on the historical causes of the evacuation, St Kilda is a tantalising subject for poets. Edwin Morgan's 'Lady Grange on

St Kilda', published in 1984, was inspired by the true story of an eighteenth-century woman exiled to Hirta by her husband so that she couldn't disclose his Jacobite sympathies. The contemporary poet Robin Robertson has written movingly about the human ecology of the islands and the 1930 evacuation in 'Leaving St Kilda', published in 2010. In a poem from 1980 called 'St Kilda's Parliament: 1879–1979', Douglas Dunn imagines a photographer recollecting the island a century after he visited it to photograph the St Kildans. Every morning the men of the island would gather to decide upon the work to be done that day – the 'parliament' of Dunn's poem. His elegy for St Kilda contrasts this remote peasant community with the technologically advanced, war-mongering civilisations of twentieth-century Europe. His implication is that St Kilda offered an alternative, more egalitarian, environmentally sustainable model for society, and he would probably agree with Martin Martin's sentiment, recorded at a time when this fragile society hadn't yet begun to diminish, that its people were: 'happier than the generality of mankind, as being almost the only people in the world who feel the sweetness of true liberty'.

❦ 7 ❦

THE NORTH

The Great Glen to Shetland

Loch Ness

One of the most obvious landmarks on the map of Scotland is the Great Glen, a series of lochs and valleys which bisects the country from Fort William to Inverness. It's possible to sail the entire length of the Great Glen, from Loch Linnhe on the west coast to the Moray Firth, the estuary that spills into the North Sea, via the Caledonian Canal. The canal was built in the early nineteenth century by Thomas Telford so that ships could cross Scotland rather than sailing round its perilous northern coast; instead of digging a canal the breadth of Scotland, Telford linked the Great Glen's lochs together. This was no mean feat, as the canal doesn't follow a level route – at one point a sequence of eight canal locks called Neptune's Staircase raises boats 20 metres over a distance of half a kilometre. Robert Southey, poet laureate from 1813 to 1843, visited Neptune's Staircase during its construction and described it not only as 'the greatest piece of such masonry in the world', but also as Britain's 'greatest work of art' because of the skill with which natural watercourses were harnessed for human use.

The Great Glen's fame lies not in Telford's engineering genius, however, but in something altogether more elusive: the Loch Ness Monster. Loch Ness is long and narrow, but is one of the deepest bodies of water in Britain. It never freezes and it holds more water than all the freshwater lakes of England and Wales combined. The earliest surviving account of the Loch Ness Monster is from the sixth century and concerns Saint Columba, founder of the monastery at Iona, who is said to have rebuked the monster in the name of God after it attacked one of his followers. The story was written up a century later by his biographer, Adomnán. Since then, the monster appears to have become more placid, with reported sightings but few documented assaults. Some witnesses have said the monster was a serpent, or the last of the water-dwelling dinosaurs. Others have claimed it was an eel, a giant slug, an endemic species of fish or a mammal. In their social history of interwar Britain, *The Long Weekend* (1940), the writer Robert Graves and his collaborator Alan Hodge point to 1933 as the beginning of the Loch Ness Monster boom:

> Theories multiplied, and so did efforts to trace the monster [. . .] Someone then tried to detect its presence with hydrophones; someone else reported having seen it cross the road with a sheep in its mouth. An old woman disappeared and her body was later discovered on the moors; she was said to have been carried off. Mutilated carcases of sheep were found on the shores of the loch, and the tooth-marks in them were pronounced to be the monster's.

In the 1960s some dedicated monster-seekers founded the Loch Ness Phenomena Investigation Bureau, whose volunteers scanned the surface of the water in hope of a sighting. John McPhee, writing in *The Atlantic* in 1970, studies the watchers while they study the loch; his article was later republished as the title essay in *Pieces of the Frame*. One of the most determined members of the bureau tells McPhee:

> I shall never rest peacefully until I know what it is. Some of the largest creatures in the world are out there, and we can't name them. It may take ten years, but we're going to identify the genus. Most people are not as fanatical as I, but I would like to see this through to the end, if I don't get too broke first.

Nearly 50 years on, studies of varying technological sophistication haven't yet turned up any more information about this legendary creature. Photographs are invariably grainy and generally suggest that the monster is of the genus *tractor tyre*. The Loch Ness Monster Exhibition Centre at Drumnadrochit, on the northern shores, is one of the best places to begin a search, and on days when the water is too rough for a reliable sighting, the stunning ruins of Urquhart Castle, overlooking the loch, are much easier to find.

Inverness and Culloden

Perhaps Samuel Johnson, stopping in Inverness on his way to the Hebrides with James Boswell, was overcome by the same spirit of zoological inquiry as the monster-watchers. According to an anecdote included in the 1936 edition of Boswell's *Tour to the Hebrides*, Johnson bewildered some fellow drinkers at an inn with a demonstration of the habits of an animal which had only recently become known to British science, the kangaroo: 'He stood erect, put out his hands like feelers, and, gathering up the tails of his huge brown coat so as to resemble the pouch of the animal, made two or three vigorous bounds across the room!' Inverness is a thriving city, positioned on the banks of the River Ness not far from the head of the loch. Although it's one of the smallest of Scotland's seven cities, it's by far the largest settlement in the Highlands, and its population is growing. Just to the east of the city is Culloden Battlefield, where the Jacobite rising led by Bonnie Prince Charlie was crushed on 16 April 1746. The battle lasted just an hour, with the Hanoverian troops enjoying a numerical advantage and fighting on ground much better suited to their artillery, infantry and cavalry than it was to their less well-drilled opponents. The Jacobites had been on the retreat since December and, exhausted and hungry, they were ill-prepared to face the Hanoverian army. The battlefield was quickly strewn with dead and wounded Jacobites: at least 1,500 were killed, compared to only 50 Hanoverians.

After the battle, as Magnus Magnusson puts it in his 2000 book *Scotland: The Story of a Nation*, the government troops began 'a systematic process of murder, mutilation and almost inconceivable brutality which has remained an ugly and ineradicable blot on the annals of British arms'. Many survivors as well as bystanders, including women and children, were slaughtered by the ruthless victors. Wounded combatants were stripped naked and left on the moor. The playing of bagpipes, the wearing of tartan and the carrying of arms were prohibited; the Highland clan system was shaken to the core. Culloden is the last battle to have been fought on British soil.

Neglected and used for timber forestry for many years, the battlefield has now been restored into something resembling the landscape that the opposing forces would have seen on the day of the battle: heathery moorland and bog. The site is run by the National Trust for Scotland, whose modern visitor centre offers a comprehensive introduction to the events and historical context of the battle. On the field itself are gravestones commemorating each of the clans who fought, as well as a six-metre memorial cairn erected in 1881. The moor is quiet, and visitors often describe it as haunting and atmospheric.

People tend to invest places like Culloden with a lot of historical baggage, expecting to see indications of Highland heritage on every hummock and to hear the wind whispering the names of dead clansmen. In reality, the landscape is reticent when it comes to its bloody history, and even the monuments look small in this relatively bare and wild setting. How does a contemporary Scottish novelist respond to Culloden, a place which has been so mythologised? At the end of Alan Warner's *The Man Who Walks*, a modern-day drifter called Macushla is crawling across Culloden Moor, having been beaten up. Ahead of him a figure is lying in the grass: 'He could near touch the leg of the man. Oh Christ, it was wearing a kilt! [. . .] He reached, took the foot, tugged. The leg came away and sped up to his face. A long plastic leg, its moulded

calf reflecting the sun. It was a mannequin in a kilt!' Macushla
has crawled into a Hollywood film set, with kilted mannequins
arranged like the bodies of fallen soldiers on the moor. There is
'scattered weaponry and even an entire fake horse corpse'. On the
horizon, instead of the Hanoverian artillery, are the lights and
cameras of the film producers: 'the deep burn of high-fired movie
lights, flanked by battalions of reflectors, were blasting down on
reality, fighting the natural light with overwhelming, colonising
superiority, determined to force a vision on the mundane and
curse the consequences.' Warner's vision of Culloden is Beckett-
like in its absurdity, with the novel's disoriented anti-hero crossing
a landscape where global media culture is repackaging history
with dummies dressed in tartan. Natural light is overpowered by
artificial lamps; fact is clouded by fiction. Warner creates a surreal
landscape and in the process pokes fun at the clichés involved in
commercial uses of history.

The main artery linking the cities of the Central Belt with Inverness is the A9, a busy route that continues north as far as Scrabster,
about 110 miles beyond Inverness on the north coast. Michel Faber,
a Dutch-born, Highland-based writer, makes unforgettable use of
the A9 in his sci-fi horror *Under the Skin*, published in 2000. A
young woman named Isserley cruises the road looking for lone male
hitchhikers, preferably young and muscular: 'she spotted a tall,
rangy backpacker holding a cardboard sign that said THURSO. He
looked fine. After the usual three approaches, she stopped for him,
about a dozen yards ahead of where he stood. In her rear-view mirror
she watched him bound towards the car shrugging his backpack off
his broad shoulders even as he ran.'

Isserley's obsession with hitchhikers isn't what you might expect.
Her car's passenger seat contains a pair of needles, controlled by a
toggle on the steering wheel, which inject a powerful sedative into
her unsuspecting passengers. As the novel progresses, the shocking
truth about her motivations is revealed: she's an alien hunter, trained
to pick up solitary men whose disappearance won't warrant much

investigation. She takes her unconscious prey to a farmhouse in the Highlands, where they are processed as livestock to feed her species. Her own appearance has been altered by surgery in an attempt to make her look not only human, but also sexually alluring to her prey. The look isn't entirely successful: one victim thinks of her as 'Half Baywatch babe, half little old lady'. However, the more contact she has with humans, the more she comes to think and feel like one herself. *Under the Skin* is by turns a graphic satire on meat production, a moving account of someone wrestling with their identity, and a paean to the A9. Jonathan Glazer's 2013 film adaptation, starring Scarlett Johansson, distils the action into an utterly unsettling and profound meditation on what it is to be human.

Glenfinnan

One of the most enticing road signs in the Highlands is situated at the northern end of Fort William, directing drivers to the 'Road to the Isles'. This leads to Mallaig, a fishing port where ferries depart for Skye, South Uist and the Small Isles. It's a scenic drive, but the most rewarding way to get from Fort William to Mallaig is via the West Highland Line: as well as regular services, a steam train called *The Jacobite* travels this route. The most dramatic point on the journey is the high sweeping curve of the Glenfinnan Viaduct. Completed in 1901, with 21 supporting arches and a span of over 300 metres, the viaduct is another example of the technical virtuosity required to establish transport links across the Highlands. The Glenfinnan Viaduct has long been an attraction in its own right, but its popularity soared when it was used as a location in three of the Harry Potter films. Students on their way to Hogwarts School of Witchcraft and Wizardry cross here on the Hogwarts Express. The viaduct's cinematic highlight undoubtedly comes in *Harry Potter and the Chamber of Secrets*, when Harry and Ron Weasley pursue the train in a flying Ford Anglia. Judging by

17 Crossing the Glenfinnan Viaduct by steam train

the number of passengers on *The Jacobite* dressed as witches and wizards, there may well be a magical school hidden in one of the glens near the West Highland Line.

Long before Harry Potter cast his spell over millions of readers, and even before the construction of the railway, Glenfinnan attracted pilgrims. This is because, on 19 August 1745, Bonnie Prince Charlie mustered his supporters and raised his standard at Glenfinnan as a sign that he had launched his bid to regain the British and Irish throne for the Stuart dynasty. His forces surged southwards, taking Edinburgh and crossing into England on 8 November. After marching as far south as Derby, the decision was made to turn back and consolidate control of Scotland rather than attempting to seize London. Their retreat eventually led to Culloden. In 1815 a monument was erected on the banks of Loch Shiel. A column with the figure of a solitary kilted Highlander on top, the monument is surrounded by a stone stockade mounted with plaques in Gaelic, Latin and English paying tribute to the men who 'fought and bled in that arduous and unfortunate enterprise'.

Glenelg and Wester Ross

The Sound of Sleat lies between Mallaig and Skye and flows into the inlets of Loch Nevis and Loch Hourn. Glenelg, the village from which Boswell and Johnson sailed to Skye, lies at the north of the sound: a tiny community-run ferry still crosses to the island from Glenelg. Not far to the south of Glenelg a forest track leads to the horseshoe-shaped Sandaig Bay. Even by the standards of the Highlands this is a quiet corner of the country, somewhere it would be impossible to stumble across by accident: getting here involves driving on miles of potholed road and then following a footpath that includes stepping stones and an intimidating rope bridge. Gavin Maxwell moved to Sandaig after the collapse of his basking shark fishery and set up home in a lighthouse keeper's cottage which had long been deserted. He fell in love with the beauty and seclusion of the place, celebrating it in his classic book *Ring of Bright Water*, published in 1960. In the book he gave Sandaig the name Camusfeàrna, Gaelic for 'The Bay of Alders'.

Ring of Bright Water sold over a million copies, capturing the hearts of its readers, not merely because of Maxwell's vivid descriptions of the landscape and wildlife of the west coast of Scotland, but also because of his beloved companions at Camusfeàrna – two otters named Mijbil and Edal. Both had been captured abroad, in the Middle East and Africa, but Maxwell's custody of them was, arguably, a benevolent attempt to take them out of the wild animal trade. Maxwell's bond with these animals is captivating: he's affectionate and intimate, but he never loses sight of their wildness. In one enthralling scene, Mijbil catches a flounder in the bay and presents it to Maxwell:

I was in no hurry to take the gesture at its face value, for, as I have said, one of the most aggressive actions one can perform to a wild animal is to deprive it of its prey, but after perhaps half a minute of doubt, while Mij redoubled his invitation, I reached down slowly and cautiously for the fish, knowing that Mij would give me vocal warning if I had misinterpreted him. He watched me with the plainest approval while I picked it up and began a mime of eating it; then he plunged off the rock into the sea and sped away a fathom down in the clear water.

Maxwell doesn't gloss over darker moments of his life at Camusfeàrna, and Mijbil's death at the hands of a road mender wielding a pick is a heartbreaking scene. It was after Mijbil's death that Maxwell acquired Edal, and the latter stages of the book tell of his growing relationship with Edal's different personality. Tragedy was never far away from Maxwell's life, however, and in 1968 the cottage at Sandaig was destroyed by fire. Edal was killed in the blaze. A year later Maxwell died of cancer. At Sandaig there now stand two memorials: one to Edal and one to Maxwell, a large boulder positioned where his writing desk used to sit. The Bright Water Visitor Centre, in the Skye village of Kyleakin, pays tribute to the author and highlights the conservation work that he inspired.

On the mainland a few minutes' drive north from the Skye Bridge is Plockton, one of the prettiest of Scotland's villages, in a sheltered location on the banks of Loch Carron. Plockton is a popular stopping point for holidaymakers, but has a distinctive appeal because its seafront was a location for the cult 1973 film *The Wicker Man*. The region of Wester Ross stretches north from Loch Carron to above Ullapool, an area of imposing mountains and small coastal settlements. The village of Applecross perches on the coast opposite Raasay and is reached by the Bealach na Bà, a dizzying pass through cloud-covered hills, with steep gradients and hairpin bends. Another village, Torridon, sits in the shadow of the vast face of Liathach, a five-mile ridge of crags and jagged pinnacles.

Ullapool is located on the shore of Loch Broom, a cosmopolitan town with a thriving arts scene, including a book festival and a contemporary music festival. Much of Wester Ross's cultural life centres on the Ceilidh Place, Ullapool's restaurant, bar, inn, music venue, bookshop and local affiliate of the Scottish Poetry Library. Ullapool fish and chips are among the best in the country, and the village is the perfect base for exploring Wester Ross as well as being the departure point for the Lewis ferry. Fans of George R. R. Martin's *Game of Thrones* fantasy series have speculated that its continent of Westeros is named after Wester Ross, and the landscape around Ullapool wouldn't look out of place in Martin's books. Like Westeros, the region has had its fair share of warring clans and brutal murders, but Martin's fans may be disappointed by the lack of sword fighting, or indeed crime of any sort, in this part of Scotland today.

The Black Isle

While the west coast of north Scotland is a network of sea lochs, cliffs, islands and rivers, the coastline on the east is smoother, with only a handful of firths, or estuaries, carved into the land. Just above Inverness the A9 crosses the Beauly Firth at the Kessock Bridge. The waters around this part of the coast are among the best places in Europe to watch dolphins, which are regularly seen from the Whale and Dolphin Conservation Centre at the north end of the bridge. The Kessock Bridge leads to the Black Isle – not, in fact, an island at all, but a peninsula whose gentle slopes are one of the few fertile districts in the Highlands. The Black Isle's shallow bays, pockets of deciduous woodland and chequerboard of fields are a balm to travellers overwhelmed by the rocky peaks and tumbling cliffs of the west. Further relief comes with the local tipple: the Black Isle Brewery makes beer from its own organic barley and is one of Scotland's best-loved small brewers.

Cromarty, the picturesque little town at the eastern corner of the Black Isle, is well preserved without being overly quaint, and its strand is prime dolphin-watching territory. Hugh Miller, one of the nineteenth century's leading palaeontologists, was born in Cromarty in 1802. Miller was a hirsute, plaid-wearing, pistol-carrying stonemason with a broad Highland brogue and a questioning intellect, a self-taught geologist who also had a penchant for poetry. In 1829 he published *Poems Written in the Leisure Hours of a Journeyman Mason*, a collection that, judging by the title, was never destined to become a bestseller. But in 1841 another work, *The Old Red Sandstone*, established him as one of the century's leading writers on natural history. In this book Miller takes his readers on a voyage of discovery, his sense of wonder evident as he describes chiselling away at cliffs and studying the fossils he finds. He may have been a frustrated poet, but his literary ability shines through:

> In the Chimaera Borealis, a cartilaginous fish of the Northern Ocean, the spine seems placed in front of the weaker rays just, if I may be allowed the comparison, as in a line of mountaineers engaged in crossing a swollen torrent, the strongest man in the party is placed on the upper side of the line, to break off the force of the current from the rest.

Miller had a collection of over 6,000 fossils – stonemasonry was an ideal trade for acquiring specimens – and these now form the basis of the National Museum of Scotland's collection. Miller's work as a stonemason took its toll on his health and in the 1850s his physical and mental condition declined dramatically. Depressed and fearing the onslaught of insanity, he shot himself on Christmas Eve 1856. His funeral in Edinburgh attracted a huge crowd, and a monument was erected in his hometown – a raised statue of him looking out towards the North Sea, where there's now an oilfield named after him.

Miller gazed into the deep past, discovering prehistoric creatures whose remains were preserved in rock. But the Black Isle is also famous for a figure renowned for his ability to look into the future. This is Kenneth Mackenzie, the Brahan Seer, a man endowed with second sight – the prophetic ability once much prized in Gaelic-speaking communities. Mackenzie's ability to predict events that had not yet come to pass won him acclaim across the Highlands in the seventeenth century. Walking on Culloden Moor a century before the battle that decimated the clans, he pronounced that the best blood of the Highlands would be shed there. He saw a vision of boats sailing round the back of Tomnahurich Hill on the outskirts of Inverness – land where the Caledonian Canal would later be dug. He said that the clans of the north would flee their territories because of an army of sheep, a prophecy later understood to refer to the Highland Clearances. On a day-to-day level he also predicted deaths and births, including that of a child with four thumbs.

The Seer worked as a labourer on the Brahan Estate, seat of the Mackenzie earls of Seaforth. His downfall came when the wife of the third earl ordered him to tell her whether her husband, who had travelled to Paris, was safe and well. He replied that the Earl was 'on his knees before a fair lady, his arm round her waist' – not an illogical theory, but not a prudent revelation either. The Countess was humiliated and had the Seer put to death at Chanonry Point, a low promontory on the Moray Firth near the village of Fortrose. Close to the lighthouse at the point, in a landscape almost entirely composed of sea and open Highland skies, a boulder marks the place where the Brahan Seer is said to have died. He was pitched head-first into a barrel of boiling tar with knives driven into its sides. The truth behind the Brahan Seer's life remains elusive – proof that he even existed, let alone made his prophecies, is unreliable. There are still plenty of believers, however, and the Brahan Seer's place in the folk history of the Highlands is assured.

The Far North: Assynt to Cape Wrath

No one has written as consistently and affectionately about the far north-west of Scotland as Norman MacCaig. The poet, who died in 1996, spent most of his working life as a teacher in Edinburgh, but every summer he holidayed in Assynt, a coastal parish about halfway between Ullapool and Cape Wrath. A journey through Assynt can take your breath away; a more prolonged stay invites the sort of intimate observation and celebration that MacCaig made the hallmark of his deft lyric poetry. The mountains of the district's hinterland stand isolated, carved by glaciers into strange shapes that are instantly recognisable. The Assynt coast is serrated with sea lochs and bays, and its rivers and moors teem with wildlife. Assynt is sparsely populated, like all of the northern region of Sutherland: by one calculation, there is one person for every 40 hectares of the parish.

Assynt cast its spell on MacCaig, who returned again and again to the settlements of Achmelvich and Inverkirkaig, near the principal village of Lochinver. A flick through his extensive body of work is the best introduction to the place a traveller could wish for. Poems such as 'Midnight, Lochinver', 'On the North Side of Suilven', 'Above Inverkirkaig' and 'A Man in Assynt' bring the landscape, people and ecology to life with both charm and emotional depth. 'A Man in Assynt', one of MacCaig's most ambitious poems, is a roll-call of mountains and lochs, villages and resident wild species. The poet turns his attention to the adders, wildcats, falcons and ravens that dwell in the 'frieze of mountains' that includes Canisp, Cul Beag, Suilven and Stac Polly. The poem isn't merely a picturesque account of the landscape, however; MacCaig's anger is directed at absentee landowners whose estates have no regard for the needs of the crofters and fishermen who live here. At the heart of the poem is the question as to who owns a landscape: wealthy landlords, the tenants who work on it, visitors who fall in love with it, the wild creatures who hunt and graze on it or, ultimately, no one and nothing, since its stones predate all of these claims. The poem was published in 1969; since then sections of Assynt have been bought by a community trust, part of an ongoing reform of land ownership in the Highlands and Islands.

MacCaig's poetry is seldom as explicitly political as it is in 'A Man in Assynt'. Often his meditations turn inwards, and this is nowhere more apparent than in a late poem, 'On the Pier at Kinlochbervie', published in his 1988 collection *Voice-Over*. Kinlochbervie is the last village of note on the west coast – beyond it there are only a few clustered farms before the end of the road. Standing on the pier at the small harbour, the speaker of the poem, his mind on his own mortality, longs for answers to the deepest metaphysical questions. Instead of the loneliness and isolation he feels at this remote location, he desires an 'extreme of nearness', a sense of intimacy and shared belonging with other people and with the natural world.

Belonging is also the theme at the heart of Andrew Greig's 2010 memoir *At the Loch of the Green Corrie*, an account of his search for a small body of water in Assynt where Norman MacCaig, a keen angler, used to fish. According to Greig, not long before his friend MacCaig

18 *A loch-side in the north-west – the landscape of Norman MacCaig's poetry*

died he told him, 'I should like you to go fishing for me at the Loch of the Green Corrie,' but declined to tell him where exactly this loch was to be found. Greig's book is a dreamy mix of reflections upon the Highland landscape, encounters with old friends of MacCaig, and gentle literary criticism. Greig is also a poet, and his fascination with language adds colour to his memoir: the lochans (pools) of Assynt are 'sprinkled over the moor like bits of broken windshield'; the colours of these waters range from 'darkest slate to acid lime green'. Despite his lyricism, he points out a truth that can disappoint those travellers who arrive seduced by their map's tantalising Gaelic names, but are unprepared for the tough reality of small, isolated communities: in many Highland villages, 'the name is far lovelier than the place.'

When Greig finally locates the Loch of the Green Corrie, hidden away from the road behind the curved cliffs of Glas Bheinn, he finds that it's 'one of the most frustrating' places to fish in the Highlands. His attempts to hook a trout here are enjoyable but unsuccessful, and at last he resolves to find himself a loch of his own, a symbolic departure from living under the influence of the older poet. On the shore of Loch Dubh Leallan Mhurchaidh ('the black loch of Murphy's hillock'), Greig reaches for a fly and prepares to cast a line. Like MacCaig's poetry, his prose hovers between the literal and the metaphysical world:

> I tied it on the bob dropper, the one nearest to me, and wearily, cheerfully stood up. I saw my reflection making ready to cast [. . .] Outer and inner world, the world doubled and made ambivalent, for it is easy to mistake one for the other though both are real. The two worlds hinge at the shoreline where MacCaig's poetry stands. Where any one of us stands.
>
> Lures wetted, I began fishing my last loch of the day.

Sure enough, his line jerks and he reels in a trout. Afterwards he gratefully lets it slip back into the water and heads home having fulfilled his promise to MacCaig.

Beyond Kinlochbervie, accessible only by a footpath leading over four miles of moorland, is Sandwood Bay. A mile-long beach of pinkish sand, bookended by cliffs and a towering sea stack, Sandwood is often described as the most special beach in Britain, one of the few parts of a crowded island where solitude is almost guaranteed. Legends abound here: a rocky outcrop halfway along the beach is rumoured to be the best place in the country to see a mermaid; the ghost of a black-bearded sailor, killed in one of the many shipwrecks on the north-west coast, is said to frequent the towering dunes. Even on a busy day only a few walkers share this expanse; its inaccessibility by car is such that in 2009, when a microlite plane crashed on the beach, the aircraft had to be dismantled and carried off in pieces.

Sandwood Bay is the setting for one of the most memorable scenes in James Robertson's epic 2010 novel *And the Land Lay Still*. The book is a state-of-the-nation account of twentieth-century Scotland: war and the welfare state, Thatcherism and devolution, deindustrialisation, urban regeneration and rural depopulation are all touched upon in this sprawling story of photographers, politicians, drop-outs, Scottish nationalists, spies, landowners and labourers. The lives of this disparate cast are loosely connected through the wanderings of an elusive drifter, a man broken by his confinement in a Japanese prisoner-of-war camp. One day this man, Jack Gordon, disappears from his suburban life, walking out on his wife and daughter. For the rest of his life he roams all over Scotland, collecting pebbles he finds along the way. Towards the end of the book, and at the end of his life, Jack reaches Sandwood Bay and knows that this is his final resting place:

> You followed a track and the track led through great dunes to a bay. The wind had the last warmth of the south in it and drove spume and veils of sand across the beach. The great ocean roared and crashed beside you. Gull feathers and the empty armour of crabs scurried before your steps. [. . .] You stopped, looked back.

Nobody. You were alone in the vast expanse of land meeting water. You trudged on, your steps heavy now as you counted them down, the last of all the millions you had taken.

Jack stops just above the high tide mark, lies down and, exhausted and delirious, swallows the pebbles he has carried here from every part of Scotland. It's a long time before his skeleton is found, with the pebbles piled under his ribs.

Beyond Sandwood Bay, at the north-western limit of the mainland, is Cape Wrath. It's a wild place with lofty, wave-battered cliffs, dominated by seabirds. The name doesn't refer to the ferocity of the sea, but derives from the Norse word for 'turning point', referring to the cape which Viking navigators would steer round as they headed for the Hebrides. For generations of sailors, however, the cape was indeed considered wrathful, a turbulent jumble of rocks where many ships were lost. In 1814 Robert Stevenson, engineer grandfather of Robert Louis Stevenson, surveyed the cape with a view to constructing a lighthouse to guide fearful mariners; the light first shone on Christmas Day 1828. Robert Stevenson was accompanied by Sir Walter Scott, whose journal entry captures the drama and danger of the place:

> It is a high promontory, with steep sides that go sheer down to the breakers, which lash its feet [. . .] There the foam of the sea plays at long bowls with a huge collection of large stones, some of them a ton in weight, but which these fearful billows chuck up and down as a child tosses a ball.

The Far North: Strathnaver and Caithness

Sutherland covers most of the north coast of Britain and was a territory belonging to the Norse earls of Orkney from around the ninth to the twelfth century. The region's name is Norse for 'southern land'. Today most of the population of Sutherland lives in coastal villages and the hinterland is eerily quiet. Nowhere is this more evident than in Strathnaver, a broad, fertile valley running from Altnaharra to Torrisdale Bay, about a third of the way east from Cape Wrath to John O'Groats. Strathnaver has a long history of human habitation, with evidence of Neolithic tombs dating from 6,000 years ago, as well as later remains of Bronze and Iron Age constructions. A broad and fertile valley, it's little surprise that ancient communities were drawn here. It's now surely one of the saddest places in the country, sparsely populated and still haunted by the Highland Clearances.

In the early nineteenth century the valley belonged to the Countess of Sutherland and her husband the Marquis of Stafford, and they were determined to 'modernise' and make their estate more economically lucrative. Their factor was Patrick Sellar, a zealous proponent of 'progress', responsible for evicting tenants and replacing them with sheep. The people of Strathnaver were relocated to mean and inhospitable areas on the coast; allegations were made that Sellar had set fire to homes while people were inside, and that he had destroyed their crops. He became a hate figure for victims of the Clearances and their descendants, including the heirs of those forced to emigrate; rumours persist of Canadian sightseers stopping to relieve themselves on Sellar's grave at Elgin Cathedral. Sellar appears in Iain Crichton Smith's *Consider the Lilies*, published in 1968. The novel tells the story of an old woman, a widow with a son in Canada, who is evicted by Sellar. The opening, which would appear whimsical if it wasn't for its context, is chilling:

> Her name was Mrs Scott and she was an old woman of about seventy. She was sitting on an old chair in front of her cottage when she saw the rider. The rider was Patrick Sellar, factor to the Duke of Sutherland, and he wasn't riding his horse very well, though he felt that in his position he ought to have a horse. He was an ex-lawyer, and horses aren't used to that kind of law. Also, it was

a white horse which was one of the reasons why the old woman paid such particular attention to it.

Sellar tells Mrs Scott she must leave her home and move to the coast. She doesn't understand: why would the Duke want her simple stone cottage? When Sellar leaves, she turns to the Church for an explanation and assistance, but the minister is only concerned with currying favour with the Duke and does what he can to make her eviction inevitable. Perplexed and lonely, menaced by the presence of Sellar in the valley, she has to come to terms with the fact that the institutions she trusted – her aristocratic landlord, her Church – no longer treat her as they should.

In one scene Mrs Scott sees an emigrant ship bound for Canada and recalls the rumours she's heard about long voyages in overcrowded boats, of 'emigrants being promised good work and having to fell trees and cultivate stony land at low rates of pay', of 'exiles dying of exposure'. While many Highlanders were moved from their farming communities to the Scottish coast, others emigrated. In *No Great Mischief*, published in Britain in 2000, Canadian novelist Alistair MacLeod tells the story of the Clearances from the opposite end of the voyage, following the Gaelic-speaking descendants of Calum MacDonald, who settled in Nova Scotia in 1779. Fiercely aware of their history, these emigrants struggle to make this new land their home, retaining the language and culture of the Highlands into the twentieth century.

In fiction, eastern Sutherland is a lonely, formidable, yet occasionally wondrous region of glens and hunting lodges. In Elspeth Barker's 1991 novella *O Caledonia*, the fictional manor of Auchnasaugh is situated in this 'gaunt place' where the wind moans through pine woods and people 'kept themselves to themselves in those hills and in the village'. A similar sense of the vast and empty Sutherland landscape exists in Kirsty Gunn's magisterial *The Big Music*, published in 2012. In the novel a glen inland from the village of Brora is the ancestral home of a dynasty of bagpipers schooled in *ceòl mór* ('big music'), the grandest form of Gaelic music. The novel is written in fragments supposedly collected as an archive, and the reader has to piece these fragments together to form a narrative. Gunn's writing is evocative, and the land itself is a character in the work. Characters appear tiny against the hills and the sky, and Gunn imagines nature speaking to its insignificant human inhabitants: 'The hills only come back the same: *I don't mind*, and all the flat moorland and the sky. *I don't mind* they say, and the water says it too, those black falls that are rimmed with peat, and the mountains in the distance to the west say it.'

Caithness, another former fiefdom of the Norse earls of Orkney, lies at the north-eastern corner of the Highlands. The landscape is less mountainous than much of the Highlands, with glistening rivers weaving their way across the open moors. Fishing villages line the coast, evidence of a once-strong herring industry that has receded across the east of Scotland. Neil Gunn, one of the country's leading novelists in the early twentieth century, was born in the Caithness village of Dunbeath in 1891. His fiction has a Zen-like spirituality and an intimate, lyrical sensitivity to the natural world. In a few sentences he encapsulates the environment and history of his childhood home. In his 1941 essay 'My Bit of Britain' he writes:

> These small straths, like the Strath of Dunbeath, have this intimate beauty. In boyhood we get to know every square yard of it. We encompass it physically and our memories hold it. Birches, hazel trees for nutting, pools with trout and an occasionally visible salmon, river-flats with the wind on the bracken and disappearing rabbit scuts, a wealth of wild flower and small bird life, the soaring hawk, the unexpected roe, the ancient graveyard, thoughts of the folk who once lived far inland in straths and hollows, the past and the present held in a moment of day-dream.

The novel which established Gunn's reputation as a leading Scottish modernist was *Highland River*, first published in 1937. It tells the story of a young boy, Kenn, who explores the Caithness landscape, following a river inland until he reaches its source; the river is a physical location but also a symbol of consciousness and memory. A photographic essay following Kenn's journey up Dunbeath Water can be seen at Dunbeath Heritage Centre, which also contains a wealth of information about the author. This small museum is housed in the former village school, where Gunn himself was educated, and where Kenn in *Highland River* lets his mind wander as his teacher lectures on concerns that are culturally remote to the village children: the wives of Henry VIII, the industries of the English cities. A formative moment comes for Kenn when he catches a huge salmon in a river pool, wrestling with it until, soaked through, he heaves it from the water. His mother, looking up from housework, sees her son heaving it home, 'face down, hands knotted behind his head, dripping wet and staggering. The salmon's nose was under his right ear, its tail was sweeping the ground behind.' Kenn is understandably delighted with his achievement. Gunn is commemorated by a statue at Dunbeath harbour of a boy carrying a salmon larger than himself.

Orkney

The islands to the north of Scotland have a different character to the mainland. For five centuries they weren't part of Scotland at all, but were the dominions of Norse kings. In 1469 King James III of Scotland married the ten-year-old Princess Margrethe of the dual kingdom of Norway and Denmark. Her father, King Kristian, mortgaged Orkney and Shetland to the Scottish Crown as part of her dowry until he could pay a lump sum of 60,000 florins. He was never able to raise the cash, and so Scotland acquired two extensive archipelagos which to this day have a distinctly Norse heritage. Orkney and Shetland aren't easily confused, however. Orkney (with around 70 islands) is mostly flat and fertile; Shetland (with over

100) is more rugged, with poorer soil. Not for nothing is there a saying that an Orcadian is a farmer with a boat, while a Shetlander is a fisherman with a croft. The southern reaches of Orkney are divided from Scotland by the narrow but exceedingly tempestuous Pentland Firth; Shetland is a further 50 miles north, and closer to Iceland than it is to London.

Reading the *Orkneyinga Saga*, written around the year 1200 by an unnamed Icelandic author, leaves one with little doubt of the Norse heritage of the Northern Isles. This medieval chronicle centres on Orkney, conquered by Vikings in the ninth century and subsequently controlled by the earls of Orkney. It tells of power, treachery, miracles, mythical ancestors, warfare and alliances between the earldom and the Church. Many of the events in the *Saga* took place in locations that can be easily visited today and they provide fascinating insights into the Orkney of the past.

The large central island of Orkney is called Mainland, where the principal towns of Kirkwall and Stromness are situated. By the twelfth century Kirkwall (the name means 'Church Bay') was already a busy market town. In 1137 work began on Kirkwall's St Magnus Cathedral, which was dedicated to a pious Earl of Orkney canonised posthumously in 1135. According to the *Saga*, the motives behind the construction were as much to do with political machinations as piety. The unpopular Earl Rognvald was advised to raise a great cathedral and dedicate it to the beloved Magnus, his uncle, in order to win the favour of the Orcadians. His father Kol tells him: '[L]ook for support where men will say the true owner of the realm granted it you, and that's the holy Earl Magnus [. . .] you'll build a stone minster at Kirkwall more magnificent than any in Orkney [. . .] and provide it with all the funds it will need to flourish.' Whether or not the story of Kol's plan is true, the cathedral is indeed magnificent. The yellow and red sandstone building still dominates the Kirkwall skyline and its vast interior contains many reminders of Orkney's Viking past.

Further west on Mainland is Maeshowe, one of the most significant Neolithic buildings still standing in Europe. It was constructed about 5,000 years ago, with an entrance passage which is perfectly aligned with the sun at the winter solstice. From the outside it's just a grassy mound, but this chambered cairn was used for burial and perhaps other ceremonial purposes. It's the Neolithic equivalent of St Magnus Cathedral, a building that would have required considerable labour, resources and architectural expertise. Standing inside, imagining Stone Age people coming here with their dead, is a disquieting experience. Some Vikings found it unsettling too. In the twelfth century Norsemen broke in here and carved graffiti and pictures on its walls: their vandalism is now part of its history, and the messages they inscribed make up one of the biggest collections of runes in the world. According to the *Orkneyinga Saga*, two of those who spent the night here went insane.

From Maeshowe it's only a short distance to two other breathtaking prehistoric monuments, the Ring of Brodgar and the Stones of Stenness. These henge monuments are also incredibly ancient:

19 Part of the Ring of Brodgar, Orkney

Stenness is thought to have been built about 5,400 years ago, making it slightly older than Stonehenge. Brodgar is a circle of 60 standing stones laid out on moorland. It's common to find yourself the only visitor at Brodgar, alone in the midst of its towering pinnacles, and the grandeur of the ring is awe-inspiring. The stonemason and palaeontologist Hugh Miller, visiting in 1846, described the stones as 'an assemblage of ancient druids, mysteriously stern and invincibly silent and shaggy'.

About halfway up the west coast of Mainland is another Neolithic site, the village of Skara Brae. In 1850 a storm uncovered a group of houses which date from about 5,000 years ago. A walkway now leads from house to house, allowing visitors to look down into rooms formerly inhabited by the ancient society living around the time that Maeshowe, Brodgar and Stenness were built; the Skara Brae families may even have helped in these constructions. There are beds, tables, chairs and even 'dressers' made of stone. In 'Skara Brae' the contemporary poet Michael Longley describes the 'exploded view' of homes and hearths of lives now otherwise forgotten.

The leading modern chronicler of Orkney is George Mackay Brown, who died in 1996. A poet, novelist and regular columnist for the *Orcadian* newspaper, Brown spent nearly all of his life in Stromness, the harbour town on the south-west of Mainland. His work revolves around Orkney's history and culture. In the verse prologue to his first collection of poems, *The Storm* from 1954, he declared that he would sing of his native islands. Stromness is the centre of his poetic world, renamed Hamnavoe in his writing after its Viking name. In poems such as 'Hamnavoe', about the rounds of his postman father, and 'Hamnavoe Market', about the exploits of a group of lads attending the fair, he brings to life a vibrant town, rich with tradition. As you walk the narrow cobbled streets that wind down to Stromness harbour, it's easy to imagine that Brown's verse is a documentary of his life, but in reality he generally wrote about the Orkney of the past, capturing a way of life that by his own lifetime had just about disappeared.

Nowhere is the theme of loss more evident in his work than in his writing about the township of Rackwick on the island of Hoy, the second-largest Orkney island. Brown first visited Rackwick in 1946 and was enchanted, as he recalls in the 1981 book *Portrait of Orkney*:

> We drove in a farmer's lorry between dark hills, and suddenly a sea valley was there, between immense red cliffs. I had not thought there could be a place so beautiful. It seemed like 'the island-valley of Avilion' where King Arthur was taken to heal him of his grievous wound. The valley was touched with sadness. One by one the little crofts were falling into ruins [. . .] the shore, like the tilth and pasture, was empty of the fishing boats that had once been the valley's chief food-gatherers.

20 *The low-lying islands of Orkney*

Brown went on to write a whole collection of poetry, *Fishermen with Ploughs*, about Rackwick. His writing is spare and lucid, touched with wonder and lightened by gracious good humour. It's typical of Brown to lament the changes modernity has wrought in Orkney; like Edwin Muir and Eric Linklater, Orcadian writers of the generation before him, Brown can never quite shake the feeling that the perfect, pastoral islands of the past no longer exist. A few homes remain at Rackwick today, but visitors mostly come to savour the pebbly beach or to walk to the Old Man of Hoy, the 137-metre sea stack that stands close to Rackwick Bay. The composer Peter Maxwell Davies moved to Rackwick in the 1970s and set numerous works by Brown to music, including six poems from *Fishermen with Ploughs*.

Shetland

In about 325 BC a Greek explorer, Pytheas, sailed from the Mediterranean in search of the mythical island of Thule in the far north, thought to be near the edge of the world. His account of the voyage, *Concerning the Ocean*, was one of the key works of ancient geography. Sadly the book is now lost, and speculations about its content can only be surmised from quotations and criticism in other works, such as Pliny the Elder's *Natural History*. Pytheas's record of his travels was seen by some ancient writers as fanciful – no mean feat in the world of Pliny, Herodotus and Aristotle – but it seems likely that he spent time in Orkney and Shetland researching questions such as how far north could people live, did daylight ever extend to 24 hours, and did the inhabitants of Thule really steal gold from the nests of gryphons. As Gavin Francis writes in *True North* (2008), about his own modern-day journey to Europe's icy periphery, Pytheas claimed to have sailed six days north from Britain, eventually arriving at Thule. Historians have debated ever since about where this island is: Iceland is the most likely place.

However, regulars at the Thule Bar in Lerwick, the archipelago's capital, have been known to boast that their island is the mythical land that captivated Pytheas's Greek readership.

Over 2,000 years after Pytheas, another writer made an unlikely journey to Shetland. This was Hugh MacDiarmid, poet and leading light of the Scottish Renaissance, who in 1933 took his wife and young son and settled on Whalsay, one of Shetland's smaller inhabited islands, where they lived until 1942. MacDiarmid and his family rented a four-room cottage at Sodom – the Norse name, Sudheim, was anglicised rather absurdly by the Ordnance Survey. MacDiarmid was in poor physical and mental health, suffering a nervous breakdown in 1935, and he often struggled to make ends meet on Whalsay. Concerned neighbours were known to leave gifts of food to help them survive. MacDiarmid's stay on Whalsay was nevertheless one of the most productive periods of his writing career. Among the works he completed were the collection *Stony Limits and Other Poems*, the non-fiction *The Islands of Scotland* and his ostentatiously intellectual autobiography *Lucky Poet*. Much of this work reveals the mental strain he was under. One of his most highly praised poems is 'On a Raised Beach', published in 1934 in *Stony Limits*. It's a long, dense piece, with sections written in such arcane vocabulary that impenetrability seems to be MacDiarmid's sole purpose. Inspired by the poet's three-day stay on uninhabited West Linga, near Whalsay, it describes a barren landscape that is as much an illustration of the poet's emotional state as it is a meditation on geology and physical isolation. At its more lucid moments it's a painfully honest account of depression: 'I can feel all that can perish perishing in me.'

MacDiarmid was concerned with the depopulation and deprivation he witnessed in Shetland, but his fears have been allayed to an extent by the discovery of oil in the sea near the islands. The centre of this oil industry is the terminal of Sullom Voe, on the Shetland mainland, which has its own small place in Scotland's literary history. In Ian Rankin's *Black and Blue*, published to widespread acclaim in 1997, Detective Inspector John Rebus is on the trail of a murderer he suspects might be Bible John, a notorious (real-life) Glaswegian serial killer active in the 1960s. Rebus's investigation leads him to Sullom Voe, and then on to a North Sea oil platform, where he discovers a series of connections between a murdered oil worker and a group of environmental protestors. Rebus, never entirely comfortable outside his Edinburgh haunts, doesn't see much of Shetland and dismisses it as 'miles of bugger all'. He passes towns that serve as dormitories for oil workers, mere hamlets before the terminal was built in the late 1970s. Sullom Voe itself, located in an area that would otherwise be described as a wilderness, is 'a sci-fi city transported to prehistory'.

Hugh MacDiarmid complained that, excepting his own work, Shetland had produced little poetry of note. Today, Shetland-born Robert Alan Jamieson writes poems in the Shetlandic dialect he grew up speaking. Many of these are collected, along with English translations, in *Nort Atlantik Drift*, published in 2007. Award-winning poet Jen Hadfield, born in Cheshire in 1978, lives in Shetland and the language, weather and wildlife of the islands loom large in her work. MacDiarmid would be pleased to know that Shetland now holds its own in Scotland's literary scene.

❧ 8 ❧

ABERDEENSHIRE
AND PERTHSHIRE
History and Legend

Aberdeen

With a population of a quarter of a million, Aberdeen is the largest city outside Scotland's Central Belt. Scotland's North Sea coast has been settled for at least 8,000 years and in 1179 and 1319 royal charters established Aberdeen as one of Scotland's most important municipalities. Its university was founded in 1495, making it the fifth oldest in the United Kingdom, and trade with northern Europe thrived here: Daniel Defoe, writing in *A Tour through the Whole Island of Great Britain* in 1724, declared that 'the people of Aberdeen are universal merchants.' The city was also one of the chief beneficiaries of Britain's herring boom in the early twentieth century. With trade came wealth and, during the expansion of the city from the eighteenth century onwards, many of Aberdeen's new civic and religious buildings were made from local granite, giving rise to nicknames such as the 'Granite City' and the 'Silver City by the Sea'. Aberdeen's cool grey buildings glisten in the sun, but on a rainy winter's day one can be forgiven for thinking the city centre bleak. Lewis Grassic Gibbon, in a 1934 essay included in *Scottish Scene*, finds in the city's austere architecture a corollary of its atmosphere:

It has a flinty shine when new – a grey glimmer like a morning North Sea, a cold steeliness that chills the heart. Even with weathering it acquires no gracious softness, it is merely starkly grim and uncompromising. [. . .] Not only are there no furbelows [adornments] possible in this architecture, there is amid it, continually, the uneasy sense that you may not rest here, you may not lounge, you cannot stand still and watch the world go by . . . Else presently the warders will come and move you on.

In another essay, Gibbon personifies Aberdeen as 'a thin-lipped peasant woman who has borne eleven and buried nine'; he also wrote a novel, *Grey Granite*, set in a fictional, depression-era city resembling Aberdeen, where worker unrest and socialist demonstrations are rife.

More recently, Aberdeen has been the chief beneficiary of another bounty from the North Sea: oil. Around 50,000 people in the area work in the oil industry or related services, and 'black gold' has made Aberdeen one of Britain's wealthiest cities. It also has the busiest heliport in the world, shuttling workers to and from oil platforms. In Ian Rankin's crime novel *Black and Blue*, the city's Duthie Park, famous for its winter gardens, plays host to an anti-oil protest concert; the headliners are fictitious superstars called the Dancing Pigs, named after the band Rankin sang in as a teenager.

Aberdeen's literary history is long and significant, featuring writers who in their time here had a marked influence on Scottish literature. The earliest of the celebrated Aberdonian bards is John Barbour, born in around 1325. As well as serving as archdeacon of Aberdeen, he became a member of the royal household of King Robert II, founder of the Stewart (later spelled 'Stuart') dynasty. Barbour's output was sycophantic: in addition to 'The Stewartis Original', a now-lost poem which concocted a regal pedigree for Robert, Barbour was commissioned by the King to write *The Bruce*, a 13,550-line narrative poem in Scots, celebrating Robert the Bruce as a national hero. Few now read Barbour's *magnum opus* in full, but it contains lines about independence which are still frequently quoted in relation to Scottish politics. The first line of the four below is inscribed on a wall in Makars' Court, Edinburgh:

> A! Freedom is a noble thing!
> Freedom makis [allows] man to have liking [contentment].
> Freedom all solace to man givis,
> He livis at ease that freely livis!

One of Scotland's leading Renaissance poets, Arthur Johnston, was born in rural Aberdeenshire in around 1579 and educated at King's College, Aberdeen, where he was appointed lord rector in 1637. He spent much of his working life on the Continent, and his use of the international language of the day, Latin, means that his poetry is seldom given the attention it deserves. His work was, however, praised by Samuel Johnson in *A Journey to the Western Islands of Scotland.* Well-travelled and cosmopolitan, like the earlier Scottish Latin poet George Buchanan, Johnston nevertheless wrote many poems in praise of the Scottish towns which he loved, including Aberdeen, Glasgow, Edinburgh and St Andrews. His verse epistle 'To Robert Baron' depicts the slog of agricultural labour with a delicate poetic touch, as Robert Crawford reveals in his 2006 translation: 'with my writing hand / I haul the stones from new-ploughed fields.'

The most famous writer with a connection to Aberdeen is George Gordon, Lord Byron. In 1785 Captain John 'Mad Jack' Byron, the profligate son of an admiral, married Catherine, the laird of Gight in Aberdeenshire. It didn't take long before he had squandered his wife's considerable wealth – much of it went towards paying debts – but Mad Jack nonetheless spent the next few years moving from place to place in order to evade his creditors. His son George was born in London in 1788, but Catherine soon relocated to Aberdeen, where she was intermittently joined by her husband. John died in Valenciennes, France, in 1791; in his will he charged his three-year-old son with 'pay[ing] my debts, legacies, and funeral expenses'. For about four years, until he inherited the title of Lord Byron in 1798, George attended Aberdeen Grammar School, an institution dating back to the thirteenth century. On Skene Street, in front of the school's granite façade, there stands a bronze statue of Byron. Eric Linklater, who attended Aberdeen Grammar School from 1913 to 1916, wrote in his autobiography, *The Man on my Back*, that seeing the figure of Byron out of the classroom window 'undid the schoolroom teaching that literature must be a solemn thing'. One of the school's houses is also named Byron, an audacious choice of role model for its pupils.

Byron and his mother moved to London after his accession to the family title, and by the time of his death in 1824 his reputation as a rake, rebel and poet of prodigious ability was assured. Following the runaway success of his poem *Childe Harold* in 1812 he became one of the celebrities of Regency London, frequenting exclusive clubs and the most fashionable of soirées. He engaged in numerous affairs, sometimes with a reckless disregard for the conventions of polite society; one lover, Lady Caroline Lamb, famously described him as 'mad, bad and dangerous to know'. Speculation continues to this day that he was the father of a daughter borne by Augusta, his half-sister, in 1814. Byron died in Greece during the country's campaign for independence from the Ottoman Empire.

Despite spending much of his adulthood in London and continental Europe, Byron recalled Scotland with affection. In the tenth canto of *Don Juan*, Byron's masterpiece and perhaps the greatest comic poem in the English language, the poet turns to his northern origins, referencing tartan, Aberdeen's two rivers, Macbeth's murdered rival and the nostalgic song still sung at Hogmanay, the Scottish New Year celebration:

> But I am half a Scot by birth, and bred
> A whole one, and my heart flies to my head,

As 'Auld Lang Syne' brings Scotland, one and all,
Scotch plaids, Scotch snoods, the blue hills, and clear streams,
The Dee, the Don, Balgounie brig's black wall,
All my boy feelings, all my gentler dreams
Of what I then dreamt, clothed in their own pall,
Like Banquo's offspring – floating past me seems
My childhood in this childishness of mine:
I care not – 'tis a glimpse of 'Auld Lang Syne'.

The Aberdeenshire Coast and Countryside

South of Aberdeen is the district of Kincardineshire, also known as the Mearns. Lewis Grassic Gibbon was born James Leslie Mitchell in 1901 and grew up in the Mearns village of Arbuthnott. He adopted his mother's maiden name as his *nom de plume* for his finest work, the trilogy of novels collectively known as *A Scots Quair* ('quair' being the Scots word for a book). Gibbon boasted that he came from authentic peasant stock, and his father expected that as his son grew up he would help with the work on their holding, a small patch of land from which it was difficult to scrape a living. But as a young man Gibbon rejected what he saw as the drudgery of farm labour. After stints working as a journalist and in the British armed forces, he became a full-time writer in 1929. He is yet another Scottish novelist who died young: a perforated ulcer, which he blamed on years of army food, caused his death in 1935 at the age of 33. Overwork was more likely the exacerbating factor; in the last year of his life alone he published six books. His work spanned the genres of literary fiction, science fiction, anthropology and, in *Scottish Scene*, co-authored with Hugh MacDiarmid, political broadside.

The first novel in *A Scots Quair*, titled *Sunset Song*, was published in 1932 and is regarded by many critics as the best Scottish novel of the twentieth century. It's written in a unique lyrical style, fusing the rhythm of the Scots language with a vocabulary that's largely

English, resulting in a book that sounds quintessentially Scottish but is widely accessible. *Sunset Song* tells the story of a young woman, Chris Guthrie, growing up in the Mearns just before the First World War. It's a time of great upheaval: traditional methods of farming are being challenged by mechanisation and modern commerce, and with the outbreak of war many men of fighting age enlist, some never to return, including Chris's husband. Chris's adolescence, marriage, widowhood and experience as a mother form the core of the book. Gibbon, perhaps drawing on his own experience, is acute on the village gossip that surrounds her at every stage. The other protagonist of the novel is the land itself: the red clay fields that Chris's father, like Gibbon's own, struggles to keep fertile; the moors, blanketed in heather and the yellow-flowering broom; the circle of standing stones that is a symbol of continuity with the peasantry of the ancient past and that, in the final chapter, is given a new role as a memorial to those who died in the Great War.

In the subsequent volumes in the trilogy, *Cloud Howe* and *Grey Granite*, Chris becomes more removed from her childhood home as she relocates first to a small town and then to a sprawling industrial city. *Sunset Song* reads perfectly well as a standalone novel, the book in which Gibbon perfected his distinctive style and created characters and settings of great vitality. Gibbon's love–hate relationship with his agricultural upbringing infuses the novel, and Chris, like the author, is torn between a commitment to her family farm and the world of books and education. Despite her academic success at school, Chris comes to discover a close, almost spiritual, attachment to the land and to the people who have worked it for generations, and this above all is what makes *Sunset Song* captivating:

> You hated the land and the coarse speak of the folk and learning was brave and fine one day; and the next you'd waken with the peewits crying across the hills, deep and deep, crying in the heart of you and the smell of the earth in your face, almost you'd cry for that, the beauty of it and the sweetness of the Scottish land and

skies. You saw their faces in the firelight, father's and mother's and the neighbours', before the lamps lit up, tired and kind, faces dear and close to you, you wanted the words they'd known and used.

With its frank treatment of sexuality, incest and childbirth, *Sunset Song* scandalised some members of the Mearns community; elsewhere in Scotland, and internationally, it was a critical and commercial success. For inhabitants of Arbuthnott there was no doubt that Gibbon was spreading malicious gossip about the village – although Gibbon names it Kinraddie in his novel, it maps closely to Arbuthnott, including the Norman-era Church of Saint Ternan with its 'fine glass windows'. Gibbon's ashes were later interred in the corner of the church's graveyard, marked by a granite memorial in the form of an open book. The people of Arbuthnott are less ambivalent towards *Sunset Song* these days, and the nearby Lewis Grassic Gibbon Centre is a small, friendly museum dedicated to the village's most famous son.

Aberdeen is blessed with miles of sandy beach which becomes wilder as you go north out of the city. About 20 miles to the north is Cruden Bay, a village fringed by another sandy cove, home to a famous golf course and, possibly, a vampire. In the 1880s and 1890s Bram Stoker visited Cruden Bay several times whilst working on *Dracula*, and he stayed at the Kilmarnock Arms, a small hotel near the shore that's still popular today. When the novel was published in 1897 it became an immediate bestseller; it's a tale of insanity, sexual repression and the supernatural which still haunts the cultural imagination. On a rocky headland just to the east of Cruden Bay is Slains Castle. The castle, built in 1664, was still inhabited in Stoker's time, but in 1920s the roof was removed to avoid taxes, and the building is now a bleak and sinister husk. There's no record that Stoker used Slains as a model when he came to devise a lair for his aristocratic vampire, but local tradition unashamedly claims it as the author's inspiration for Castle Dracula. In the opening chapter of *Dracula* Jonathan Harker records his first impression of the villain's forbidding Transylvanian home: 'I became conscious of the fact that the driver was in the act of pulling up the horses in the courtyard of a vast ruined castle, from whose tall black windows came no ray of light, and whose broken battlements showed a jagged line against the moonlit sky.' Harker's narrative could easily describe Slains, and with every passing winter the castle looks more and more the part. Few readers of *Dracula* would feel comfortable standing before this Scottish castle under the light of a full moon.

North of Cruden Bay, where the coast curves west towards Inverness, lie the thriving fishing ports of Fraserburgh and Peterhead. Inland, across a patchwork of fields and farming villages, is the small town of Huntly. This is the birthplace of George MacDonald, the nineteenth-century children's fantasy writer whose work influenced J. R. R. Tolkien and C. S. Lewis.

Between Fraserburgh and Inverness is Elgin, the largest town in the district of Moray and a royal burgh since the twelfth century. Elgin was a favourite with the Scottish kings of the twelfth and thirteenth centuries, who enjoyed hunting in the nearby forests; its renowned cathedral dates from this time. Founded in 1224, Elgin Cathedral has a colourful history. It was completed destroyed by fire in 1270, rebuilt, and then burned down again in 1390 by Alexander Stewart, the son of King Robert II, known as the Wolf of Badenoch because of his cruelty and brutality. The cathedral then survived as a place of worship until the Reformation, but in the 1560s, by order of Scotland's Privy Council, the lead was stripped from the roof to be sold. The subsequent history of the building is a story of falling towers and quarrying by builders looking for a supply of cheap stone.

The novelist Jessie Kesson, who was born in a workhouse in Inverness in 1916, grew up in the now-demolished Kelby's Close, adjoining Elgin's handsome High Street. She was raised in slum conditions by her mother, who was almost certainly a prostitute, until at the age of eight she was sent to an orphanage when her mother contracted syphilis. Kesson went on to excel at school before entering domestic service. In later life she lived in London, working as a producer on BBC radio plays and for the long-running *Woman's Hour*. Her fiction features intelligent women fighting to reconcile their desires with the reality of living in a patriarchal society that constricts their opportunities. In her semi-autobiographical novel *The White Bird Passes*, published in 1958, Kesson draws on her own Elgin childhood:

> Lady's Lane was a tributary of High Street, one of many such tributaries of long, narrow wynds that slunk backwards from the main street, gathering themselves into themselves, like a group of women assuring each other proudly, 'We keep ourselves to ourselves', and, at the same time, usually knowing more than most people of what is going on around.
>
> If you rushed down High Street in a hurry, you wouldn't notice Lady's Lane at all, so narrowly and darkly does it skulk itself away, but Lady's Lane would most certainly see you.

In and Around the Cairngorms

Inland from the relatively flat and arable coast around Aberdeen and Elgin are the Cairngorms, the largest mountainous plateau in Britain. The granite massif is so extensive that, exceptionally for Scotland, it has a subarctic climate, battered by blizzards and gales during the winter and retaining snow during the summer months. Around the fringes of the plateau are some of the country's largest natural woodlands, and the rivers gushing down from the hills are an integral component in the prized Speyside whiskies distilled in seemingly every village. The Cairngorms National Park, the largest of its kind in Britain at 4,528 square kilometres, encompasses the mountains, rivers, forests and villages. In terms of rugged grandeur, the Cairngorms can't match the West Highland peaks of Glencoe and Torridon, or the dramatic knife-edge ridge

21 The Cairngorm mountains, seen from the banks of Loch Morlich

of the Skye Cuillin. But the plateau has its own mystique, with unique flora and fauna living in some of the most isolated glens and mountain passes in the country.

In *The Living Mountain*, written in the 1940s but not published until 1977, Nan Shepherd meditates upon the character of the Cairngorms. Shepherd spent most of her life in Cults, a village three miles from Aberdeen, where her family moved a month after her birth in 1893. She studied at the University of Aberdeen and lectured in English at Aberdeen College of Education; between 1928 and 1933 she published three novels, to critical acclaim. The manuscript of *The Living Mountain* sat in a drawer for 30 years, but since the turn of the century it has come to be recognised as one of the masterpieces of twentieth-century nature writing, a philosophical, poetic, earthy and yet spiritual essay on the Cairngorms, their climate and their wildlife, and what they mean to the people who visit them. Shepherd loved these mountains, walking in them until she knew them intimately: 'Summer on the high plateau can be delectable as honey; it can also be a roaring scourge. To those who love the place, both are good, since both are part of its essential nature. And it is to know its essential nature that I am seeking here.' Shepherd's portrait of the Cairngorms isn't a hillwalker's guide. She explains that the more time she spends in the hills, the more she wants to savour their nuances of colour and smell, to taste water from their streams and above all to listen: 'The sound of all this moving water is as integral to the mountain as pollen to the flower. One hears it without listening as one breathes without thinking. But to a listening ear the sound disintegrates into many different notes – the slow slap of a loch, the high clear trill of a rivulet, the roar of spate.'

On birds and trees, on fellow walkers and even on mosses, Shepherd's prose is equally brilliant. Reading *The Living Mountain*, like walking the slopes of the Cairngorms, can be a rapturous experience. And on winter days when roads to the hills are blocked by snow and the battering winds of the plateau make standing up, let alone walking, impossible, Shepherd's book is the ideal consolation for those who have attempted to know these mountains in person but have been defeated by the elements.

Aviemore is the primary village in the Cairngorms, a Mecca for outdoor sports enthusiasts coming here to ski or mountain bike. It's a busy place, with shops and restaurants, a welcoming pub on the banks of the River Spey, and even a nightclub. Between Aviemore and the slopes leading up to the plateau is the Rothiemurchus Estate, home to an ancient woodland containing rare species such as the capercaillie, a magnificent member of the grouse family known for its clucking call and its elaborate mating dance. Hidden away in the forest is Loch an Eilein, surely one of the prettiest lochs in Scotland. Aged pines ring its shores, and a little way from the north bank is an islet almost entirely covered by the remains of a thirteenth-century castle. In the distance rises the great wall of the mountains.

In her *Memoirs of a Highland Lady*, published in 1898, Elizabeth Grant of Rothiemurchus brings to life the intricacies of managing the estate in the early nineteenth century. Grant's memoir is a lively account of the life of a wealthy young woman of the time, faced with the ordeal of a broken engagement, her family's financial difficulties and the need to marry well; she spends her early life touring resorts and spas, and enjoying time in Edinburgh and London as well as on her family estate of Rothiemurchus. When she was 23 her father's legal and political career collapsed and the family settled at Rothiemurchus for the next seven years. Her *Memoirs* contains spirited explanations of forestry as well as the goings-on of neighbouring gentry. It was written between 1845 and 1854 for the amusement of Grant's family, and she has the ability to make everyday lives and pieces of gossip enthralling. Her book touches on famous names: Walter Scott and his family receive scathing criticism – he is 'dull and listless' in company and his wife is 'very silly and foolish' – while Shelley, whom she knew when he was an undergraduate, is 'very insubordinate' and 'slovenly in his dress'. She is more positive when writing about Rothiemurchus, including Loch an Eilein, and she's not afraid to mingle fact with legend:

22 Rothiemurchus Forest, clad in winter snow

The people said there was a zigzag causeway beneath the water, from the door of the old castle to the shore, the secret of which was always known to three persons only. We often tried to hit upon this causeway, but we never succeeded. A great number of paths crossed the forest, and one or two cart roads; the robbers' road at the back of Loch an Eilein, 'the lake of the island,' was made by Rob Roy for his own convenience when out upon his cattle raids.

An exposed, 18-mile pass called the Lairig Ghru weaves through the heart of the Cairngorms, connecting Aviemore with the village of Braemar. From the north the mouth of the pass is unmistakable: a V-shaped dip in the mountain range. On either side rise the shoulders of the mountains: these include Ban Macdui, the second highest summit in Britain, described by Nan Shepherd as a mist-covered giant; and Bod an Deamhain, a peak which, according to legend, gained its euphemistic English name of Devil's Point when John Brown, ghillie to Queen Victoria, declined to supply her with the literal translation of Devil's Penis. In days gone by the Lairig Ghru was used by cattle drovers and bandits, but now its main traffic is hikers braving the boulder-strewn, wind-blasted path, which in winter can quickly become blocked by snowdrifts. Braemar registers some of Britain's coldest winter temperatures and can be cut off in bad weather. A webcam is permanently focused on the snow gate which is used to close the road in and out of the village.

Robert Louis Stevenson spent the summer of 1881 in Braemar, hoping that the cool mountain air would ease his consumption. The weather was poor, and he was often confined to the cottage he and his family had rented on Glenshee Road, the main thoroughfare bisecting the village. It was here, in an effort to entertain his stepson Lloyd Osbourne, that Stevenson started to write the novel that made his name, *Treasure Island*. As he claims in 'My First Book', published in the *Idler* in 1894 and later reprinted as part of *Essays in the Art of Writing*, the idea for the story began when he drew Lloyd the map of an imaginary island:

[T]he shape of it took my fancy beyond expression; it contained harbours that pleased me like sonnets; [. . .] the future characters of the book began to appear there visibly among imaginary woods; and their brown faces and bright weapons peeped out upon me from unexpected quarters, as they passed to and fro, fighting and hunting treasures, on these few square inches of a flat projection. The next thing I knew I had some papers in front of me and was writing out a list of chapters.

Stevenson spent a lot of his childhood at coastal lighthouse sites and was to live out his final years on the island of Upolu in Samoa. Perhaps it was a longing for the sea that spurred him to create a fictional island while living in one of the most inland villages in Scotland. He completed *Treasure Island* while residing in an even more landlocked location – a sanatorium in Davos, Switzerland (where Thomas Mann was later inspired to write *The Magic Mountain*).

A few minutes from Braemar is Balmoral, the Highland retreat of Queen Victoria, a fairytale castle in the Scottish Baronial style popularised by Walter Scott's Abbotsford. The castle's turrets and ivy-clad walls, situated within wooded, riverside grounds, make an impressive sight when viewed from the surrounding hills; the estate and castle are also open to visitors. Lying in a fertile valley, it's as romantic a setting as Victorian culture could conceive of, and has understandably been cherished by generations of royals.

To the west of the Cairngorms, on the outskirts of the village of Kingussie, is the stately home and sporting estate of Balavil. The house was built in 1790 by James Macpherson, a crofter's son from nearby Ruthven, who acquired fame and then notoriety with the publication of *Fragments of Ancient Poetry* in 1760 and *Fingal* in 1761. In 1759 Macpherson met John Home, a popular dramatist, in the Borders spa town of Moffat. Home asked his Highland acquaintance to recite some ancient Gaelic poetry to him and was sufficiently impressed with Macpherson's translations that he used his contacts to help him publish some of these texts. *Fingal* purported to be Macpherson's translation of a Gaelic epic about the eponymous third-century hero, as composed by the hero's son, the warrior-poet Ossian. This ancient bard was lauded as a Celtic Homer and caused a sensation at home and abroad; urbane Europeans such as Goethe and Napoleon were swept away by the stirring landscapes and passionate rhetoric of his verse. Macpherson claimed to have collected Gaelic originals through extensive research in the Highlands, and to have merely rendered them into English. It eventually became apparent, however, that Macpherson, whilst working from a few fragmentary originals, had invented most of the ancient poetry himself. Macpherson's literary con arguably gave him all the training he needed for his later career as a political journalist and pamphleteer – the eighteenth-century equivalent of a spin doctor. His 'translations' haven't weathered any better than his literary reputation and seem turgid and overblown to many modern readers, but it's easy to see how works such as *Fragments of Ancient Poetry* inspired the more florid excesses of the Romantic movement:

> I sit by the mossy fountain; on the top of the hills of winds. One tree is rustling above me. Dark waves roll over the heath. The lake is troubled below. [. . .] Sad are my thoughts alone. Didst thou but appear, O my love, a wanderer on the heath! thy hair floating on the wind behind thee; thy bosom heaving on the sight; thine eyes full of tears for thy friends, whom the mist of the hill had concealed! Thee I would comfort, my love, and bring thee to thy father's house.

Dunkeld, Birnam and Scone

About 60 miles south of Balavil on the A9, where the uplands of the Cairngorms and Breadalbane level out and meet the lush farmlands of rural Perthshire, is the Hermitage at Dunkeld. The Hermitage is a stone folly overlooking the Black Linn waterfall on the River Braan, built in 1758 for the Duke of Atholl. Surrounding the folly is a woodland garden containing some of the tallest trees in the country. In 1783 the folly was renamed Ossian's Hall and decked out as the supposed home of the Celtic bard. It is now owned by the National Trust for Scotland and in 2007 the Hermitage was refurbished with mirrored artwork and secret handles in the spirit of the Duke's early attempts to dramatise this Ossianic setting. As with many of the 'Romantic' destinations in Scotland, the Hermitage was visited by Queen Victoria, Turner and Mendelssohn. William Wordsworth also visited it in 1814, and in his poem 'Effusion in the Pleasure-Ground on the Banks of the Bran, near Dunkeld' he pours out his misgivings about the artificial folly and its decor, the woodland of imported trees, and the allusions to a fabricated bard:

> Thus (where the intrusive Pile, ill-graced
> With baubles of theatric taste,
> O'erlooks the torrent breathing showers
> On motley bands of alien flowers
> In stiff confusion set or sown,
> Till nature cannot find her own,
> Or keep a remnant of the sod
> Which Caledonian Heroes trod)
> I mused; and, thrusting for redress,
> Recoiled into the wilderness.

A final spot of pilgrimage for admirers of Ossian is Sma' Glen, a small, scenic valley between Dunkeld and Crieff, a town about 15 miles to the south-west. At the northern end is Ossian's Stone, a monolith over two metres high said to mark the bard's final resting place. The story goes that when General Wade was building a military road past the glen in the eighteenth century his men had to move this boulder, and underneath they found a cavity containing ashes, bone and charred heather, which locals reburied ceremoniously, suspecting they were the remains of the warrior-poet. Whatever the truth of this story, Sma' Glen is a fitting place for a poet to be memorialised, a quiet spot off the beaten track and, like much of Perthshire, less intimidating and barren than the glens further north. In the 1981 film *Chariots of Fire* Sma' Glen was used as the location for the Highland athletics meeting in which Eric Liddell runs in his tweeds and braces.

About five miles to the east is the village of Logiealmond, where John Watson was the Free Church minister for some of the 1870s. In 1894, under the pseudonym Ian Maclaren, Watson published *Beside the Bonnie Briar Bush*, a collection of sentimental stories about rural life which became a bestseller, shifting almost a million copies in Britain and America. It remains one of the leading examples of the kailyard school of literature popular at the time; writers like Lewis Grassic Gibbon and Ayrshire's George Douglas Brown were soon publishing their own brutal ripostes to kailyard nostalgia.

On the other side of the A9 from the Hermitage is Dunkeld, a vibrant town with a long history. A monastery was built here in the sixth century, and in 849 Kenneth MacAlpin, the first ruler of the unified kingdom of Scotland, had Saint Columba's relics brought here from Iona to protect them from Viking raiders. From this time on, Dunkeld was one of the country's main ecclesiastical centres: Dunkeld Cathedral, sections of which are still in use as a parish church today, was begun in the twelfth century; the bell tower and nave are now conserved ruins. Gavin Douglas, poet and translator of Virgil's *Aeneid* into Scots, was Bishop of Dunkeld from 1516 to 1520 (he had earlier been the provost of St Giles' Cathedral in Edinburgh). This was an era marked by infighting among the Scottish nobility: his appointment met with influential opposition, and according to one eyewitness Douglas was fired upon from the cathedral's steeple as he arrived in Dunkeld for his inauguration. In 1689 the entire town was destroyed during the Battle of Dunkeld, part of the first Jacobite rising led by John Graham, Viscount Dundee, known to his supporters as Bonnie Dundee.

An even greater tale of violent political struggle is associated with this area, however. Dunkeld is adjoined to a village called

Birnam, which is on the opposite bank of the Tay; technically they're a single town, Dunkeld and Birnam. Birnam was built in the nineteenth century but it's name has had a special place in Scottish history – and indeed in Western culture – for much longer. In William Shakespeare's play *Macbeth*, a prophecy is made which involves the bloodthirsty king, Birnam Wood and Dunsinane, a nearby fortified hill:

> Macbeth shall never vanquished be until
> Great Birnam Wood to high Dunsinane Hill
> Shall come against him.

While this is initially interpreted as a guarantee of security, a way of saying that Macbeth will remain king until the impossible happens and a forest moves, his downfall comes when his rival Malcolm commands his army to march on the stronghold of Dunsinane using boughs from Birnam as camouflage. Thus Birnam Wood comes to Dunsinane, and Macbeth is killed in the ensuing fight.

Shakespeare was notoriously liberal with history in *Macbeth*, and while his bloodthirsty tragedy was a success, both in his lifetime and in the centuries since, it has probably damaged the reputation of a decent king for all time. Macbeth became king of Scotland in 1040 when he defeated Duncan I in battle, probably at Pitgaveny near Elgin. While Shakespeare depicts Duncan as a benevolent and much-loved ruler, he was in reality an immature king, prone to reckless military enterprises. Macbeth, despite also killing Duncan's father, the abbot of Dunkeld, was generally perceived as a pious and generous monarch, a patron of the Church who gave money to the poor. He unsuccessfully fought Earl Thorfinn of Orkney for control of Caithness and Sutherland and is thought to be the Scottish king referred to as Karl Hundason in the *Orkneyinga Saga*. On 27 July 1054 Macbeth was defeated by Malcolm Canmore, later to become King Malcolm III, in a battle probably fought at Dunsinane. Macbeth's authority was weakened but, contrary to Shakespeare's dramatic account, he wasn't killed at this battle. Instead he was killed three years later in a last stand at Lumphanan, 25 miles inland from Aberdeen.

A short walk from Birnam village, along a path signposted as Oak Road, is the Birnam Oak, a venerable tree whose branches are propped up by stilts. It has a circumference of over seven metres and is said to be the last remnant of the wood taken up as camouflage by Malcolm's soldiers. Although it's easy to believe that the oak was part of an ancient woodland, it's highly unlikely that it was even a sapling in 1054. About 20 miles to the south-east, near the hamlet of Collace, is the flat green top of Dunsinane Hill. It's an easy walk through farmland to reach the hill, and on the summit earthworks are easily visible, indicating the former presence of a fort. Dunsinane is a fine vantage point with wide views of the surrounding land, and may have first been fortified in the Iron Age. By Macbeth's time it's less likely that there was an active fort here, and the battle was almost certainly fought on the plain below the hill.

None of this archaeological speculation is as vivid, of course, as the image of Shakespeare's tragic hero ensconced in his hilltop retreat, surveying the approaching woods. In 1970 John McPhee, staff writer for the *New Yorker*, set out to find Dunsinane and recorded his explorations in the essay 'From Birnam Wood to Dunsinane', later collected in his book *Pieces of the Frame*. At the time there were fewer signposts for literary pilgrims than there are today and a bemused farmer, whose land included the hill, has to direct him to the top. McPhee, pointing out that the only descriptions of Dunsinane given by Shakespeare are the vague epithets 'high' and 'great', argues that if the playwright had ever seen it, his prodigious eloquence would have done it fuller justice:

The summit was flat and oval, and Macbeth's floor plan was evident there, for the foundation protruded in lumpy ridges under the turf. The castle was no cramped little broch. It was a hundred and twenty feet wide and two hundred and twenty-five feet long

– just slightly larger than the Parthenon [. . .] Macbeth apparently did not do things by halves. The view from the summit over the patchwork Scottish countryside was extraordinary. It is a virtual certainty that Shakespeare never set eyes on Dunsinane. If he had, he would have described it.

Another visitor to the Birnam area was a writer whose tales are similarly concerned with greed and ambition, although on a somewhat smaller scale than *Macbeth*. This is Beatrix Potter, whose hero Peter Rabbit is almost undone by greed. Potter grew up in London, but every summer her family spent long holidays in the Dunkeld area, staying at Dalguise House (now an outdoor activity centre) and Eastwood House, a villa with wooded riverside gardens on the banks of the Tay opposite Birnam (still available for holiday rental). On these vacations Potter developed a fascination for the natural world. Encouraged by Charles McIntosh, a Dunkeld naturalist, she studied the plants and wildlife of Perthshire and became particularly knowledgeable about fungi; her expertise was such that in 1897 her paper on the germination of fungal spores was read at the Linnaean Society in London. Perth Museum and Art Gallery houses some of her intricate drawings of Eastwood fungi.

Eastwood is more famous, though, as the birthplace of her most well-known children's story, *The Tale of Peter Rabbit*. When Potter was on holiday she would send illustrated letters to the children of her last governess. One of these letters, to Noel Moore in 1893, contained a story about a rabbit, later extended into a book and issued by Potter herself in 1901. The day after she wrote to Noel, she sent his brother Eric a letter about a frog named Mr Jeremy Fisher, another tale that would later be published as a book. In 1905 Potter moved to the Lake District, where she kept a prize-winning flock of Herdwick Sheep and purchased thousands of acres of land with the royalties from her books and accompanying drawings. She eventually gave much of her land to the National Trust. Although the Lake District is the region most closely associated with Potter, her early experiences in Perthshire were a significant influence on her interests and writing. The Birnam Institute, the arts centre serving the local area, has an authoritative exhibition on her time in the area, and a nearby garden features the local flowers and fungi which captivated her. This charming garden is also populated by her characters: footpaths lead past Jeremy Fisher's pond, Mrs Tiggy-winkle's house and Peter Rabbit's burrow.

Not far to the south of Dunkeld and Birnam, on a green and pleasant stretch of the Tay, is the city of Perth, Scotland's principal town in the Middle Ages. When Kenneth MacAlpin unified the western Scots kingdom of Dál Riata and the eastern Pictish kingdom of Fortriu in the early 840s, he (or possibly one of his successors – the history of this period is hazy) established Scone as the capital of this new Scottish kingdom. Pronounced 'Skoon', the modern village lies just beyond the northern reaches of Perth; in Kenneth's time it was a Pictish settlement. Kenneth brought with him the Stone of Destiny, used in the inauguration of kings. It's a fairly unprepossessing sandstone block, on which rulers were seated as part of their coronation ceremony. In 1296 it was taken to London by Edward I of England in order to symbolise his conquest over the Scottish nation; later it was incorporated into the throne in Westminster Abbey on which the kings and queens of England – and later of the United Kingdom – were crowned. The practice continues to this day, although since 1996 the Stone of Destiny has been loaned back to the people of Scotland and is displayed in Edinburgh Castle. There's also a replica at Scone Palace. In 1950 the stone was stolen from Westminster Abbey by four Scottish students in a nationalist gesture; after hiding it for over a year they left it in the ruins of Arbroath Abbey for the authorities to collect. The daring escapade was later the subject of *The Taking of the Stone*, a book published in 1991 by ringleader Iain Hamilton (who went on to be an eminent lawyer) and eventually adapted into a film, *The Stone of Destiny*, starring Charlie Cox, Billy Boyd and Robert Carlyle.

❦ 9 ❦

Dundee, Angus and Fife

Dundee

In his 1934 travel book *The Heart of Scotland*, Greenock-born novelist George Blake wrote that Dundee was 'an East Coast town with a West Coast temperament'. Established as a royal burgh in 1190, Dundee's rapid expansion in the nineteenth century, like that of Glasgow and the smaller towns in Ayrshire and Lanarkshire, was predicated upon mills, factory labour and slums. Dundee's industrial specialisms were known collectively as the 'three Js': jute, jam and journalism. The processing of jute – the coarse fabric used as sacking in a huge range of contexts, including for the covers of American pioneer wagons – dominated the city and relied upon cheap female labour. But by the middle of the twentieth century the industry was in terminal decline. The grand brick mill buildings were empty and the city fell into a malaise which it took decades to recover from. Dundee's other two primary trades were also chastened in the twentieth century, although the city's magazine and comic book publishers have survived. Among the famous comics to have come from Dundee are *The Beano*, *The Dandy*, and the Scottish favourites *The Broons* and *Oor Wullie*. Characters such as Dennis the Menace adorn the city's buses; a statue of Desperate Dan stands in the centre of town, his huge belly gleaming in bronze. Today a more modern form of narrative entertainment, computer gaming, has given Dundee another industry to be proud of. Clusters of game designers have joined a new generation of comic book artists and graphic novelists in the city and among the games developed by

Dundee companies are the hugely popular *Minecraft* and *Grand Theft Auto* franchises.

Dundee is the most beautifully situated city in Scotland, laid out below a hill on the north bank of the Firth of Tay. The water glistens in the estuary; seals haul themselves onto sandbanks and the whole panorama is visible as you enter the city on the road and rail bridges from the south. In a 1935 essay titled 'Angus and Mearns', Fionn MacColla, novelist and Scottish nationalist, paid tribute to this setting whilst condemning the conditions in which its population lived:

> Nature intended Dundee to be a dignified and gracious city, for the site is one of the most magnificent in Europe. But as men have made it it stands today perhaps the completest monument in the entire continent of human folly, avarice, and selfishness; a perfect object-lesson in what results from the divorce of economic life from ethics.

As you cross the road bridge into Dundee, one of the most conspicuous sights is a three-masted wooden sailing ship moored in its own dock. This is the *Discovery*, purpose-built for Captain Robert Falcon Scott's Antarctic expedition of 1901–4. The chief promoter of this expedition was Sir Clements Markham, president of the Royal Geographical Society. In *I May Be Some Time*, his 1996 book about Britain's polar expeditions, Francis Spufford argues that Markham and Scott were driven by idealism and patriotism as they prepared for the *Discovery*'s mission:

> So Scott presented himself for service, susceptible (as his sister said) to 'the romance of ice and snow', ignorant till he educated himself of the technical aspects of exploration, but sensitive to the impalpable relationship between ice and England; so Markham's brain-child the *Discovery* sailed, 485 tons of purpose-built ship, freighted with a nostalgia which had got out of hand, a reverie

trying to be real. Absorbed in the erection of idols, Markham had effectively restricted the equipment the *Discovery* might use in the Antarctic to those he remembered in boyhood.

Despite these weaknesses, Scott's expedition was deemed a success. Its team of naval officers and scientists charted large tracts of the continent, recorded meteorological conditions and, whilst not actually reaching the South Pole, nevertheless got further south than anyone else had before. This provided the impetus for Scott's doomed return to Antarctica in 1910, which culminated in his death in 1912 along with four of his companions. The *Discovery* had been sold by the admiralty, so he set sail in a converted Dundee whaler, the *Terra Nova*. While the *Terra Nova* returned to commercial fishing afterwards and later foundered off the coast of Greenland in 1943, the *Discovery* lives on in well-kept retirement, the centrepiece of Dundee's Discovery Point museum. A 30-year project to regenerate Dundee's waterfront is currently underway, and will have as its focal points the *Discovery* and a branch of the Victoria and Albert Museum. Soon Dundee's riverside, to quote Fionn MacColla, will be as 'dignified and gracious' as nature intended; this city's future seems far brighter than its past.

Dundee's most famous poet, William Topaz McGonagall, has a reputation for hapless perseverance that rivals Captain Scott's, but without the redeeming heroism. He recited his poetry in theatres and pubs, where his rhymes in favour of teetotalism were received with hilarity rather than annoyance. When it came to poetic metre, metaphor and basic imagination, McGonagall was unaware of his shortcomings. Audiences paid to hurl abuse at him as he read his work. He was the victim of hoaxes: he received a letter purportedly from 'King Theebaw, of Burmah and the Andaman Islands', conferring upon him the title of 'Sir Wm. Topaz McGonagall, Knight of The White Elephant', and he subsequently used the title with pride. He also applied to Queen Victoria for patronage and walked to Balmoral on foot in the hope of performing before her. And yet, despite his ineptitude, McGonagall's poetry is strangely compelling. His twentieth-century champions included the comedians Spike Milligan and Billy Connolly; the contemporary poet W. N. Herbert, Dundee's first official makar (poet laureate), is also an admirer.

For McGonagall, a great opportunity to celebrate his city in verse came when the Tay Rail Bridge was opened in 1878. At the time its two-mile span made it the longest bridge in the world. His poem 'Railway Bridge of the Silvery Tay' is a piece of uniquely engineering-based doggerel:

> Beautiful new railway bridge of the silvery Tay,
> With your strong brick piers and buttresses in so grand array;
> And your thirteen central girders, which seems to my eye,
> Strong enough all windy storms to defy.

Later in the poem comes one of the unlikeliest couplets in Scottish poetry:

> The New Yorkers boast about their Brooklyn Bridge,
> But in comparison to thee it seems like a midge.

McGonagall's eye misled him, however. In December 1879 disaster struck when the central sections of the bridge collapsed in a gale, taking with them a train and causing the deaths of all on board – at least 59 people. McGonagall sat down to compose a new poem, 'The Tay Bridge Disaster', mourning this event. Quoting the initial number of fatalities reported in the media, the opening stanza aspires to be a tragic echo of his earlier poem:

> Beautiful Railway Bridge of the Silv'ry Tay!
> Alas! I am very sorry to say
> That ninety lives have been taken away
> On the last Sabbath day of 1879,
> Which will be remember'd for a very long time.

Happily, Dundee's contemporary literary scene has developed somewhat since McGonagall. Among the writers who hail from the city are W. N. Herbert, award-winning poet Don Paterson, fiction writer A. L. Kennedy and the versatile James Meek, a journalist, non-fiction writer and novelist. Romance novelist Rosamunde Pilcher, a native of Cornwall who has sold over 60 million books (and started as a Mills and Boon writer), moved to Dundee after marrying a jute industry executive in 1946. Kate Atkinson studied at the University of Dundee and in her 2001 novel *Emotionally Weird* the institution features prominently: the book begins with a murder mystery that, it transpires, is the coursework of a Dundee creative-writing student. Kirsty Gunn, the New Zealand-born author of *The Big Music*, is a real-life professor of creative writing at the university. John Burnside, the acclaimed Scottish poet, fiction writer and memoirist, was a writer-in-residence here before becoming a professor in creative writing at the nearby University of St Andrews. His short story 'Slut's Hair', from the 2013 collection *Something Like Happy*, is a brutal story of domestic violence set in a Dundee tenement. Local farmer James Oswald is one of a number of crime writers based in the area – like Edinburgh and Glasgow, Dundee has a seamy side that lends itself perfectly to the genre. With such a diverse range of writers coming from or operating in the city, Dundee is now beginning to rival Edinburgh and Glasgow for the title of Scotland's hottest literary city.

On the eastern side of Dundee is Broughty Ferry. It's frequently described as a suburb but has the feel of a distinct town. In former days jute barons had mansions here and fishermen lived in cottages by the shore; today it's a place for pleasant afternoons strolling the beach and esplanade and for leisurely lunches in its bars and bistros. Between 1812 and 1814 Broughty Ferry was the home of Mary Wollstonecraft Godwin, who later married the poet Percy Bysshe Shelley. She was a precocious girl, described by her father, the radical philosopher William Godwin, as 'singularly bold, somewhat imperious, and active of mind'. Broughty Ferry wasn't necessarily the best place for her to showcase her creative talents. Two years later she returned to London, where she fell in love with the charismatic Shelley, who was five years older than her and already a published poet. Despite Godwin's best efforts, they eloped to the Continent, leaving Shelley's wife Harriet in England. As we have already seen, Harriet drowned herself in 1816, and Percy married Mary a few weeks later.

The genesis of Mary Shelley's novel *Frankenstein* is almost as famous as the book itself. In 1816 Mary and Percy spent time near Lake Geneva with Lord Byron and his physician John Polidori. One evening, confined indoors by bad weather, Byron suggested that each member of the party write a ghost story. This prompt provided the inspiration for *Frankenstein*, published in 1818. To this day it's one of the most enduring fables of scientific overreaching ever written, with the obsessive Victor Frankenstein and his hideous but maltreated creation living on in all manner of films, theatre productions and even cartoons. In her introduction to the 1831 reissue of the book, Mary Shelley wrote that Broughty Ferry inspired her to create imaginary worlds:

> [M]y habitual residence was on the blank and dreary northern shores of the Tay, near Dundee. Blank and dreary on retrospection I call them; they were not so to me then. They were the eyrie of freedom, and the pleasant region where unheeded I could commune with the creatures of my fancy. I wrote then – but in a most common-place style. It was beneath the trees of the grounds belonging to our house, or on the bleak sides of the woodless mountains near, that my true composition, the airy flights of my imagination, were born and fostered.

Angus

To the north and east of Dundee is Angus, a region of farming villages and fishing towns. The underappreciated Angus glens lead into the southern Cairngorms, less visited than many other parts of rural Scotland but dramatically beautiful nonetheless. On the coast above Dundee is Arbroath, a town perhaps most famous today as the home of the Arbroath smokie, a whole haddock hot-smoked to give it a deep and earthy flavour; freshly prepared, a smokie is as warming as a peat fire on a cold afternoon. However, Arbroath has a far greater claim to national significance. Arbroath Abbey was founded in 1178 by King William I, 'the Lion', and until the Reformation was one of Scotland's most distinguished monasteries. It was here in 1320 that Bernard, abbot of Arbroath and chancellor to King Robert I (Robert the Bruce), drafted one of the most important documents in Scottish history, the Declaration of Arbroath. Six years earlier, Bruce's victory over England's Edward II at the Battle of Bannockburn had proved a decisive moment in Scotland's First War of Independence. Endorsed by the nobles of Scotland, the Declaration of Arbroath entreated Pope John XXII to recognise Bruce and his successors as kings of an independent Scotland. After keeping them waiting for nine years, the Pope gave his assent. It's a stirring document, written in the tone of a great piece of political oratory: 'As long as but a hundred of us remain alive, never will we on any conditions be brought under English rule. It is in truth not for glory, nor riches, nor honours, that we are fighting, but for freedom – for that alone, which no honest man gives up but with life itself.' The surviving copy is held at the National Archives in Edinburgh, battered and fragile but still heartfelt and convincing. When the nationalist students who stole the Stone of Destiny from Westminster Abbey in 1950 left it in the ruins of Arbroath Abbey for the authorities to collect, the location was symbolic of Scotland's independent past.

When you stand at Arbroath seafront a light can be seen 11 miles out to sea. This is Bell Rock Lighthouse, built in 1811 on a shallow reef by the king of Scottish lighthouse builders, Robert Stevenson. It's an awesome construction, a tall white tower rising 35 metres from the water: at high tide the base is thoroughly submerged. Turner painted the lighthouse in a storm, with the North Sea waves reaching almost to the top as if trying to throttle the building. In the 1860s the children's author R. M. Ballantyne, best remembered for *The Coral Island*, stayed with the lighthouse keepers for two weeks before writing his 1865 adventure *The Lighthouse*.

Beyond Arbroath, the next sizeable town along the coast is Montrose, which sits at the head of a large lagoon called the Montrose Basin, a haven for migrating birds. Three miles of sandy beach run north from the town, rarely warm enough for sustained sunbathing but nevertheless a glorious place, with big skies, wildflowers growing in the dunes, and the colours of the sea fluctuating from aquamarine to gunmetal. Montrose was the childhood home of Willa Anderson, later Willa Muir, one of Scotland's leading literary intellectuals in the early twentieth century. She was a novelist, critic and, with her husband Edwin Muir, a translator. She was the senior partner in their translations of European literature, notably the long-definitive English versions of Franz Kafka's *The Castle*, *The Trial* and *Metamorphosis*. In her 1968 memoir, *Belonging*, she wrote that even at the age of three, 'I did not feel that I belonged whole-heartedly in Montrose.' Nevertheless the Muirs lived in Montrose intermittently in the decade following their marriage in 1919; they also spent time in St Andrews, a few miles south in Fife. Muir draws on her Montrose childhood in *Living with Ballads*, her landmark study of oral poetry published in 1965. The opening chapter recounts the songs she and her classmates would sing in the playground and she argues that these are a form of balladry because of their strong rhythms, simple formulaic patterns of imagery and subject matter, and oral transmission from one generation to the next.

Whilst living and writing in Montrose in the 1920s the Muirs met Christopher Murray Grieve, reporter-editor of the weekly *Montrose Review* between 1919 and 1929. It was during his stay in the town that Grieve gave birth to his pugnacious, nationalistic alter ego Hugh MacDiarmid, the pseudonym under which he published a prodigious amount of poetry as well as non-fiction concerned with

Scottish politics and culture. His collections of imagist Scots poetry, *Sangshaw* and *Penny Wheep*, date from this time, and many of his contemporaries considered these his greatest literary achievement. He also wrote his long modernist poem *A Drunk Man Looks at the Thistle* in the town, and the inebriated Scottish everyman of the title is a resident – as far as he can remember – of Montrose. MacDiarmid and Edwin Muir enjoyed a cordial relationship at first, but this soured when Muir argued in *Scott and Scotland* in 1936 that Scots was 'a language for simple poetry' – a comment that MacDiarmid, given his own poetic accomplishments, presumably felt was too close to the bone. Nevertheless MacDiarmid, ever the talented self-promoter, felt able to reflect in a late essay, titled 'The Angus Burghs', that 'In a very real sense in the 'Twenties Angus (and particularly Montrose) was the cultural centre of Scotland. There was something in the atmosphere and lay-out of Montrose very conducive to creative work [. . .] These were indeed great times in Montrose and will live in Scottish literary history.'

Another writer connected with Montrose is Violet Jacob, who was born in 1863, the daughter of the laird of nearby Dun – the family's château-inspired house is now owned by the National Trust for Scotland. Her family had owned land in the area since 1375 and she drew on their colourful history in her work, with the character of David Logie in her 1911 novel *Flemington* based on an ancestor living in the aftermath of the 1745 Jacobite rising. Jacob was one of several Angus writers to have been inspired by Scotland's oral tradition, and her short stories, like her poems, often capture the menace and eroticism of the ballads. In her short story 'The Debatable Land', published in 1922 in *Tales of my Own Country*, a rootless young woman finds work in the cottage of a widow. The widow's son tries to rape her and as she flees from him she finds herself in a clearing where a gypsy has set up camp. With his help she hides in his tent until her pursuer has gone. At the end of the story, knowing that she's no longer safe in the widow's house, she heads once more for the clearing:

The pine-scent came up from under her feet as she trod and down from the blackness overhead. [. . .] In and out of the shadows she went, her goal the clearing among the whins in the debatable land. As the steeple of distant Montrose, slumbering calmly between the marshes and the sea, rang one, she slipped out of the bushes and, going into the tent, awakened the sleeping man.

Jacob spent her final years near Kirriemuir, a town about 30 miles inland from Montrose, in the heart of Angus. Kirriemuir was the birthplace of J. M. Barrie, whose most famous work is his 1904 play *Peter Pan* (he also published the story in novel form). Barrie was born in the town in 1860 at 9 Brechin Road, a house now run as a museum to the author's life and work. Another building associated with Barrie, Moat Brae House in Dumfries, is acknowledged as the inspiration for Neverland and in 2017 a Neverland-themed garden, as well as a National Centre for Children's Literature and Storytelling, will open on the site.

In his biographical novel *Margaret Ogilvy*, published in 1896, Barrie pays tribute to his mother, one of the enduring influences in his life. It was from her, Barrie claimed, that he heard the stories about Kirriemuir life that he later turned into popular fiction. In *Margaret Ogilvy* he also describes how mechanisation changed Kirriemuir, a weaving town whose cottage industry was rapidly transformed into factory mass production with a female (and therefore cheaper) workforce. Barrie's father had been a handloom weaver, but in his fifties suddenly had to change profession. In *Margaret Ogilvy* Barrie captures the impact of industrial change on the families of Kirriemuir:

[E]very morning at half-past five the town was wakened with a yell, and from a chimney-stack that rose high into our caller [fresh] air the conqueror waved for evermore his flag of smoke [. . .] as quickly as two people may exchange seats, the daughter, till now but a knitter of stockings, became the breadwinner, he who had been the breadwinner sat down to the knitting of stockings; what had been yesterday a nest of weavers was to-day a town of girls.

Kirriemuir is renamed Thrums in the book, after the spare threads that handloom weavers kept beside them to make running repairs: Barrie's fictional creation is literally a town full of loose ends. Despite snippets of social history, the novel has a saccharine edge. Barrie used Thrums as the setting for much of his fiction, which is often described as being part of the kailyard trend in Scottish literature. In his writing small-town Scottish life is quaint and innocent; the titles of his books give a taste of their sentimentality: *Auld Licht Idylls*, *A Window in Thrums*, *The Little Minister* and *Sentimental Tommy*. Despite his use of his hometown as a literary resource, Barrie left for London in 1885 to seek his fortune. Here he wrote *Peter Pan* as well as the other two plays that brought him success in 1902, *The Admirable Crichton* and *Quality Street*; although not as famous as *Peter Pan*, the latter lives on as the inspiration for a brand of chocolates.

North Fife

Fife lies south across the Tay Bridge from Dundee, and in his poem 'At Falkland Palace', published in *Northlight* in 1988, Douglas Dunn alludes to 'Fife's lyric hills'. Above the village of Falkland are the Lomond Hills, the two highest points in Fife which are visible for miles around. Compared to the grand ridges of the Highlands, the hills seem domestic, surrounded by stone farmhouses and, a few miles away, the tidy harbour villages on Fife's eastern coast. The Fife peninsula was once the breadbasket of Scotland and is still a thriving agricultural district today. It's a region of gently undulating fields which flush red with poppies in summer; hedgerows and woodlands border the farmland. Fife as a whole, to adapt Dunn's phrase, could be described as a 'lyric landscape'.

23 Fife's 'lyric landscape'

One of the largest towns in the north of Fife is Cupar, seat of the medieval earls of Fife. Cupar Castle, built by the earls, is no longer standing, but a busy market town grew up around it and by 1357 it had its own grammar school. Among the boys likely to have been educated here was the poet and playwright Sir David Lyndsay, the son of a local landowner, born in around 1490. By 1511 Lyndsay was a member of the court of King James IV, a great patron of the arts whose reign saw a flourishing of Scottish culture. James died in 1513 at the calamitous Battle of Flodden, in which much of the Scottish nobility was wiped out by a superior English force led by the Earl of Surrey. His son James V was hastily crowned king despite being scarcely a year old. In 1542 Lyndsay, whose writing celebrated the virtues of the previous king, was knighted by James V.

In 1552 Lyndsay's play *Ane Satyre of the Thrie Estaitis* (*A Satire of the Three Estates*) was performed at Castle Hill in the centre of Cupar. Part medieval morality play, part satire on sixteenth-century politics, Lyndsay's drama features the interaction of the three powerful groups governing Scotland – the aristocracy, the clergy, and the merchant class; John the Commonweal, a representative of the commoners, also has a role. The plot involves a king using Parliament to eradicate vices in his realm, and the characters representing sensuality, wantonness and other vices are hanged towards the end. *The Thrie Estaitis* is the oldest surviving Scottish play and continues to be performed today in productions that connect Lyndsay's satire with contemporary politics. Another of Cupar's claims to literary fame is the brief mention of the town in Mary Shelley's *Frankenstein*. Victor Frankenstein, having promised to construct a mate for his monster, travels through Edinburgh, Cupar, St Andrews and Perth on his way to Orkney, where he begins his labours in a hut on a remote island.

Nine miles east of Cupar is Auchtermuchty, a town with its own connection to Gothic literature. Auchtermuchty features in an anecdote told in James Hogg's 1824 novel *The Private Memoirs and Confessions of a Justified Sinner*. The 'sinner', the over-zealous Calvinist Robert Wringhim, hears a story about the devout churchgoers of Auchtermuchty. In the midst of a religious revival in the town an old man, Robin Ruthven, is sitting on the slopes of West Lomond Hill when he hears voices – crows – whom he discerns are from 'some ither warld than this'. The birds plot to bring ruin down upon 'the lean crazy souls o' Auchtermuchty'. The next day the town's minister is gone and his mysterious replacement, clothed in black, preaches a message that is 'awful in the extreme'. The new preacher prophesies that the townsfolk will be given up to the Devil unless they reject their previous beliefs and become radically austere in their worship. As the narrator of this story observes: 'The inhabitants of Auchtermuchty were electrified – they were charmed; they were actually raving mad about the grand and sublime truths delivered to them by this eloquent and impressive preacher of Christianity. [. . .] Nothing in the world delights a truly religious people so much as consigning them to eternal damnation.' People travel from afar to hear the new minister, but this hell-fire preacher is not as pious as he seems; rather he is a demon from hell. Robin Ruthven saves the townsfolk from this supernatural threat when he lifts the preacher's gown to reveal a pair of cloven feet. Ever since then, the narrator quips, Auchtermuchty congregations have kept a firm eye on the feet of anyone who delivers a passionate sermon.

Not far to the south of Auchtermuchty is Falkland, one of the best-preserved historical villages in Fife. Its narrow streets are lined by old stone walls and its palace – built for James V in the 1530s and now open to the public – is a Renaissance mansion with luxurious gardens and orchards. Local legend tells, however, that the walled garden is haunted by the ghost of a woman named Jenny Nettles. According to a ballad written down in the eighteenth century, she committed suicide rather than be rejected by her community for bearing an illegitimate child. Falkland is the home of another ballad heroine, Kynd Kittock, a grandmother with a prodigious thirst. 'The Ballad of Kynd Kittock' is often ascribed to William Dunbar, a contemporary of Sir Robert Lyndsay who is chiefly remembered for his 'Lament for the Makars'. Written in Scots, Dunbar's is a surreal and riotous poem. After Kynd Kittock dies of thirst she makes for an 'alehouse near heaven' where 'she never ate but drank her fair measure and more'. She then sneaks in through the gate of heaven without Saint Peter seeing her, but God sees her entering and 'laughed his heart sore'. She lives contentedly in heaven for a time, looking after the Holy Mother's hens, but after seven years grows tired of heavenly ale, which she finds too sour. So she leaves heaven to have a sly mug of ale, but when she returns, Saint Peter is guarding the way, wielding a club and hitting her on the head.

St Andrews and the East Neuk of Fife

St Andrews is on the coast of north-east Fife, a town with several claims to national, and even international, significance. For the majority of its summer visitors, it's the home of golf, which has been played on the flat links land bordering the dunes since at least the sixteenth century, although according to one legend, local shepherds were knocking stones into rabbit holes with sticks in the twelfth century. But St Andrews's influence extends beyond golf. In the eighth century the relics of Saint Andrew, one of Jesus's disciples and Scotland's patron saint, were said to have been brought here. Work was begun on the town's great cathedral in 1160 and completed 150 years later, by which time it was easily the largest church in Scotland. In the Reformation, St Andrews was one of the centres of religious revolution: firebrand cleric John Knox preached here, and monuments to Protestant martyrs indicate their execution sites throughout the town. The University of St Andrews, founded between 1410 and 1413, is the oldest in Scotland and the third-oldest in the English-speaking world.

Even though St Andrews Cathedral is now a ruin, its remaining spires still dominate the skyline and the three medieval streets that pointed pilgrims to their destination form the bustling centre of the

24 *The ruins of St Andrews Cathedral, seen from the town harbour*

modern town. Near the cathedral is the town's prestigious boarding school, St Leonards, and close by is a tidal swimming pool widely believed to have been the model for the pool in Enid Blyton's Malory Towers series; Darrell Rivers, the central character in the series, goes on to study at the University of St Andrews. On a clifftop nearby is St Andrews Castle, which was the residence of the cathedral's bishops and archbishops from the twelfth century onwards. Like the cathedral, the castle was a casualty of the Reformation, but also of the elements because in 1801 the remains of the Great Hall fell into the sea. It's little wonder that the Australian poet Les Murray, writing for the year 2000 commemoration of Scots poet Robert Fergusson, describes the town as a 'Reformation bombsite'.

Fergusson is one of the many poets to have studied or taught at St Andrews. Historians believe both David Lyndsay and William Dunbar studied here, as did Gavin Douglas, who later occupied St Andrews Castle while laying claim to the bishopric of St Andrews. These poets would all have been students in the late fifteenth or early sixteenth centuries, but it's in the last 100 years that St Andrews has come into its own as a literary destination. In the 1930s a wealthy American called James H. Whyte opened the Abbey Bookshop opposite the cathedral ruins. From here he published the *Modern Scot*, an influential magazine that championed Scottish writers, including Edwin Muir and Hugh MacDiarmid, as well as support-ing Scottish nationalism. MacDiarmid lived in St Andrews for a time, as did Willa and Edwin Muir. Willa Muir was a graduate of the university, and the Muirs moved there in 1935 in the hope that they'd find inspiration in its cobbled streets and intellectual gather-ings. As it turned out, the perennially melancholy Edwin wrote little poetry there and in his autobiography, some of which was written in the town, he complained, 'We could find no one to talk to.'

Another former student of St Andrews is Alastair Reid, whose study of Classics was interrupted by his conscription into the navy in the Second World War. The son of a Church of Scotland minister from Galloway, Reid enjoyed a fairly itinerant existence after military service. In the 1950s he lived in Spain, where he assisted Robert Graves in his translation of Suetonius' *The Twelve Caesars*. Reid later had a relationship with Graves's 'muse', Margot Callas, and this unsurprisingly brought the men's friendship to an end. Reid went on to become a staff writer for the *New Yorker* and, as well as publishing his own poems and essays, he won widespread admiration for his translations, especially of Pablo Neruda and Jorge Luis Borges. While his literary talents were acclaimed, his colleague at the *New Yorker* Muriel Spark once remarked that he was the 'second worst dressed man in New York'. Intriguingly, she never revealed who the worst dressed man was.

In 1970 Reid rented Pilmour Cottage on the outskirts of St Andrews, 'an expansive country house' standing in 'a conspicuous clump of elm, oak, and sycamore trees, screened by an umbrella of resident crows, and facing the sea, some five hundred yards across the golf courses'. The cottage is still there, now somewhat absorbed into a complex of golf-related buildings, but even in Reid's time there was an 'unending plod of golfers', as he recalls in 'Digging up Scotland', collected in the 2008 volume *Outside In*. Reid notes that St Andrews is a self-contained place: 'As we settled into St Andrews, the outside world grew hazy and remote', an experience shared by students who to this day describe the town as a 'bubble'. In April 1971, when Borges visited Reid in St Andrews, the Argentinean writer was in his seventies, blind, and deeply moved by visiting Scotland. He had long been an admirer of its literature, particularly the ballads and the novels of Robert Louis Stevenson. Around the kitchen table, he recited ballads to Reid and his son. An undergraduate named Jay Parini, later to become a leading American poet, novelist and critic, was responsible for escorting Borges around town. On one memorable occasion, Parini took Borges for a walk on West Sands, a two-mile stretch of sand where the famous opening sequence from *Chariots of Fire* was later filmed. Borges, addressing the North Sea, recited the Anglo-Saxon poem 'The Seafarer'.

St Andrews in the early twenty-first century has once again become a hotbed of literary talent, with novelists, playwrights and, especially, poets lecturing in creative writing at the university. Many of Britain's leading poets have taught here, including John Burnside, Robert Crawford, Douglas Dunn, Kathleen Jamie, Don Paterson and Jacob Polley. For readers of contemporary poetry, this is a stellar list, and between them these writers have won every major British poetry award (some several times over). It's little wonder that, with so many poets in the vicinity, St Andrews is home to StAnza, an annual five-day poetry festival that attracts poets from all over the world. Also based nearby is the poet Thomas A. Clark, whose minimalist meditations on the natural world are both perceptive and poignant. Work by most of these contemporary writers, as well as by many others who have been inspired by the town over the centuries, is collected in Robert Crawford's eclectic 2005 anthology *The Book of St Andrews*. St Andrews is the setting for the historical crime novels of Shirley McKay and for T. F. Muir's modern hard-boiled stories. The bestselling Val McDermid is perhaps the most prominent crime writer to have set a novel here: in her 2003 book *The Distant Echo* four drunken students find a corpse beside a Pictish graveyard on the outskirts of town.

The coast turns west below St Andrews, and its string of villages face south into the Firth of Forth. This area is known as the East Neuk of Fife, a district of fields, beaches and old stone harbours piled with lobster creels. The hills and villages of East Lothian can be seen across the water and the Bass Rock sits in the Firth, gleaming white in the sunlight. Looking over the Firth from the East Neuk, it's easy to imagine that this is a prehistoric scene: in certain lights no human structures are visible, only the dark Lothian coast and the islands looming before it. The coastline of the East Neuk forms part of the Fife Coastal Path, and the beaches and craggy bays between St Andrews and Elie make for some of the best low-level walking in Scotland. Among those to have explored the area are two characters from Muriel Spark's novel *The Prime of Miss Jean Brodie*. Jenny and

Sandy, on holiday in Crail, take their secret notebook to a cave – of which there are several between Crail and Anstruther – in order to write a fictional erotic correspondence between Miss Brodie and her suspected lover.

Fishing was the main industry of the East Neuk in its heyday, and although the number of boats has declined considerably, there is still plenty of local seafood to savour in the villages. At Crail's tiny harbour lobsters and crabs are landed daily and can be eaten freshly cooked at the water's edge. Pittenweem's fish market supplies fish to much of Scotland and beyond, and its underrated fish and chip shop is a rival to the more celebrated fish bars of nearby Anstruther. Many Scots travel to this peaceful corner of the country for summer holidays, but the East Neuk also hosts a world-class classical music festival, and the Pittenweem Art Festival showcases the area's thriving visual arts community every August. In recent years a vibrant music scene has grown up in Anstruther, and its alternative folk musicians – from local heroes King Creosote and James Yorkston to the household name K. T. Tunstall – have put the East Neuk on the UK music map.

25 Lobsters for sale at Crail harbour

Crail is the most northerly of the East Neuk's harbour villages, a quiet place with an exciting Cold War past. Three miles away under the fields is an underground bunker, designed as a retreat for the nation's leaders in the event of a nuclear attack; the bunker was taken off the Official Secrets list in 1993 and is now a popular tourist attraction. Even closer to the village is another, less well-known, piece of Cold War history, with intriguing connections to leading twentieth-century writers. On the northern edge of the village is Crail Airfield, which in the 1950s became the base of the Joint Services School for Linguists. The brightest conscripts on national service were sent here to undertake intensive tuition in Russian language and culture. Trainees also learned espionage techniques, giving the airfield a reputation as something of a spy school. Among the graduates from this training programme were Alan Bennett, Dennis Potter and Michael Frayn, who all went on to become successful dramatists, writing for stage and television. The airbase is now derelict, the concrete shells of its buildings slowly disintegrating.

South Fife

At the south-western end of the East Neuk is Largo Bay, a wide arc-shaped curve in the Fife coast. Gannets from the Bass Rock can be seen diving in the water, and seals and porpoises are sometimes visible from the shore. At the eastern end of the bay are Elie and Earlsferry, former fishing villages now so popular with visitors they've been described as 'Edinburgh-on-Sea'. At the western end it's somewhat different, with the small industrial towns of Leven and Methil marking the way to Kirkcaldy, once the world centre of the linoleum industry. At the centre of the arc of Largo Bay is Lower Largo, which still – just about – retains the feel of the other fishing villages, with their distinctive stone architecture and golf links.

In 1676 Alexander Selkirk, the man who was to become the inspiration for Daniel Defoe's *Robinson Crusoe*, was born in Lower

Largo. Selkirk was a rebellious figure, once rebuked in church for his 'indecent carriage' (behaviour). Leaving Fife in disgrace, he became a mariner, and in 1703 sailed to Brazil on the *Cinque Ports*. When the ship's captain died in Brazil, his replacement found Selkirk antagonistic and in the autumn of 1704, after many arguments, Selkirk requested to be put ashore on the South Pacific island of Juan Fernández. The castaway lived on this uninhabited island for over four years before being rescued by Captain Woodes Rogers in February 1709. Selkirk made a curious spectacle, clothed in goat skins and, through lack of practice, scarcely able to form comprehensible words. Back in Britain in 1712 Rogers published *A Cruising Voyage Round the World*, in which he described how Selkirk managed to cope with being marooned for so long:

> He had with him his clothes and bedding, with a firelock, some powder, bullets, and tobacco, a hatchet, a knife, a kettle, a Bible, some practical pieces, and his mathematical instruments and books. He diverted and provided for himself as well as he could; but for the first eight months had much ado to bear up against melancholy [. . .] he built two huts with pimento trees, covered them with long grass, and lined them with the skins of goats [. . .] he said he was a better Christian while in this solitude than ever he was before.

Daniel Defoe is likely to have read Rogers's book, and may even have met Selkirk himself. Certainly, Robinson Crusoe's situation is similar to Selkirk's, although Defoe shifts the action to the Caribbean and adds in the dramatic twists that make his novel, published in 1719, one of the best-loved works of British fiction. Crusoe's vision of a strange footprint on the sand is one of the most arresting moments in Defoe's book: 'It happened one day, about noon, going towards my boat, I was exceedingly surprised with the print of a man's naked foot on the shore, which was very plain to be seen in the sand. I stood like one thunderstruck, or as if I had seen an apparition.' Selkirk struggled to settle back into life in Britain. At his family home in Lower Largo he constructed a cave for himself where he could imagine he was still alone. Halfway along the village's Main Street is a statue in honour of the castaway and at the seafront the Crusoe Hotel is a shrine to Selkirk and his fictional counterpart, complete with a 'Juan Fernández Bar' where a mysterious footprint is outlined on the floor.

Compared to the compact villages of the East Neuk, Kirkcaldy is a sprawling metropolis. Known locally as the 'lang toun' because of the length of its High Street, it stretches uphill from the shore of the Firth of Forth, where fragments of pottery, remains from another of the town's industries, litter the beach. The economist Adam Smith was born here in 1723, growing up on High Street. Although his career took him to the universities of Oxford, Edinburgh and Glasgow, he returned to the town of his birth in later life. He wrote his 1776 treatise *An Inquiry into the Nature and Causes of the Wealth of Nations*, one of the founding texts of capitalist economics, while living in Kirkcaldy High Street. Smith's reputation in his hometown has wavered over the last two and a half centuries. During the 1980s Smith's writing came to be associated with factory closures and neo-liberal economics. About that time Mario Vargas Llosa, the Peruvian novelist who would later win the Nobel Prize, visited Kirkcaldy hoping to visit locations associated with the economist. He left empty-handed. Visitors today looking for landmarks associated with Kirkcaldy writers may find it more fruitful to visit the town's football stadium, Starks Park, which has a stand named after Kirkcaldy-born crime writer Val McDermid.

Fifteen miles west of Kirkcaldy, not far from the Forth Road and Railway bridges, is Dunfermline, another Fife town with a long ecclesiastical history. In the twelfth century King David I supported the construction of the town's great abbey, bringing stonemasons from Durham Cathedral to work on the building. Later Scottish kings, including Robert the Bruce, were interred here. Since the Reformation sections of the abbey have fallen into ruin, although a grand neo-Gothic parish church now stands on the location of the original nave. In 1835 Andrew Carnegie was born within sight of Dunfermline Abbey, the son of a handloom weaver whose cottage industry, like that of J. M. Barrie's father in Kirriemuir, was being mechanised, leaving many redundant. The Carnegies emigrated to Pittsburgh in the United States in 1848 and Andrew worked his way up to the top of the steel industry, becoming the world's wealthiest industrialist by the time of his retirement in 1901. He was a contradictory figure, quashing unions but supporting the education of workers, and acquiring a vast fortune only to give it away in later life. Carnegie's philanthropy endowed, amongst other things, Scottish libraries and university scholarships. Like many Scots of his background, Carnegie admired the poetry of Robert Burns, and Burns's egalitarianism may have influenced Carnegie's thinking about wealth and charity. Carnegie was generous towards the town of his birth: among his gifts to Dunfermline is Pittencrief Park, a 30-hectare garden that was once a private estate but was bought by Carnegie and gifted to the people of the town.

About 400 years before Carnegie, another act of philanthropy took place when Richard Bothwell, abbot of Dunfermline, established a school for poor scholars in the town. Its teacher was Robert Henryson, who is now celebrated as one of the greatest of the 'makars' of the fifteenth and sixteenth centuries: he is one of the dead bards mourned in William Dunbar's poem 'Lament for the Makars'. Little's known about Henryson, except that he studied at the University of Glasgow and died in about 1490. He was a virtuosic poet, writing in Scots and influenced by Chaucer. In his greatest poem, *The Testament of Cresseid*, he tells the story of a Trojan woman, Cresseid, who has been abandoned by her Greek lover Diomeid. Returning to her father, she curses the gods, who subsequently put her on trial for blasphemy. They punish her by destroying her beauty and afflicting her with leprosy, so that she becomes an outcast and has to resort to begging. In the scene that lies at the heart of the poem she is given alms by Troilus, her first lover. They fail to recognise each other, but later Cresseid discovers her benefactor's identity and sends him the ring that was the first gift he ever gave her. After her death the stricken Troilus erects a monument to her memory. Henryson's account of the mythological lovers is sympathetic and moving, told in concise language, and sensitive to the moral plight of the heroine. The poem is framed by an opening scene in which the narrator, striving to keep a cold Scottish winter at bay, lights a fire and reaches for a good book:

> I mend [added fuel to] the fyre and beikit me about [warmed
>   myself by it],
> Than tuik [took] ane drink, my spreitis [spirits] to comfort,
> And armit me weill fra the cauld thairout. [from the cold outside]
> To cut the winter nicht and make it short
> I tuik ane quair [book] – and left all other sport [activities] –
> Written be worthie Chaucer glorious,
> Of fair Cresseid and worthie Troilus.

The narrator then picks up where Chaucer's story leaves off, imagining Cresseid's tragic end. In a further Scottish twist on the classical myth, Henryson's depiction of the leper colony where Cresseid ends up may well have been inspired by a similar colony near St Andrews which attracted sufferers from a wide area in Henryson's time. For a while *The Testament of Cresseid* was attributed to Chaucer himself, although it is now recognised as one of the masterpieces of early Scottish literature. In the twenty-first century Irish poet Seamus Heaney wrote a modern English version of *The Testament*, bringing it to a wider contemporary audience.

Six miles from Dunfermline are the road and rail bridges that cross the River Forth, linking the towns of North Queensferry and South Queensferry and connecting Edinburgh with Fife, Dundee and Aberdeen. The Forth had long been crossed by ferries, including, from 1850, a specially designed ferry transporting rail carriages. In 1878 construction began on a railway bridge designed by Thomas Bouch, designer of the ill-fated Tay Bridge. When the latter collapsed in 1879 Bouch's plans were abandoned and John Fowler and Benjamin Barker were commissioned to build a crossing guaranteed to remain rigid and stable in all conditions. The resulting bridge was made from 53,000 tons of red-painted steel, its cantilevered profile rising and falling in the three humps that give it its iconic appearance. Alasdair Gray, in his novel *1982 Janine*, published in 1984, mixes Scottish iconography perfectly when he describes a 'railway bridge crawling across like a steel Loch Ness monster'. Iain Banks sets part of his 1986 novel *The Bridge* in a fantastical world called the Bridge, in which the railway crossing is hundreds of miles long and supports an entire society that lives in its arches and pillars.

At the southern end of the bridges is South Queensferry, the location of the seventeenth-century Hawes Inn, the hostelry from which David Balfour begins his enforced journey in Robert Louis Stevenson's *Kidnapped*. Here Balfour is enticed onto a boat bound for America, and it's only when the ship runs aground off Mull that he can make his way back to South Queensferry in pursuit of his stolen inheritance. Stevenson doesn't mention whether or not David stopped at Hawes on his return to enjoy a well-earned mug of ale, but for the modern-day literary traveller the inn is the perfect place to relax after a journey around Scotland.

26 The Forth Rail Bridge

AUTHOR PROFILES

This section includes brief biographies of writers mentioned above, but is a non-exhaustive list. Further information on many of these writers is available in the books listed in the bibliography.

Iain Banks (1954–2013)
Born in Fife, Banks became a cult figure upon the publication in 1984 of *The Wasp Factory*, a dark and twisted novel set in the Highlands of Scotland. His 1992 novel, *The Crow Road*, was adapted by the BBC into a television series. Many of his mainstream novels are set in Scotland, but he also wrote science fiction. *Raw Spirit*, his book about whisky, is the ideal lay-person's introduction to Scotland's national drink.

John Barbour (*c.*1325–95)
Not much is known about Barbour's early life, but in 1356 he was appointed archdeacon of Aberdeen and later served as an auditor at the royal court. At the request of King Robert II he wrote *The Bruce*, an epic poem celebrating the role of Robert I (Robert the Bruce) in the early fourteenth-century Wars of Independence. The poem paints Robert I in a positive light and influenced later Scottish poets, historians and patriots.

Sir James Matthew Barrie (1860–1937)
J. M. Barrie was born in Kirriemuir, Angus, the ninth child of a handloom weaver. After graduating from the University of Edinburgh, he moved to London and quickly forged a career as a novelist and playwright. His fiction included *Auld Licht Idylls* and *A Window in Thrums*, which were based on his mother's reminiscences about small-town Scottish life. His 1904 play *Peter Pan* became a record-breaking success.

James Boswell (1740–95)

The son of the Lord Auchinleck, Boswell is most famous for his biography of Dr Samuel Johnson. Boswell toured the Highlands and Islands of Scotland with Johnson in 1773; both men later published accounts of their travels. Boswell's book, *The Journal of a Tour to the Hebrides*, is as concerned with his companion as it is with the islands they visited.

Dan Brown (1964–)

An American thriller writer, Brown's 2003 bestseller *The Da Vinci Code* captivated millions with its potent mix of symbols, codes, mythology and Catholic conspiracy. Towards the end of the novel crucial revelations are made at Rosslyn Chapel, a fifteenth-century church south of Edinburgh known for its ornate, symbolic ornamentation.

George Mackay Brown (1921–96)

Apart from a few years in Edinburgh as a mature student, Brown spent his entire life in the town of Stromness, Orkney. Here he dedicated himself to writing poems, short stories, novels and pieces of journalism about the Orkney archipelago, celebrating its Norse heritage, traditional industries and tight-knit communities. His 1994 novel *Beside the Ocean of Time* was shortlisted for the Booker Prize, but it's in poems like 'Hamnavoe Market' and 'The Year of the Whale' that his finely wrought lyricism is at its most vivid.

John Buchan (1875–1940)

Buchan was a hugely ambitious and successful man, who became a member of Parliament and governor general of Canada. He also found time to write popular thrillers, including *The Thirty-Nine Steps*. He was given the title of Lord Tweedsmuir in 1935: the Scottish Borders, near the River Tweed, was the location of childhood holidays and also the setting for Richard Hannay's adventures in *The Thirty-Nine Steps*.

Robert Burns (1759–96)

Scotland's most famous poet. Born near Alloway in Ayrshire, the son of a tenant farmer, Burns published *Poems, Chiefly in the Scottish Dialect* to acclaim in 1786. Upon achieving literary success, Burns moved to Edinburgh, where he mingled with Scotland's literati and caroused in taverns. As well as his own compositions, Burns collected old Scottish songs, recording and adapting them into such famous lyrics as 'Auld Lang Syne'. In 1788 he moved back to the south-west of Scotland, working as a farmer and later an exciseman until his death in Dumfries. Alloway is the setting for 'Tam o' Shanter', his masterpiece, and is now home to the Robert Burns Birthplace Museum.

George Gordon, Lord Byron (1788–1824)
Romantic poet and libertine whose maternal ancestors were landowners in Aberdeenshire. He spent much of his childhood in Aberdeen and attended the city's grammar school, where a statue now commemorates him. He left Scotland soon after succeeding to the title of Lord Byron in 1798; in his comic tour de force *Don Juan* he pays tribute to his Scottish ancestry.

Karel Čapek (1890–1938)
Czech novelist best remembered for coining the term 'robot'. In 1924 he travelled to the United Kingdom and recorded his impressions of the country in *Letters from England*. Despite the title, he travelled widely in Scotland, and his opinions range from praise of Edinburgh's grandeur to horror at the industrial cityscape of Glasgow.

Thomas Carlyle (1795–1881)
One of the leading intellectuals of the nineteenth century, Carlyle was born in Ecclefechan, Dumfriesshire. He married Jane Welsh and in 1825 they moved to Craigenputtock in the Borders, where they were visited by Ralph Waldo Emerson.

Catherine Carswell (1879–1946)
Modernist novelist born and brought up in Glasgow. Carswell worked as a literary reviewer and corresponded with D. H. Lawrence; her 1920 novel *Open the Door!* about a young woman growing up in middle-class Glasgow has a Lawrentian emphasis on nature and the emotions. Carswell's Glasgow is vibrant, exciting and artistic, much like the modern-day city.

John Davidson (1857–1909)
Born in Renfrewshire, Davidson grew up in Greenock and draws on the sights and sounds of the industrial town in his poetry. He moved to London in 1890 and published plays, fiction and poems, which were praised by W. B. Yeats. Debt and illness led to his suicide in 1909. His writing, pioneering in its incorporation of scientific ideas and imagery, was subsequently championed by Scottish modernists, including Hugh MacDiarmid.

Elspeth Davie (1918–95)

Novelist and short-story writer who was born in Ayrshire but spent much of her life in Edinburgh. Davie worked as an art teacher, and her experiences in that profession, as well as her ability to capture the essence of Edinburgh, inform *Creating a Scene*, her 1971 novel about a downtrodden art teacher and his precocious pupils.

Thomas De Quincey (1785–1859)

English essayist best known for *Confessions of an English Opium Eater*. De Quincey moved to Edinburgh in the hope of becoming a regular writer for the prestigious *Blackwood's* magazine. In order to avoid creditors he frequently resided in Holyrood Sanctuary, a haven for debtors. He died in Edinburgh and is buried in St Cuthbert's Churchyard, Princes Street.

Roger Deakin (1943–2006)

English writer, documentary-maker and environmental activist. His 1999 book *Waterlog*, about wild swimming in Britain's lakes and rivers, was a bestseller and an influence on the 'new nature writing' of the early twenty-first century. Deakin plunges through the pools and lochs of the Isle of Jura in one chapter of *Waterlog*, but meets his match when he attempts to swim in the Corryvreckan, the notorious whirlpool off the island's coast.

Daniel Defoe (1660–1731)

Businessman, political pamphleteer, novelist and spy. In 1706 he was sent to Edinburgh to report on opinion in the run-up to the Act of Union between Scotland and England. In 1727 he published *A Tour Through the Whole Island of Great Britain*, which included his impressions of Scotland's landscape and culture. His famous novel *Robinson Crusoe* is based on the story of Alexander Selkirk, a sailor from Lower Largo in Fife.

Gavin Douglas (*c*.1474–1522)

Son of the Earl of Angus, Douglas was born in Tantallon Castle on the East Lothian coast. He entered the priesthood, becoming provost of St Giles' in Edinburgh in 1503 and bishop of Dunkeld in 1515. Douglas was also a poet, and his translation of Virgil's *Aeneid* is one of the masterpieces of Scots-language literature.

Sir Arthur Conan Doyle (1859–1930)

Born in Edinburgh, Conan Doyle studied medicine at the University of Edinburgh. One of his teachers was Joseph Bell, whose meticulous deductions about patients were to inspire Conan Doyle when he came to invent his famous detective Sherlock Holmes. Although he wanted to be remembered as an author of historical fiction, his reputation rests almost entirely on his deerstalker-wearing sleuth.

William Dunbar (*c.*1460–*c.*1520)

In the early sixteenth century Dunbar served as court poet to King James IV. He was the leading light of the 'golden age' of Scottish culture that ended with James's death at the Battle of Flodden in 1513. His melancholy poem 'Lament for the Makars' is a roll-call of dead poets with a haunting refrain about the poet's own fear of death.

Douglas Dunn (1942–)

Contemporary poet born in Inchinnan, Renfrewshire. Dunn studied at the University of Hull, where he was influenced by Philip Larkin. Many of his collections have a Scottish emphasis, including *St Kilda's Parliament*, published in 1981. He lectured at the University of St Andrews in Fife, and the region features in his 1988 collection *Northlight*. He also edited *Scotland: An Anthology* and *The Faber Book of Twentieth-Century Scottish Poetry*.

Jennie Erdal (1951–)

Contemporary Scottish novelist, based in Fife. Her memoir, *Ghosting*, published in 2004, is an unforgettable account of life as a ghost-writer. Erdal's first novel published under her own name is *The Missing Shade of Blue*, much of which is set in and around the University of Edinburgh; the narrator is a French translator of the philosopher David Hume, who lived and worked in the city.

Michel Faber (1960–)

Born in the Netherlands, Faber moved to Scotland in 1993 and is often considered a Scottish novelist: he has won many of the country's literary awards and is published by leading Edinburgh publisher Canongate. His debut novel *Under the Skin* was published in 2000, part sci-fi horror and part satire on the ethics of eating meat. In this book the A9, the main road north from Perth, becomes the hunting ground for an alien who preys on unsuspecting hitchhikers.

Ian Hamilton Finlay (1925–2006)

Avant-garde poet and artist who was a leading figure in the international 'concrete poetry' movement of the 1960s. In 1966 Finlay and his wife Sue moved to a farmhouse near Dunsyre in Lanarkshire. Over the next 40 years they turned the surrounding land into Little Sparta, a garden filled with sculpture and engraved poems. The artworks situated in Little Sparta explore conflict, revolution and classical philosophy, but the atmosphere of this beautiful garden is meditative, peaceful and charming.

Susan Fletcher (1979–)

Contemporary English novelist who was enchanted by the landscape and history of Glencoe and lived there while researching her novel *Witch Light*, the story of a young woman who finds refuge in the glen, only to witness the Glencoe Massacre of 1692. Fletcher's novel provides a vivid impression of life in this remote, impoverished place in the seventeenth century.

Lewis Grassic Gibbon (1901–35)

Modernist novelist whose 1932 book *Sunset Song* is one of the most lauded of Scottish novels. Born James Leslie Mitchell, he grew up in the rural parish of Arbuthnott. He became a full-time author in 1929, writing no fewer than 18 books before his death at the age of 33. *Sunset Song* is set in a fictionalised version of Arbuthnott, and the novel is both an honest examination of farming life and an experiment in language and narrative style.

W. S. Graham (1918–86)

Born in the shipbuilding town of Greenock, Graham trained as a structural engineer before studying literature and becoming a poet. After 1943 he lived in Cornwall and was a member of the county's artistic community. In many of his poems he writes about the west of Scotland with affection and with the guilt of a self-imposed exile, as in the heartbreaking 'Loch Thom'. Graham's poetry is influenced by his engineering background and some of his best poems are about the coastal landscapes of Scotland and Cornwall.

Elizabeth Grant of Rothiemurchus (1797–1885)

Victorian memoirist famous for *Memoirs of a Highland Lady*, recollections of life on her Highland estate of Rothiemurchus, near Aviemore. Rothiemurchus contains some of Scotland's oldest woodlands, and today its picturesque lochs attract many visitors.

Alasdair Gray (1934–)

Scottish post-modern novelist and artist whose novel *Lanark* made a huge impact upon its publication in 1981. A sprawling tome that combines genres including science fiction and social realism, *Lanark* paints a dystopian picture of Glasgow, with many of the city's landmarks (such as Glasgow Cathedral and the Necropolis) reimagined as the sinister centres of a bleak futuristic metropolis.

Andrew Greig (1951–)

Novelist, non-fiction writer and poet who grew up in Fife and now lives in Edinburgh and Orkney. His memoir, *At the Loch of the Green Corrie*, describes his attempts to fish in a remote loch in the Assynt region of the Highlands, and his relationship with an older generation of Scottish poets, most notably Norman MacCaig.

Kirsty Gunn (1960–)

Prize-winning contemporary novelist and short-story writer, born in New Zealand but now based in Scotland. Her novel *The Big Music* was published in 2012 and is set in Sutherland, in the far north of Scotland. Gunn's intricate novel about a family of bagpipe virtuosi is, like the music it describes, complex and rich.

Neil M. Gunn (1891–1973)

Modernist novelist from Dunbeath in Caithness. Some of his fiction is historical and much of it is concerned with life in the small fishing and crofting communities of the Highlands. *Highland River*, arguably his greatest novel, is a lyrical and psychologically intense story about a young man moving from childhood to adulthood around the time of the First World War. Gunn's writing melds folklore, ancient history and a Zen-like attunement to Highland landscapes.

George Campbell Hay (1915–84)

Poet who wrote in Gaelic, Scots and English and also translated European poetry into all three languages. The son of novelist John MacDougall Hay, he grew up in Tarbert, Argyll, and during the Second World War tried to avoid conscription by hiding in this fairly depopulated region. After being caught, he served in North Africa, and some of his best writing is the war poetry to come from this experience; he also writes with local insight about the Argyll fishing communities among which he grew up.

John MacDougall Hay (1879–1919)

Novelist and Church of Scotland minister born in Tarbert on the banks of Loch Fyne. His first novel, *Gillespie*, is a tough, unsentimental portrait of an Argyll fishing village riven by poverty and gossip. He died aged 40, having published one further novel; his son was the poet George Campbell Hay.

Robert Henryson (*c.*1420–*c.*1490)

Little is known about Henryson's life, but he worked for a time as a schoolmaster in Dunfermline and was one of the poets mentioned in William Dunbar's 'Lament for the Makars'. His Scots poem *The Testament of Cresseid* extends the story told in Chaucer's *Troilus and Criseyde*, framing it with the voice of a narrator struggling to entertain himself on a miserable Scottish winter evening.

Archie Hind (1928–2008)

Writer from the East End of Glasgow who only completed one novel, *The Dear Green Place*. This powerful novel is based on Hind's own experience of combining creative ambitions with employment that would support his family. Published to critical acclaim in 1966, it's an evocative portrait of Glasgow in that period, as well as one of the best accounts of the struggles of a working-class writer.

James Hogg (1770–1835)

Romantic novelist and poet born in the Ettrick Forest in the Scottish Borders, where he worked as a shepherd. At the age of 40 he moved to Edinburgh, and pursued a literary career. Hogg's most famous work is *The Private Memoirs and Confessions of a Justified Sinner*. A subversive satire of Scottish Calvinism and Enlightenment rationality, one of the book's most memorable scenes involves a ghostly apparition seen from the crags of Arthur's Seat in Edinburgh.

Gerard Manley Hopkins (1844–89)

Poet who converted to Roman Catholicism and became a Jesuit priest. In 1881 he was temporarily posted to Glasgow, where he worked as a curate. During an excursion to Loch Lomond he stopped at the hamlet of Inversnaid and, inspired by the sound and movement of a river as it cascaded into the loch, composed the poem 'Inversnaid', one of the most vivid verbal portraits of a waterfall ever written.

David Hume, (1711–76)

Edinburgh-born philosopher who became a leading figure in the eighteenth-century Scottish Enlightenment. His religious scepticism was a barrier to an academic career, but his writings nevertheless went on to influence many Western philosophers, including Immanuel Kant and A. J. Ayer. In later life he was a neighbour of James Boswell in Edinburgh's Lawnmarket.

Violet Jacob (1863–1946)

Born near Montrose, Angus, the daughter of the laird of Dun. Her novels, short stories and poems are often set in the north-east of Scotland and influenced by the language, folklore and ballad tales of the region.

Kathleen Jamie (1962–)

Award-winning contemporary poet and essayist. Jamie grew up near Edinburgh and has taught creative writing at the universities of St Andrews and Stirling. In collections such as *The Tree House* and *The Overhaul* her poetry is meditative and lyrical, attentive to the natural world and sensitive to modern environmental concerns. She also considers Scotland's ecology and history in her entertaining and profound essays, collected in *Findings* and *Sightlines*.

Robin Jenkins (1912–2005)

Novelist who worked as a teacher in Glasgow and Argyll, as well as in Afghanistan, Malaysia and Spain. His bleakly comic novels are set in Scotland and involve subtle moral conflicts: *The Changeling*, about a well-meaning teacher who brings a pupil from a Glasgow slum on a family holiday to Argyll, explores the identity crises of both pupil and teacher while also capturing the atmosphere of postwar Glaswegian holidays in the Firth of Clyde.

Dr Samuel Johnson (1709–84)

England's pre-eminent man of letters in the eighteenth century. In 1773 he travelled to the Highlands and Islands of Scotland with James Boswell; their trip became an iconic literary journey. Two years after the voyage Johnson published *A Journey to the Western Islands of Scotland*.

Arthur Johnston (*c*.1579–1641)

Born in Aberdeenshire, Johnston was educated at Kings College, Aberdeen, and was made lord rector there following a long period in continental

Europe. Along with George Buchanan, he is the most celebrated of Scottish poets to have written in Latin, and his best poems celebrate Aberdeen and its surrounding countryside.

John Keats (1795–1821)
Romantic poet born in London. After qualifying as a physician and apothecary, Keats undertook a walking tour of Scotland in 1818. He visited the cottage where Robert Burns was born, sailed to the Hebrides, and climbed Ben Nevis. Keats wrote poems and letters at every stage of his tour, which ended with an Inverness doctor recommending he return home due to exhaustion.

James Kelman (1946–)
Glasgow-based novelist who won the 1994 Booker Prize for *How Late It Was, How Late*, a stream-of-conscious account of a blind, downtrodden, foul-mouthed Glaswegian man. Kelman's work is almost always set in Glasgow, and although novels such as *The Busconductor Hines* and *Kieron Smith, Boy* don't describe the city's landmarks in any detail, he captures the soul of the city better than anyone else.

Jessie Kesson (1916–94)
Novelist born in Inverness and brought up in nearby Elgin. From an impoverished upbringing she eventually became a BBC radio producer. Her novel *The White Bird Passes* is a semi-autobiographical account of a young woman struggling to overcome material and psychological pressures while living in the backstreets of Elgin.

Eric Linklater (1899–1974)
Prolific novelist who lived for several years in Orkney and came to be associated with the Scottish Renaissance of the 1920s and 1930s. In 1933 he was the National Party of Scotland candidate in the East Fife by-election; he satirised his unsuccessful campaign a year later in the novel *Magnus Merriman*, an entertaining and still-relevant political farce featuring wry observations about Edinburgh and earthy descriptions of farming life in Orkney.

Sir David Lyndsay (*c.*1490–1555)
Son of a landowner who lived near the Fife market town of Cupar, Lyndsay was a member of the royal courts of James IV and James V; he

was knighted by the latter in 1542. His play *Ane Satyre of the Thrie Estaitis* was first performed in Cupar in 1552. *Ane Satyre* is the oldest surviving Scottish play.

Alexander McArthur (1901–47)
A baker from Glasgow's Gorbals district, McArthur wrote novels about slum life while he was unemployed in the early 1930s. One of these novels sufficiently impressed Longmans publishers that they commissioned a journalist, H. Kingsley Long, to help McArthur turn it into a bestseller. Published as *No Mean City* in 1935, it sold around a million copies and helped cement Glasgow's reputation for gangs, knife crime and shocking poverty.

Norman MacCaig (1910–96)
Poet who worked as a teacher in Edinburgh and spent his summers in Assynt in the north-west Highlands. Much of his poetry is set in one or other of these locations and ranges from deft studies of city life to lyrical meditations on the natural world. MacCaig's Assynt poems, concerned with the mountains, lochs, villages and wildlife of the region, are essential reading for any traveller to the north-west.

Hugh MacDiarmid (1892–1978)
The pseudonym of Christopher Murray Grieve, modernist poet, political activist and leading light in the twentieth-century Scottish Renaissance. MacDiarmid's poems in Scots, from the lyric poems in the collection *Sangshaw* to the ambitious long poem *A Drunk Man Looks at the Thistle*, reinvigorated the language with modern issues and ideas. His later poems in English are the collages of an intellectual magpie, referencing philosophy, science, politics and many other subjects. A founder member of the National Party of Scotland, he was an outspoken commentator on Scottish affairs. Montrose, Biggar and the Shetland island of Whalsay are among the places connected with his life and work.

Robert Macfarlane (1976–)
One of the leading figures in the 'new nature writing' genre, Macfarlane's acclaimed books about British cultural history and landscape include *The Wild Places* and *The Old Ways*. The Highlands and Islands feature prominently in his writing.

William Topaz McGonagall (1825–1902)

A handloom weaver from Dundee, McGonagall was in his fifties when he was gripped by a 'strong desire to write poetry'. His invariably clunky verse reported on the major issues of the day, from the collapse of the Tay Railway Bridge to the conversion of Loch Katrine into a reservoir.

William McIlvanney (1936–2015)

Novelist from Kilmarnock, Ayrshire. His novel *Docherty*, about a family of Ayrshire coal miners, is a powerful and perceptive account of working-class life in the early twentieth century. *Laidlaw* is a gritty crime thriller featuring a detective inspector who reads existentialist philosophy. Published in 1977 and set in down-at-heel corners of Glasgow, *Laidlaw* influenced the next generation of Scottish crime writers.

Duncan Ban Macintyre (1723?–1812)

Born in Glen Orchy on the eastern edge of Argyll, Macintyre worked as a gamekeeper and forester. His long Gaelic poem 'In Praise of Ben Dorain' is a virtuosic tribute to the mountain that dominates the glen: a rhythmical, musical composition that is alive to the subtleties of the mountain environment. Compelled to leave the glen in the 1760, Macintyre settled in Edinburgh, where he served in the city guard. A memorial to him stands in Edinburgh's Greyfriars Kirkyard.

Sir Compton Mackenzie (1883–1972)

Although brought up in England, Mackenzie became increasingly enamoured with Scotland in the 1920s. In 1925 he bought the Shiant Islands, a small, rocky archipelago east of Harris; in 1933 he relocated to Barra, the Hebridean island which inspired his comic novel *Whisky Galore*. He was a founder member of the National Party of Scotland and at his Barra home he played host to many writers, artists, nationalists and romantics.

Bernard MacLaverty (1942–)

Contemporary novelist from Belfast, Northern Ireland, who now lives in Glasgow. His novel *Grace Notes*, about a young composer struggling to earn her living while raising a child, is set in the city and on the Hebridean island of Islay. While MacLaverty brings these two very different places to life, it's the depth of character and the exhilarating descriptions of music that make *Grace Notes* unforgettable.

Sorley MacLean (1911–96)

Influential Gaelic modernist poet born on the island of Raasay and educated on Skye. Much of MacLean's poetry is about the landscapes and history of these two islands. His poem 'Hallaig', set in a ruined township on Raasay, is his most popular work; *The Cuillin*, about Skye's jagged mountain range, is a wide-ranging poem that alludes to Scottish history, European politics, Marxism and psychology.

Louis MacNeice, (1907–63)

Anglo-Irish poet who in 1937 was commissioned to write a travel book about the Outer Hebrides. Finding Hebridean hotels and cuisine rather basic, and surprised by the extent to which Gaelic (which he didn't speak) was the language of the islands, MacNeice produced *I Crossed the Minch*. The book is a study in boredom as much as a guide to the Scottish islands and occasionally features breathtaking descriptions of the Hebrides.

Kevin MacNeil (1972–)

Poet and novelist who grew up in the Outer Hebrides. His novel *The Stornoway Way* is a foul-mouthed, whisky-fuelled riposte to the notion that Hebridean life is all pastoral tranquillity and Celtic mysticism. MacNeil has also edited *These Islands, We Sing*, an anthology of Scottish island poetry.

John McPhee (1931–)

American non-fiction writer and staff writer at the *New Yorker* magazine. McPhee's ancestors emigrated from Colonsay in the Inner Hebrides, and in 1969 McPhee lived on the island for several months. His book about the island, *The Crofter and the Laird*, is filled with illuminating details about Colonsay's history, culture and mythology. In other essays, collected in *Pieces of the Frame*, McPhee writes about the whisky industry, the Loch Ness Monster and the legendary castle of Macbeth, all in immaculate, wry prose.

James Macpherson (1736–96)

Poet and literary fraudster. Macpherson collected Gaelic poems in the Highlands. When he published the poem *Fingal*, he claimed that he'd discovered and translated an epic about the titular third-century Celtic hero, composed by Fingal's son Ossian. The poem was hugely successful and influenced the emerging Romantic movement, but it transpired that most of *Fingal* was Macpherson's own invention.

Martin Martin (*c.*1660–1719)

Early Scottish travel writer and a native of Skye. Martin's *A Late Voyage to St Kilda* was published in 1698, followed by *A Description of the Western Islands of Scotland* in 1703. Samuel Johnson claimed that Martin's *Description* was the inspiration for his own tour of the Hebrides in 1773. Martin's eclectic observations, punctuated with plenty of outlandish superstitions, are never less than enthralling.

Gavin Maxwell (1914–69)

Writer and naturalist, born in Wigtownshire. In 1944 he bought the island of Soay, south of Skye, and set up a commercial – and ultimately unsuccessful – basking shark fishery on the island. He wrote about this work in *Harpoon at a Venture*. He later settled at Sandaig, a remote cove on the mainland with views over to Skye. Here he raised two wild otters, Mijbil and Edal, the stars of his eloquent and immensely popular memoir *Ring of Bright Water*.

Hugh Miller (1802–56)

Stonemason from Cromarty in the Black Isle whose trade led to his interest in geology. Miller became one of the leading geological writers of the nineteenth century, his work characterised by simple, vivid explanations of complex ideas. As well as making his own geological discoveries, Miller's books, including *The Old Red Sandstone*, brought the subject to a wide readership.

Naomi Mitchison (1897–1999)

Prolific novelist, poet and non-fiction writer. Mitchison's long and varied career included being appointed honorary mother of a Botswanan tribe. From the 1940s until her death Mitchison lived in Carradale, a small village near Campbeltown in Argyll. Her memoir *Among You Taking Notes*, written as part of the Mass Observation project, is an earthy yet intellectual account of life in rural Argyll during the Second World War.

Edwin Morgan (1920–2010)

Poet closely associated with Glasgow, the city of his birth. He was a lecturer at the University of Glasgow and enjoyed a long poetic career in which he wrote in a number of styles, from 'concrete poetry' to conventional sonnets, as well as translating into English and Scots from a wide range of languages. In 2004 he was appointed Scotland's first makar, or national poet. Some of his writing explores Glasgow's seamier side, but light-hearted work about mythical beasts and the clichés of Scottish culture is another aspect of his large oeuvre.

Edwin Muir (1887–1959)

Born in Orkney, Muir moved to Glasgow aged 14, and the shift from a peaceful rural island to a sprawling industrial city was one of the greatest upheavals of his life. He began to write poetry in his thirties, and his work often idealises the islands he spent his childhood on. In 1919 he married Willa Anderson and they collaborated on translations of European writers, including Franz Kafka.

Willa Muir (1890–1970)

Novelist, literary critic and translator. After marrying the poet Edwin Muir, Willa Muir returned for a time to Montrose, the Angus town where she grew up; the Muirs also spent time in Germany, Italy, Austria and Czechoslovakia. Her influential *Living with Ballads*, a study of Scotland's oral culture, opens with an analysis of the playground songs she learned as a schoolgirl in Montrose.

Alice Munro (1931–)

Canadian short-story writer and winner of the 2013 Nobel Prize for Literature. Munro's ancestors emigrated from the Scottish Borders in the nineteenth century, and she is a distant relation of the Romantic novelist James Hogg. She explores this connection, and her impressions upon visiting her ancestral homeland, in *The View from Castle Rock*, a collection that hovers between fiction, memoir and family history.

Adam Nicolson (1957–)

Author of numerous non-fiction books about literature, landscape and history. Nicolson inherited the Shiant Isles (which had formerly been owned by Compton Mackenzie) from his father at the age of 21. His memoir *Sea Room* is a love song to this tiny cluster of islands, filled with striking descriptions of their natural history as well as anecdotes about the difficulties of living there.

Andrew O'Hagan (1968–)

Contemporary Scottish novelist and non-fiction writer. O'Hagan grew up in Ayrshire and studied in Glasgow. His novel *Our Fathers* is the story of a man who built tower blocks for social housing. The novel is an elegiac but unsentimental tribute to Scotland's twentieth-century socialists and trade unionists, who played a huge part in the nation's politics.

George Orwell (1903–50)

Pseudonym of Eric Arthur Blair, English novelist and essayist best known for his dystopian masterpiece *Nineteen Eighty-Four* and his haunting political fable *Animal Farm*. In 1946, looking for a quiet retreat in which to work on *Nineteen Eighty-Four*, Orwell moved to an isolated farmhouse at the northern end of the island of Jura. Plagued by ill health and grieving for his recently deceased wife, Orwell lived there for almost three years.

Beatrix Potter (1866–1943)

Children's author who spent many holidays in Birnam, north of Perth. Here she developed an interest in natural history and sent illustrated letters to children she knew. One of these letters was later extended into *The Tale of Peter Rabbit*, one of her best-loved stories. The arts centre at Birnam contains a museum dedicated to Potter.

Ross Raisin (1979–)

Contemporary novelist from Yorkshire. His second book, *Waterline*, is the story of a retired Glasgow shipbuilder grieving for his wife, who died from asbestosis contracted through washing his contaminated clothes. *Waterline* examines the decline of the once-dominant shipbuilding industry, the effect of deindustrialisation on Glasgow's working-class communities, and the male Glaswegian psyche.

Ian Rankin (1960–)

Born in Fife, Rankin is one of Britain's leading crime writers. Many of his books feature Detective Inspector John Rebus, a hard-drinking, curmudgeonly but ultimately sensitive Edinburgh cop. With locations ranging from famous city landmarks to dingy strip clubs, and featuring characters including politicians, gangsters, asylum seekers and environmentalists, Rankin's books are unsurpassed in the way they capture the mood and complexity of contemporary Edinburgh.

Alastair Reid (1926–2014)

Poet, translator and essayist. Born in Wigtownshire, Reid travelled widely following service in the Second World War, and became a staff writer for the

New Yorker. In the early 1970s Reid rented a cottage in St Andrews, Fife, and here he was visited by Jorge Luis Borges. Reid's poems and prose are collected in two volumes, *Outside In* and *Inside Out.*

James Robertson (1958–)
Scottish novelist whose 2010 book *And the Land Lay Still* is an epic saga covering much of Scottish political and cultural life in the twentieth century. Set mainly in Edinburgh, it also contains a memorable, if somewhat desolate, scene at Sandwood Bay in the far north of the country.

J. K. Rowling (1965–)
Whilst working on *Harry Potter and the Philosopher's Stone*, the first in her phenomenally successful series of children's books, Rowling lived in Leith. The streets and graveyards of Edinburgh's Old Town offer tantalising connections for dedicated Harry Potter fans.

Dorothy L. Sayers (1893–1957)
Crime writer who spent several holidays in Galloway and Kirkcudbright in the south-west of Scotland. Her 1931 whodunit *The Five Red Herrings* is set in this region and characterises it as a leisurely place populated by painters and fly fishermen. When a cantankerous artist dies in suspicious circumstances and six suspects emerge, Sayers's detective Lord Peter Wimsey has to ruffle a few feathers to separate the true killer from the red herrings.

Sir Walter Scott (1771–1832)
Romantic poet and pioneer of historical fiction. His long poems such as *The Lay of the Last Minstrel* and *The Lady of the Lake* enthralled a large readership with their combination of clan history, misty glens, tranquil lochs and luscious language. When Scott switched to writing fiction, he was even more successful, and in novels such as *Waverley* and *Rob Roy*, which were similarly full of heroic Highland clansmen and stirring landscapes, he played a significant part in the formation of Scotland's modern image. Scott's commercial success funded the building of Abbotsford House near Melrose, now a marvellous visitor attraction.

Mary Wollstonecraft Shelley (née Godwin) (1797–1851)
Romantic novelist and author of *Frankenstein*. As a teenager she lived for two years in Broughty Ferry, to the east of Dundee, and she later claimed

that her time in Tayside was an important stage in her development as a writer. After returning to London in 1814 she eloped with the poet Percy Bysshe Shelley, and during their travels on the Continent she came up with the idea for her famous novel.

Percy Bysshe Shelley (1792–1822)
Romantic poet. Three years before he eloped to Europe with Mary Wollstonecraft Godwin, he eloped to Edinburgh with Harriet Westbrook. They were married in 1811 at 225 Canongate, on the Royal Mile, and stayed in the city for several weeks.

Nan Shepherd (1893–1981)
Scottish writer whose three modernist novels, published between 1928 and 1933, are thoughtful and descriptive stories of life in the rural north-east of Scotland, where Shepherd spent her whole life. *The Living Mountain*, her lyrical, mystical, ecologically sensitive book about the Cairngorm mountains, lay in a drawer for decades before being published, but has slowly come to be recognised as one of the masterpieces of twentieth-century nature writing.

Alexander McCall Smith (1948–)
Bestselling author of the No. 1 Ladies' Detective Agency series. Based in Edinburgh, his Scotland Street novels are a gentle introduction to the city. The cafés, venues and delicatessens mentioned in the books are invariably worth visiting, for their own qualities as well as for their literary connections.

Iain Crichton Smith (1928–98)
Poet, novelist, short-story writer and playwright, working in both Gaelic and English. Smith grew up on the island of Lewis, the subject of many of his poems. His novel *Consider the Lilies*, written in disarmingly simple language, is a powerful story about the effects of the Highland Clearances in Sutherland in the nineteenth century.

Tobias Smollett (1721–71)
The son of a landowner in West Dunbartonshire, Smollett combined work as a surgeon with a literary career. His picaresque novel *The Expedition of Humphry Clinker*, published in the year of his death, is written in the form of a series of letters by characters touring Scotland and England. His memorial stands in Renton, West Dunbartonshire.

Dame Muriel Spark (1918–2006)

Often described as Scotland's leading twentieth-century novelist. Spark's masterpiece is *The Prime of Miss Jean Brodie*, the complex story of an Edinburgh schoolteacher who cultivates devotion in her pupils. A remarkable psychological character study, full of wonderful descriptions of the city, it's essential reading for visitors to Edinburgh. Spark grew up in Edinburgh, but spent much of her adult life in New York, London and Tuscany.

Robert Louis Stevenson (1850–94)

Novelist, poet and essayist, Stevenson was born in Edinburgh into a renowned family of lighthouse engineers. Troubled by ill health, he began his first book, *Treasure Island*, while convalescing in Braemar in the Highlands. In novels including *Kidnapped* and *Catriona* he set adventures in Scotland's turbulent past. *The Strange Case of Dr Jekyll and Mr Hyde*, whilst ostensibly set in London, owes a lot to Stevenson's Edinburgh upbringing.

Bram Stoker (1847–1912)

Gothic novelist of the late nineteenth century who visited Cruden Bay, Aberdeenshire, whilst working on his iconic *Dracula*. Nearby Slains Castle, an imposing clifftop ruin, is rumoured to have been Stoker's inspiration for Castle Dracula, his vampire's Transylvanian lair.

Derick Thomson (1921–2012)

Gaelic poet, translator, publisher and scholar. Thomson was born on the island of Lewis and lectured in Celtic studies at the University of Glasgow. Regarded as the leading authority on Gaelic language and culture, he was the first poet to write free verse in Gaelic, and although his writing is often concerned with the Highlands, his frame of reference is modern and cosmopolitan.

James Thomson (1834–82)

Poet from Port Glasgow, Inverclyde, who wrote under the pseudonym B. V. His dystopian long poem *The City of the Dreadful Night* is set in an unnamed, nightmarish industrial city that combines the worst aspects of Glasgow and London.

Jules Verne (1828–1905)

French novelist best known for his science fiction writing. Verne claimed Scottish ancestry, and three of his novels are set in the country. These include *Backwards to Britain*, a semi-fictional account of his 1859 travels around Scotland. In the Trossachs, Verne's protagonist turns literary tourist, relishing the fact that he's exploring the landscape made famous in Sir Walter Scott's *Rob Roy*.

Irvine Welsh (1958–)

Novelist from Leith who shot to fame with his 1993 book *Trainspotting*, later made into a successful film. A story of heroin addicts, criminals and chancers scraping by in run-down corners of Edinburgh, *Trainspotting* provides a unique, sometimes grotesque, perspective on Scotland's capital. A sign of Edinburgh's evolution is the fact that many of the book's locations have now been gentrified and redeveloped, making a *Trainspotting* tour of the city almost impossible.

Louise Welsh (1965–)

Glasgow novelist whose 2002 debut *The Cutting Room* is a crime novel set in the underworld of the city's sex trade. The book is full of famous Glasgow locations, including the Necropolis, and explores other aspects of the modern city, from its gay sub-culture to its religious sectarianism.

Virginia Woolf (1882–1941)

Leading modernist novelist associated with the Bloomsbury Group of the early twentieth century. In 1927 she published *To the Lighthouse*, set on the Isle of Skye, a place she didn't visit until several years after writing the novel.

Dorothy Wordsworth (1771–1855)

Romantic writer and diarist, sister of the poet William Wordsworth. In 1803 she and her brother made a tour of Scotland, travelling through the Borders and into the Highlands. For a while they were accompanied by Samuel Taylor Coleridge. Her journal of the trip, later published as *Recollections of a Tour Made in Scotland*, is an entertaining and illuminating piece of travel writing.

William Wordsworth (1770–1850)

Romantic poet, appointed British poet laureate in 1843. His publications include the influential *Lyrical Ballads* and the long, autobiographical poem *The Prelude*. He spent much of his life in Grasmere, in the Lake District. During his 1803 tour of Scotland, Wordsworth wrote poems about many of the landmarks he visited. He and his sister Dorothy were shown around the Borders by Walter Scott, then an aspiring poet and country sheriff.

CHRONOLOGY OF EVENTS

	Literary and Cultural Events	*Political Events*
*c.*3200 BC	Neolithic village of Skara Brae, Orkney, first inhabited.	
*c.*2800 BC	Chambered tomb of Maeshowe constructed in Orkney.	
*c.*325 BC	Pytheas travels at least as far north as Shetland and is the first Greek to write about Scotland.	
55 BC		Romans under Julius Caesar invade Britain.
AD 122		Emperor Hadrian begins construction of Hadrian's Wall.
*c.*214		Romans withdraw from Scotland.
*c.*500		The Irish 'Scoti', or Scots, colonise the west coast of Scotland.
563	St Columba arrives in Scotland and establishes a monastery on the island of Iona.	
*c.*740	Ruthwell Cross inscribed with sections of the Anglo-Saxon poem *The Dream of the Rood*.	
*c.*840		Kenneth MacAlpin unifies the east and west kingdoms of Scotland into one country.

	Literary and Cultural Events	Political Events
*c.*860		Norse earldom established in Orkney and Shetland. Western Isles also fall under Norse rule.
1040		Macbeth defeats and kills Duncan I, becoming king.
1057		Macbeth killed by Malcolm Canmore.
*c.*1200	*Orkneyinga Saga* compiled.	
1266		Western Isles ceded to Scotland by Norway.
1286		Death of Alexander III, leading to succession crisis and the Wars of Independence with England.
1296		Edward I of England invades Scotland.
1297		William Wallace leads rebellion against English; wins the Battle of Stirling Bridge.
1305		Wallace captured and executed.
1314		Robert the Bruce defeats Edward II of England at the Battle of Bannockburn.
1320	The Declaration of Arbroath, asserting Scottish independence, submitted to Pope John XXII.	
1328		Edward III of England recognises Scottish independence.
1375	John Barbour completes his epic verse history *The Bruce*.	

	Literary and Cultural Events	*Political Events*
1469		James III marries Margrethe of Denmark; Scotland acquires Orkney and Shetland as part of the dowry.
*c.*1477	Blind Harry's *Wallace*, an epic poem about the freedom fighter, is completed.	
*c.*1485	Robert Henryson writes *The Testament of Cresseid*.	
1513	Gavin Douglas completes the *Eneados*, his Scots translation of Virgil's *Aeneid*.	James IV and most of the Scottish nobility killed at the Battle of Flodden.
1552	Sir David Lyndsay's play *Ane Satyre of the Thrie Estaitis* performed in Cupar.	
1560		Scottish Parliament accepts the Reformation.
1567		Mary Queen of Scots deposed and tried in England; executed in 1587.
1603		Union of the Crowns: James VI of Scotland becomes James I of England.
1611	Premiere of Shakespeare's *Macbeth*.	
1649		Execution of Charles I.
1660		Restoration of Charles II.
1688		The 'Glorious Revolution': James II deposed; in 1689 William and Mary accept English and Scottish crowns.
1692		Glencoe Massacre.
1698– 1700		Darien colonial expedition.

	Literary and Cultural Events	Political Events
1703	Martin Martin publishes *A Description of the Western Islands of Scotland*.	
1707	Daniel Defoe active as spy and propagandist prior to Union.	Act of Union: Scotland becomes part of the United Kingdom.
1715		Jacobite rising fails after the inconclusive Battle of Sheriffmuir.
1719	Daniel Defoe's *Robinson Crusoe* published.	
1725		General Wade starts his Highland road-building project.
1745		Jacobite rising led by Bonnie Prince Charlie, which ends in defeat at Battle of Culloden in 1746.
1761	James Macpherson publishes *Fingal*.	
1773	James Boswell and Samuel Johnson travel in the Hebrides, and each later publishes a book about the journey.	
1776	David Hume, leading figure in the Scottish Enlightenment, dies; Adam Smith publishes *The Wealth of Nations*.	
1786	Robert Burns publishes *Poems, Chiefly in the Scottish Dialect*.	
1792		The 'Year of the Sheep', the first mass emigration from the Highlands to Canada during the Highland Clearances.

	Literary and Cultural Events	Political Events
1803	William and Dorothy Wordsworth tour Scotland, accompanied for part of the way by Coleridge.	
1810	Walter Scott publishes *The Lady of the Lake*.	
1814	Walter Scott publishes *Waverley*.	
1818	John Keats tours Scotland on foot.	
1822		Royal visit of George IV to Edinburgh.
1824	James Hogg publishes *The Private Memoirs and Confessions of a Justified Sinner*.	
1833	Ralph Waldo Emerson meets Thomas Carlyle at Craigenputtock.	
1859	Jules Verne tours Scotland and records his experiences in *Backwards to Britain*.	
1879		Tay Bridge Disaster, which is 'elegised' by William McGonagall.
1881	Gerard Manley Hopkins visits Inversnaid, on Loch Lomond.	
1883	Robert Louis Stevenson publishes *Treasure Island*.	
1886	Robert Louis Stevenson publishes *Kidnapped*, set in the aftermath of the 1745 Jacobite rising.	
1887	The first of Arthur Conan Doyle's Sherlock Holmes stories published.	
1904	Premiere of J. M. Barrie's *Peter Pan*.	

	Literary and Cultural Events	*Political Events*
1919		'Red Clydeside' riots in Glasgow. The British government, fearing a Bolshevist revolution, responds with tanks and armed troops.
1926	Hugh MacDiarmid publishes *A Drunk Man Looks at the Thistle*.	
1928		National Party of Scotland founded: among the founder-members are Hugh MacDiarmid and Compton Mackenzie.
1932	Lewis Grassic Gibbon publishes *Sunset Song*.	
1933	Hugh MacDiarmid moves to Whalsay, Shetland.	
1937	Louis MacNeice tours the Hebrides and writes *I Crossed the Minch*.	
1943	Sorley MacLean publishes *Dàin do Eimhir* (*Poems to Eimhir*), bringing literature in Gaelic into the twentieth century.	
1946	George Orwell moves to Jura, where he writes *Nineteen Eighty-Four*.	
1950		A group of young Scottish nationalists abduct the Stone of Destiny from Westminster Abbey.
1961	Muriel Spark publishes *The Prime of Miss Jean Brodie*.	
1966	Archie Hind publishes *The Dear Green Place*; Ian Hamilton Finlay moves to Stonypath, the croft he transformed into the 'poetry garden' Little Sparta.	

	Literary and Cultural Events	*Political Events*
1979		Referendum on the creation of a devolved Scottish Assembly, in which the majority who voted 'yes' form an insufficient proportion of the total electorate for the act establishing the assembly to be ratified.
1981	Alasdair Gray publishes *Lanark*.	
1994	James Kelman wins the Booker Prize for *How Late It Was, How Late*.	
1997	J. K. Rowling publishes *Harry Potter and the Philosopher's Stone*; Ian Rankin's *Black and Blue* makes him a crime-writing superstar.	Referendum in which Scots vote to establish a devolved Scottish Parliament.
2003	Dan Brown's *The Da Vinci Code* becomes a worldwide bestseller and starts a tourist boom at Rosslyn Chapel.	
2004	Edwin Morgan named as Scotland's inaugural makar, or national poet.	
2011		The Scottish National Party win a landslide victory in elections for the Scottish Parliament, promising a referendum on Scottish independence.
2014		Scottish Independence Referendum takes place, with 55 per cent voting to remain part of the UK.

Select Bibliography

The details listed below are for the editions I have consulted. Where useful, dates of original publication are supplied in square brackets.

Anon., *Orkneyinga Saga: The History of the Earls of Orkney*, trans. H. Pálsson and P. Edwards, London, Penguin, 1981.

Atkinson, E., *Greyfriars Bobby*, London, Puffin Classics, 1994 [1912].

Banks, I., *The Crow Road*, London, Abacus, 2013 [1992].

Banks, J. T., *Congenial Spirits: The Selected Letters of Virginia Woolf*, London, Hogarth, 1989.

Barker, E., *O Caledonia and Short Stories*, Norwich, Black Dog Books, 2010 [1991].

Barker, P., *The Regeneration Trilogy*, London, Penguin, 2014 [1996].

Barrie, J. M., *Margaret Ogilvy*, London, Hodder and Stoughton, 1896.

Brown, D., *The Da Vinci Code*, London, Bantam, 2003.

Brown, G. M., *Portrait of Orkney*, London, John Murray, 1988.

—— *The Collected Poems of George Mackay Brown*, ed. A. Bevan and B. Murray, London, John Murray, 2005.

—— *For the Islands I Sing*, Edinburgh, Polygon, 2008 [1997].

Buchan, J., *The Thirty-Nine Steps*, London, William Blackwood and Sons, 1915.

Buchanan, G. and A. Johnston, *Apollos of the North: Selected Poems of George Buchanan and Arthur Johnston*, ed. and trans. R. Crawford, Edinburgh, Polygon, 2006.

Burns, R., *Selected Poems*, London, Penguin, 1993.

Byron, G. G., *The Major Works*, ed. J. J. McGann, Oxford, Oxford University Press, 2008.

Čapek, K., *Letters from England*, trans. P. Selver, London, Geoffrey Bles, 1943.

Carlyle, T., *Reminiscences*, Oxford, Oxford University Press, 1997 [1881].

Carswell, C., *Open the Door!*, Edinburgh, Canongate, 1996 [1920].

Crawford, R., *The Bard: Robert Burns, a Biography*, London, Jonathan Cape, 2009.

Davie, E., *Creating a Scene*, London, Calder & Boyars, 1971.

Deakin, R., *Waterlog: A Swimmer's Journey through Britain*, London, Vintage, 2000.

Defoe, D., *A Tour Through the Whole Island of Great Britain*, London, Penguin, 1978 [1724].

—— *Robinson Crusoe*, London, Penguin, 2003 [1719].

Donaldson, I., *Ben Jonson: A Life*, Oxford, Oxford University Press, 2011.

Doyle, A. C., *Memories and Adventures*, London, Hodder and Stoughton, 1924.

Dunn, D., *New Selected Poems, 1964–2000*, London, Faber and Faber, 2003.

Emerson, R. W., *English Traits*, Boston, MA: Philips, Sampson & Co., 1856.

Erdal, J., *The Missing Shade of Blue*, London, Little, Brown, 2012.

Faber, M., *Under the Skin*, Edinburgh, Canongate, 2000.

Fletcher, S., *Witch Light*, London, Fourth Estate, 2011.

Francis, G., *True North: Travels in Arctic Europe*, Edinburgh, Polygon, 2010.

Galloway, J., *The Trick is to Keep Breathing*, Edinburgh, Polygon, 1991.

Gibbon, L. G., *Sunset Song*, Edinburgh, Canongate, 2006 [1932].

—— and H. MacDiarmid, *Scottish Scene*, London, Jarrolds, 1934.

Graham, W. S., *New Collected Poems*, London, Faber and Faber, 2004.

Grant., E., *Memoirs of a Highland Lady*, ed. A. Tod, Edinburgh, Canongate, 2006 [1898].

Graves, R. and A. Hodge, *The Long Weekend: A Social History of Great Britain, 1918–1939*, London, Abacus, 1995 [1940].

Gray, A., *1982 Janine*, London, Jonathan Cape, 1984.

—— *Lanark*, Edinburgh, Canongate, 2002 [1981].

Greig, A., *At the Loch of the Green Corrie*, London, Quercus, 2010.

Gunn, K., *The Big Music*, London, Faber and Faber, 2012.

Gunn, N. M., *Highland River*, Edinburgh, Canongate, 1997 [1937].

Hay, G. C., *The Collected Poems and Songs of George Campbell Hay*, ed. M. Byrne, Edinburgh, Edinburgh University Press, 2002.

Hay, J. M., *Gillespie*, Edinburgh, Canongate, 2001 [1914].

Hind, A., *The Dear Green Place* [1966] *and Fur Sadie*, Edinburgh, Polygon, 2008.

Hogg, J., *Anecdotes of Sir W. Scott*, ed. D. Mack, Edinburgh, Scottish Academic Press, 1983 [1834].

—— *The Private Memoirs and Confessions of a Justified Sinner*, Oxford, Oxford University Press, 2010 [1824].

Hopkins, G. M., *Gerard Manley Hopkins: The Major Works*, ed. C. Phillips, Oxford, Oxford University Press, 2009.

Jacob, V., *Tales of my Own Country*, Edinburgh, Kennedy & Boyd, 2008 [1922].

Jamie, K., *Findings*, London, Sort of Books, 2005.

Jenkins, R., *The Changeling*, Edinburgh, Canongate, 2008 [1958].

Johnson, S. and J. Boswell, *A Journey to the Western Islands of Scotland* [1775] *and The Journal of a Tour to the Hebrides* [1785], ed. P. Levi, London, Penguin, 1984.

Kay, J., *Trumpet*, London, Picador, 1998.

Kelman, J., *How Late It Was, How Late*, London, Secker & Warburg, 1994.

Kesson, J., *The White Bird Passes*, Edinburgh, Black and White Publishing, 2003 [1958].

Leonard, T. (ed.), *Radical Renfrew*, Edinburgh, Polygon, 1990.

Lindsay, M. (ed.), *As I Remember*, London, Robert Hale, 1979.

Linklater, E., *The Man on My Back*, London, Macmillan, 1941.

—— *Magnus Merriman*, Edinburgh, Canongate, 2001 [1934].

McArthur, A. and H. K. Long, *No Mean City*, London, Corgi, 1978 [1935].

MacCaig, N., *The Poems of Norman MacCaig*, ed. E. McCaig, Edinburgh, Polygon, 2005.

MacColla, F., 'Angus and Mearns', in G. S. Moncrieff (ed.), *Scottish Country: Fifteen Essays by Scottish Authors*, Bristol, Wishart Books, 1935.

MacDiarmid, H., *The Islands of Scotland*, London, B. T. Batsford, 1939.

—— *The Complete Poems of Hugh MacDiarmid*, ed. M. Grieve and W. R. Aitken, 2 vols, Harmondsworth, Penguin, 1985.

Macfarlane, R., *The Wild Places*, London, Granta, 2007.

McGonagall, W., *Collected Poems*, ed. Chris Hunt, Edinburgh, Birlinn, 2006.

McIlvanney, W., *Docherty*, Edinburgh, Canongate, 2013 [1975].

—— *Laidlaw*, Edinburgh, Canongate, 2013 [1977].

Mackenzie, C., *Whisky Galore*, Edinburgh, Birlinn, 2012 [1947].

MacLaverty, B., *Grace Notes*, London, Jonathan Cape, 1997.

MacLean, S., *A White Leaping Flame: Collected Poems*, ed. E. Dymock, Edinburgh, Birlinn, 2011.

MacLeod, A., *No Great Mischief*, London, Vintage, 2001.

MacNeice, L., *I Crossed the Minch*, Edinburgh, Polygon, 2007 [1938].

MacNeil, K., *The Stornoway Way*, London, Penguin, 2006.

—— (ed.), *These Islands, We Sing: An Anthology of Scottish Islands Poetry*, Edinburgh, Polygon, 2011.

McPhee, J., *Pieces of the Frame*, New York, Farrar, Straus and Giroux, 2011.

—— *The Crofter and the Laird*, Colonsay, House of Lochar, 2012.

Macpherson, J., *Fragments of Ancient Poetry*, Edinburgh, Mercat Press, 1970 [1760].

Martin, M., *A Description of the Western Islands of Scotland, circa 1695*, Edinburgh, Birlinn, 2014 [1703].

Maxwell, G., *Ring of Bright Water*, Toller Fratrum, Little Toller Books, 2009 [1960].

—— *Harpoon at a Venture*, Edinburgh, Birlinn, 2013 [1952].

Miller, H., *The Old Red Sandstone*, London, J. M. Dent & Co., 1906 [1841].

Mitchison, N., *Among You Taking Notes: The Wartime Diary of Naomi Mitchison 1939–1945*, ed. D. Sheridan, London, Phoenix Press, 2000.

Morgan, E., *Collected Poems 1949–1987*, Manchester, Carcanet, 1996.

Muir, E., *Scottish Journey*, Edinburgh, Mainstream Publishing, 1996 [1935].

Munro, A., *The View from Castle Rock*, London, Vintage, 2007.

Nicolson, A., *Sea Room: An Island Life*, London, HarperCollins, 2002.

O'Hagan, A., *Our Fathers*, London, Faber and Faber, 1999.

Orwell, G., *Nineteen Eighty-Four*, London, Penguin, 2013 [1949].

Raisin, R., *Waterline*, London, Penguin, 2011.

Rankin, I., *Black and Blue*, London, Orion, 1997.

—— *Dead Souls*, London, Orion, 1999.

—— *Fleshmarket Close*, London, Orion, 2004.

—— *The Naming of the Dead*, London, Orion, 2007.

Reid, A., *Outside In: Selected Prose*, Edinburgh, Polygon, 2008.

Richards, E., *The Highland Clearances*, Edinburgh, Birlinn, 2000.

Robertson, J., *And the Land Lay Still*, London, Penguin, 2011.

Rogers, W., *A Cruising Voyage Round the World*, London, Cassell, 1928 [1712].

Rowling, J. K., *Harry Potter and the Philosopher's Stone*, London, Bloomsbury, 1997.

Sayers, D. L., *The Five Red Herrings*, London, Victor Gollancz, 1931.

Scott, Sir W., *The Heart of Midlothian*, Oxford, Oxford University Press, 2008 [1818].

—— *Rob Roy*, Oxford, Oxford University Press, 2008 [1817].

—— *Waverley*, Oxford, Oxford University Press, 2008 [1814].

—— *The Lady of the Lake*, Glasgow, ASLS, 2010 [1810].

Shakespeare, W., *Macbeth*, Oxford, Oxford University Press, 2008 [1611].

Sheeler, J., *Little Sparta: The Garden of Ian Hamilton Finlay*, London, Frances Lincoln, 2003.

Shelley, M., *Frankenstein*, London, Penguin, 2003 [1818].

Shepherd, N., *The Living Mountain*, Edinburgh, Canongate, 2011 [1977].

Smith, A., *A Summer in Skye*, Edinburgh, Birlinn, 1998 [1865].

Smith, A. M., *44 Scotland Street*, London, Abacus, 2005.

Smith, I. C., *Consider the Lilies*, Edinburgh, Canongate, 1998 [1968].

Smith, M., *The Letters of Charlotte Brontë, Volume II: 1848–1851*, Oxford, Clarendon Press, 2000.

Smollett, T., *The Expedition of Humphry Clinker*, Oxford, Oxford University Press, 2009 [1771].

Southey, R., *Journal of a Tour in Scotland in 1819*, Edinburgh, James Thin, 1972 [1929].

Spark, M., *The Prime of Miss Jean Brodie*, London, Penguin, 2000 [1961].

Spufford, F., *I May Be Some Time: Ice and the English Imagination*, London, Faber and Faber, 2003.

Stevenson, R. L., *Edinburgh: Picturesque Notes*, London, Seeley & Co., 1900.
—— *Essays in the Art of Writing*, London, Chatto & Windus, 1920.
—— *The Scottish Novels*, Edinburgh, Canongate, 1997.
—— *Kidnapped*, London, Penguin, 2007 [1886].
Stoker, B., *Dracula*, London, Penguin, 2004 [1897].
Turner, F., *John Muir: From Scotland to the Sierra*, Edinburgh, Canongate, 1997.
Verne, J., *Backwards to Britain*, trans. J. Valls-Russell, Edinburgh, Chambers, 1992.
Walker, C. K., *Walking North with Keats*, London, Yale University Press, 1992.
—— *Breaking Away: Coleridge in Scotland*, London, Yale University Press, 2002.
Warner, A., *Morvern Callar*, London, Vintage, 1996.
—— *The Man Who Walks*, London, Jonathan Cape, 2002.
Welsh, I., *Trainspotting*, London, Vintage, 1999 [1993].
Welsh, L., *The Cutting Room*, Edinburgh, Canongate, 2002.
Woolf, V., *To the Lighthouse*, London, Penguin, 2000 [1927].
Wordsworth, D., *Recollections of a Tour Made in Scotland*, London, Yale University Press, 1997 [1874].
Wordsworth, W., *The Collected Poems of William Wordsworth*, Ware, Wordsworth Editions, 1994.

Useful Resources

Bold, A., *Scotland: A Literary Guide*, London, Routledge, 1989.
Crawford, R., *The Book of St Andrews: An Anthology*, Edinburgh, Polygon, 2005.
—— *Scotland's Books*, London, Penguin, 2007.
Crawford, R. and M. Imlah, *The New Penguin Book of Scottish Verse*, London, Penguin, 2001.
Dunn, D. (ed.), *Scotland: An Anthology*, London, HarperCollins, 1991.
—— *Twentieth-Century Scottish Poetry*, London, Faber and Faber, 2006.
Foster, A., *The Literary Traveller in Scotland*, Edinburgh, Mainstream, 2007.
Haswell-Smith, H., *The Scottish Islands*, Edinburgh, Canongate, 2008.
Irvine, P., *Scotland the Best*, 12th edition, London, HarperCollins, 2016.
Lownie, A., *The Edinburgh Literary Companion*, Edinburgh, Polygon, 2005.
Magnusson, M., *Scotland: The Story of a Nation*, London, HarperCollins, 2000.
Ward, A., *Nothing to See Here: A Guide to the Hidden Joys of Scotland*, Moffat, Pocket Mountains, 2011.

Index